ALSO BY JOHN VAN DER KISTE

Published by Sutton Publishing unless stated otherwise

Frederick III: German Emperor 1888 (1981)
Queen Victoria's Family: A Select Bibliography (Clover, 1982)
Queen Victoria's Children (1986)
Dearest Affie: Alfred, Duke of Edinburgh, Queen Victoria's Second Son, 1844–1900 [with Bee Jordaan] (1984)
Queen Victoria's Children (1986)
Windsor and Habsburg: The British and Austrian Reigning Houses 1848–1922 (1987)
Edward VII's Children (1989)
Princess Victoria Melita, Grand Duchess Cyril of Russia (1991)
George V's Children (1991)
George III's Children (1992)
Crowns in a Changing World: The British and European Monarchies 1901–36 (1993)
Kings of the Hellenes: The Greek Kings 1863–1974 (1994)
Childhood at Court 1819–1914 (1995)
Northern Crowns: The Kings of Modern Scandinavia (1996)
King George II and Queen Caroline (1997)
Kaiser Wilhelm II: Germany's Last Emperor (1999)
The Georgian Princesses (2000)
Gilbert & Sullivan's Christmas (2000)
Dearest Vicky, Darling Fritz: Queen Victoria's Eldest Daughter and the German Emperor (2001)
Royal Visits in Devon and Cornwall (Halsgrove, 2002)
Once a Grand Duchess: Xenia, Sister of Nicholas II [with Coryne Hall] (2002)
William and Mary (2003)

THE ROMANOVS 1818–1959

JOHN VAN DER KISTE

SUTTON PUBLISHING

This book was first published in 1998

This new revised paperback edition first published in 2003 by
Sutton Publishing Limited · Phoenix Mill
Thrupp · Stroud · Gloucestershire · GL5 2BU

British Library Cataloguing in Publication Data
A catalogue record for this book is available from the British Library

ISBN 0 7509 3459 X

Typeset in 10/12pt
Typesetting and orig
Sutton Publishing Li
Printed and bound in Great Britain by
J.H. Haynes & Co. Ltd, Sparkford.

Contents

Preface

'Some day, a novelist possessing the qualifications of an Emile Zola and unafraid of spending long years in research and study, should choose the history of the modern Romanoffs as a subject deserving as many volumes as the epic of the Rougon-Macquards.' So wrote Grand Duke Alexander Michaelovich, cousin and also son-in-law of Tsar Alexander III, in the first volume of his memoirs published a year before his death in 1933. To do justice to even, say, the Romanovs from 1800 onwards, would indeed take several years of research and surely just as many volumes in book form. In the present work I have chosen to confine myself broadly to the lives of Tsar Alexander II and his immediate family – that is to say, his wives, children and children-in-law. The collective tragedy of Nicholas II, Alexandra and their children has been responsible for the production of a vast library in itself during the last few years, and I have chosen to concentrate instead on the somewhat less well explored lives of the previous generation, embracing Alexander II, the Tsar Liberator who met his death at the hands of terrorists in 1881, Alexander III and his siblings, and the second family of Alexander II, his morganatic wife Princess Yourievsky, and their children, the last of whom survived the fall of the Russian Empire by over forty years. The collapse of the dynasty, the Russian revolution and execution of several members of the family are thus seen through the eyes of the surviving sons and daughters of the Tsar Liberator.

'Anything in the nature of an impartial account of the great era of the reign of Alexander II is a rarity' wrote his biographer Stephen Graham in 1935. 'Apart from a few adulatory volumes bearing an almost official stamp there is nothing that is not written in a bitter and grudging spirit.' Most of the Tsar's private papers were destroyed soon after his death on the orders of his son and successor. The volumes of biography, adulatory or otherwise, have indeed been few. S.S. Tatitchev's monumental two volume study, published in St Petersburg in 1903, has never been translated into English in its entirety, although brief extracts have been used by subsequent writers, notably in the most recent life by E.M. Almedingen (1962). Her foreword modestly admits that her book 'does not pretend to be a definitive biography', remarking that she very much doubts if such a work could ever be written, especially after the destruction of most of the Tsar's papers. Graham's book is not so much a biography as a 'life and times' study, with greater emphasis on the times. Maurice Paléologue's *The Tragic Romance of Alexander II*, as its title suggests, dwells largely on the affair between the Tsar and Princess Catherine Dolgorouky. Although factually sound it cannot resist lapsing into passages of invented dialogue from time to time, and the author is coy about his sources, citing 'the information I have gleaned here and there during my mission in Petrograd, a few letters which have since passed through my hands, and finally an intimate confidence I have recently enjoyed'.

Tsar Alexander III has received even less attention from biographers. The only English account, by a foreign correspondent of *The Times*, Charles Lowe, was published the year after his death. Lowe called his subject 'a mass of apparent contradictions', and a man whose reign 'was one painful tragedy of racial and religious persecutions, which can scarcely be paralleled out of the cruellest page of all history'. It readily acknowledges with sympathy that he was an honest man determined to govern well, but let himself be guided by the wrong people. Otherwise the nearest to a modern biography of the last Tsar but one is to be found in the first three chapters of the life of his youngest daughter, Ian Vorres's *The last Grand-Duchess*.

For the lives of the remaining Grand Dukes and Duchess, there is a plethora of relevant biographical material (if not individual biographies), plus reminiscences from members of the family, frequently at variance with each other, and often strewn with inaccuracies. Grand Duke Alexander's assertion that the future Nicholas II was the second son of Tsarevich Alexander, not the first, is but one example of the latter.

Where the true facts are not known, writers have readily supplied their own. Did Tsar Nicholas I really look with disfavour on his eldest son and heir's choice of bride in 1840, and did Tsar Alexander III do likewise in 1894? That much in the way of

Russian history was covered up at the time has not helped. Imperially appointed censors, responsible for ensuring that nothing was written or published about the dynasty that did not pay unquestioning homage to it, did their work well. As E.M. Almedingen noted in her life of Alexander II mentioned above, before 1905 'not a single sovereign of Russia had committed a single mistake, been guilty of violating his marriage vows, or been known for any other backslidings'. Even foreign correspondents were often unable to report the true facts of certain nineteenth-century events in Russia. The number of casualties at the disaster of Khodynka Field in 1896, or that of others who were killed on the same day as the assassination of Alexander II, varies in almost every account published ever since; while different interpretations as to the precise reaction to events among members of the imperial family during the harrowing last years of, say, 1916 to 1918, can be read in almost every book – be it contemporary memoirs or modern history.

One can do no better than quote the old Russian proverb from the introduction of one of the most recent – and undoubtedly one of the best – books on the last years of the dynasty, Andrei Maylunas and Sergei Mironenko's *A lifelong passion*: 'If you don't lie, you don't tell a story.' All the same, I hope that I have told the following story with as few lies as possible, while at the same pleading in self-defence that inadvertent half-truths taken from previous generations of historians and biographers, as well as the memoirs of forgetful Grand Dukes (and how much did they owe to even less knowledgeable ghostwriters?), are perhaps better than metaphorical black holes.

Modern practice is increasingly accepting the designation 'Grand Prince' as more correct than 'Grand Duke', but I have chosen to use the time-honoured latter form instead. I have also given dates in Old Style (used by Russia until 1 February 1918) and New Style simultaneously for events in Russia, but only in New Style for those occurring elsewhere.

I wish to acknowledge the gracious permission of Her Majesty The Queen to publish certain material of which she owns the copyright; the Trustees of the Broadlands Archives, the staffs of Southampton University Library, Bridgeman Art Library, and the Society for Cooperation in Russian and Soviet Studies, for the supply of illustrations. Several people have unstintingly given me considerable help while writing this book, and been tireless in replying to what has at times become an almost unending stream of lengthy letters. Robin Piguet has made valiant efforts on my behalf, in addition to the generous loan of part of his personal library, and his ever-ready encouragement. Karen Roth and Roman Golicz have both been extremely helpful in tracking down and supplying elusive material, as well as going to great efforts to answer fiendishly obscure questions. Coryne Hall, Sue Woolmans, Charlotte Zeepvat, Theo Aronson, Steven Jackson of the Commemorative Collectors' Society, Victor Pierce-Jones, and John Wimbles have also kindly provided useful advice, information and illustrations between them. The staff at Kensington Central Library have been as willing as ever to let me loose in their incomparable reserve biography collection. Last but not least, my parents, Wing Commander Guy and Kate Van der Kiste, have as usual cast a valuable eye over the manuscript in draft form; and my editors, Sarah Bragginton and Jaqueline Mitchell, have expertly seen the end result through to publication. My heartfelt thanks to all of them.

Part I: Tsar Alexander II, 1818–81

1

'A naturalness which charms'

In June 1796 Grand Duke Nicholas Paulovich of Russia was born, the third son of Grand Duke Paul and his wife Grand Duchess Maria Feodorovna. The baby's first few months coincided with the twilight era of his grandmother Empress Catherine II ('Catherine the Great'), whose reign of forty-four years was drawing to a close. She died in November and was succeeded on the throne by Paul, her mentally unstable son, whose five years as Tsar ended with a palace revolution during which he was strangled. His successor was the eldest of his four sons, who reigned for twenty-four years as Alexander I. His marriage to Princess Elizabeth of Baden gave them no sons, and their daughters died in infancy. The second son, Constantine, had divorced his first wife and his second, morganatic, marriage was childless, while the youngest son, Michael, married in 1824 but his wife produced only two daughters.

On Nicholas, therefore, depended the survival of the Romanov dynasty. With two elder brothers he had never expected to succeed to the throne, and he grew up imagining that his role would be the traditional Grand Duke's life of a soldier. In 1814 Nicholas and Michael passed through Berlin to join the Tsar's military staff. En route they met the widower King Frederick William III of Prussia, and Nicholas was captivated by his hostess, the King's daughter Charlotte; within a few months they were betrothed. When he returned to the Prussian capital for the engagement ceremony, she told him that he had come just in time to settle a most important question. The clocks of St Petersburg, she said, were three-quarters of an hour ahead of those of Berlin. Did the time go more quickly there? Gallantly he assured her 'that time passes nowhere as fast as with you'. In July 1817 they were married at the Winter Palace, St Petersburg. The groom was aged twenty-one, while his bride celebrated her nineteenth birthday that same day.

Within weeks of their marriage Charlotte, now received into the Orthodox Church and given the names Alexandra Feodorovna, was expecting their first child. A son and heir was born to them in the Kremlin on 17/29 April 1818, during Holy Week. While noting in her journal that their happiness knew no bounds, the Grand Duchess could not but feel 'slightly melancholy at the thought that the tiny helpless thing would one day have to ascend the throne'.[1]

Church bells throughout Moscow were ringing to celebrate Easter, and legend has it that as the child was born, a flock of white doves circled over the roof of the Chudov Monastery where imperial infants were traditionally christened, and where he was baptized a week later with the names Alexander Nicolaievitch. Even more poetically, observers spoke of seeing a rose-tinted cloud in the sky shaped like a diadem, similar to but richer than that of the imperial crown. Though there was surely some invention in these descriptions, to the superstitious they were good omens that the newly born Grand Duke would not merely ascend the imperial throne, but prove to be one of the most enlightened Russian monarchs of all.

The child destined to become Tsar, known by the family as *'le petit Sasha'*, spent his summers at Pavlovsk, a pleasant leafy suburb west of the capital, and winters at Anichkov Palace, St Petersburg. The parents were wise, affectionate and strict, bringing him up in spartan surroundings and a few austerely furnished rooms, with no public appearances. His grandmother the Dowager Empress was devoted to him, and for his first six years he was entrusted to the care of governesses. In 1824 a tutor, Colonel Karl Merder, took charge of his education. Merder's first report to the parents found much to praise in his pupil, but also room for improvement. His Imperial Highness was 'extremely well-mannered, thoughtful about the comfort of others, and deeply affectionate'. While quick at his lessons, he was 'rather prone to tears and reluctant to struggle with the least difficulty'.[2]

In August 1819 the couple's eldest daughter Marie was born. Their next child, a stillborn daughter, followed eleven months later. Four more Grand Duchesses followed at regular intervals: Olga, born in September 1822; another in November 1823 who only survived a few hours; Alexandra in June 1825; and Elizabeth in June 1826. By this time Tsar Alexander I had passed away. On his death on 19 November/1 December 1825, the correspondent of *The Times* observed that the Russian empire was in the strange position of having two self-denying Emperors and no active ruler.[3] Constantine was officially Tsarevich, though he was content with his post as viceroy of Poland; he had long since made it clear that he had no desire to reign, and accordingly renounced his rights to the throne. Nicholas had sworn allegiance to Constantine as Tsar, and unlike their mother he seemed unaware or reluctant to believe his brother's renunciation.

When news of Tsar Alexander I's death reached Warsaw Constantine swore allegiance to Nicholas, while the latter led the imperial guard in taking an oath of loyalty to his brother. Only when he learned of a conspiracy in the army would he accept that Constantine's renunciation was irrevocable, and that for the sake of the empire he must accept the crown. Groups of soldiers on the streets were calling for Constantine as Tsar, and though the rebellion had no proper leadership, Nicholas was aware of the risk of anarchy.

Early next morning troops and soldiers gathered at Senate Square. While disconcerted to learn that the senate had already sworn an oath of loyalty to Nicholas, they continued to demand Constantine as their Tsar. When Count Miloradovich, governor of St Petersburg, rode towards them to explain that Constantine had renounced the throne, and that he himself had seen the document of abdication, one of the ringleaders, Colonel Kakhovsky, who had sworn to kill Nicholas, shot the Count dead. Nicholas determined to meet the rebels face to face, and when officials nervously told him that several hundred officers were involved in the mutiny he brushed their protests aside, insisting that even if he was only to be Emperor for a day, he would show the world that he was worthy of the title. Riding into the square, he offered the rebels an amnesty if they promised to disperse. He did not wish to begin his reign with bloodshed, but the conspirators were in no mood for compromise. As dusk was falling, he realized that there was no alternative but to accept the advice of a general who told him to 'sweep the square with gunfire or abdicate'. The guards fired, over sixty people were killed and several hundreds injured, and with that the Decembrist conspiracy was over. Kakhovsky and four other ringleaders were sentenced to death, and around three hundred were exiled to Siberia.

At the age of seven Grand Duke Alexander Nicolaievitch became Tsarevich. A second tutor, Vasili Zhukovsky, was chosen to assist Merder in sharing the responsibility of educating the heir. Zhukovsky, the illegitimate son of a landowner from the provinces and a teenage captive taken to Russia after one of the wars with Turkey, had become one of Russia's leading poets, and was an imaginative, even radical choice. That his young charge grew up to be an enlightened monarch by Russian standards says much for the wisdom of his appointment.

Even before taking up the reins of office, he had not hesitated to risk imperial wrath by making plain his opinions of what he saw as the Tsarevich's premature first taste of pomp and splendour. In accordance with imperial tradition he was appointed colonel-in-chief to some of his father's guards regiments, although it was a token gesture and he did not appear in public with them. However he had been allowed to ride in his father's coronation parade, much to the enthusiasm of the crowds, and the Tsar's joy. Merder noticed that for some time afterwards Alexander was too excited to concentrate properly on his lessons. Bravely Zhukovsky warned the Empress that 'an over-developed passion for the art of war – even if indulged in on parade ground, would cripple the soul and the mind'. It would never do for him to end up by 'seeing his people as an immense regiment and his country as a barracks'.[4] The Tsar was angry at first, but gave way when Zhukovsky threatened to resign.

Tsar Nicholas I was always a strict father, but when the cares of state permitted he enjoyed playing with the children in the privacy of their own home; and a regular routine enabled him to spend at least two hours with them every day. He rose early, worked on various tasks, and at 10 a.m. came to the Tsarina's apartments, where he spent an hour breakfasting with his family and holding what he called '*la revue de la famille*', at which he asked each of his children to present him with a report on how the previous day had been spent, and what progress they had made with their studies and other tasks. He examined their study books himself so he could watch their progress and comment on their shortcomings as necessary, often awarding punishments and rarely giving rewards. It was his responsibility, he considered, to be stern with them as he was founding a new dynasty and thus training a new generation of Russian leaders. However any demands imposed by duty were tempered by parental warmth. He dined daily at 4 p.m. with his wife, children, and a few close friends or counsellors. The meal lasted forty-five minutes, until he left to return to his work. In the evening they might gather again for readings or informal concerts, at which the Tsar sometimes played the cornet.

The Tsarevich spent winters at the grand forbidding Winter Palace, and summers at the more homely Tsarskoe-Selo. His leisure hours were spent playing with his sisters and some of the children of commoners approved by the Empress and invited by Merder. He had no separate household; four footmen performed all domestic duties, but there were no butlers or maids. His rooms were spartan, and the classrooms in both palaces had bare floorboards and no curtains; they were merely furnished with desks, benches and bookshelves. The less forbidding playroom had a carpet, curtains and a few upholstered chairs, but no sofa or armchairs. He slept on a narrow camp bed without a pillow. Food was very plain, comprising beetroot or cabbage soup, meat cooked without relishes, boiled fish, and fruit, with special delicacies only provided at birthdays, holidays and other celebrations. Discipline at table was strictly observed; he was expected to eat everything put in front of him, and requests for a second helping were discouraged. Guests were forbidden to address the heir to the throne as 'Highness' or anything of the kind, while servants must always be treated with courtesy, and footmen were not to obey his commands or orders unless they were prefaced with 'please'.

This spartan upbringing often surprised foreign observers. When the French ambassador, le Duc de Dagouse, expected to be presented automatically to the heir after a formal audience with the Tsar in the throne room of the Winter Palace, no ceremony was suggested. He decided to ask the Tsar, who replied he would meet all the children later, probably in the park at Tsarskoe-Selo. A formal presentation would never do, as the heir would get a swollen head if an experienced and famous general was to pay him homage; 'Before everything else I am determined to have him brought up as a man.'[5] In time the Duke met Alexander and his little sisters in the park at Tsarskoe-Selo, and they invited him to cross to the children's island where they had planted all the trees and shrubs. He was enchanted by the simplicity of their miniature world and playground with its brightly painted seesaw, miniature kitchen garden, and the meal they served him of wild strawberries, lettuce and young carrots with wheat rusks served on limewood platters, with milk served in thick earthenware mugs.

From his mother, who maintained close ties with her family in Berlin, the Tsarevich inherited and retained a strong affection for Prussian ways. At the age of eleven he paid his first visit to the capital, which he enjoyed despite confessing to Merder that he often felt homesick. His maternal grandfather, King Frederick William III, had appointed him colonel-in-chief of the Third Prussian Uhlan Regiment, and until the end of his visit he refused to appear in anything except the regimental uniform. From that year he attended the annual cadet camps organized under his father's personal supervision. Every Christmas his presents were of a suitably warlike nature; in 1831 they included a bust of Peter the Great, a rifle, sword, box of pistols, parade uniform, and a set of china cups and saucers showing Russian soldiers with different arms.

While Tsar Nicholas I was very much the model of a nineteenth-century autocrat, he was prepared – if not without persuasion, sometimes against his better judgment – to allow his eldest son a relatively liberal education. Zhukovsky devised a curriculum for him whereby two young companions would share a structured school environment. They were kept away from court life and pageantry, and brought up very simply. Competition between the boys was frowned on, they were encouraged to discuss their reading and learning together, and to keep private journals. History and languages formed the core of their early studies, followed later by science, law and philosophy. As a prize for good behaviour they were allowed to put money in the poor box. The military aspect was not dispensed with entirely, but kept in perspective, with occasional drill. Sport was represented by fencing, gymnastics and riding, and every Sunday they had outings or took up handicrafts instead of formal lessons.

From boyhood Alexander was unfailingly polite, honest, keen to learn though only of average ability, sensitive and often dreamy, with a tendency to be mischievous and mentally lazy. His tutors found him emotional, erratic in his attention to studies, and often vague or hesitant when faced with difficulties; he would make an inordinate fuss about trifling problems, or cry for no obvious reason. They suspected that the unsettling circumstances of his father's accession had left him with a lasting dread of his future inheritance. When at last a brother Constantine was born in September 1827 he was relieved, as 'Papa will be able to choose him as the Heir'.[6]

Like most small boys, he preferred outdoor life to lessons. While he was fond of parades, reviews and uniforms, the more serious military aspects aroused no interest in him. When he went to camp at Krasnoe and took part in army manoeuvres for the first time in the summer of 1829, his father was concerned at an evident lack of enthusiasm, and angry with the tutors when they defended what he regarded as an imbalance in his education; he wanted more emphasis placed on military sciences. Merder was left in no doubt that Grand Dukes were meant to be soldiers first and foremost. The next Emperor, in particular, must be raised as a potential war leader, and His Majesty had no wish to see him brought up in a civilian atmosphere as if he was only fit for a professor's chair. Ironically all his younger sons showed a taste for the services; Constantine joined the Russian navy, Nicholas (born 1831) the military engineers, and Michael (born 1832) the artillery regiment. Merder knew better than to argue with his master, but as a born soldier himself with a better appreciation of human character, he saw that Grand Duke Alexander found the whole idea of war evil and abhorrent, and such a conviction formed in boyhood could not be eradicated by anything the tutors might say or do.

Little acts of kindness testified to his endearingly selfless character. On a walk with Merder along the St Petersburg canal one afternoon, the boy looked at one of the barges moored to the quay and saw an old workman on a filthy mat, groaning and shaking. He rushed across a plank, went to talk to the man, and by the time Merder caught up with them he saw his charge wiping away the old man's tears with a handkerchief. Touched by this solicitude, Merder handed the Tsarevich a gold coin from his purse, and without hesitation the boy gave it to the old man.

In the autumn of 1829 'the little school' was resumed at the Winter Palace in St Petersburg. Alexander spent Sunday afternoons and evenings with his sisters in their mother's private apartments, and Zhukovsky and Merder were asked to join them 'for a little music and tea' in the evenings. These invitations became less frequent and gradually ceased, and at Christmas presents were given with icy formality. Zhukovsky sensed that he was out of favour, and the household thought he would soon be dismissed. By March 1830 he could bear the tension no longer, and unburdened himself in a lengthy heartfelt letter to the Tsar. He could not afford to be kept in suspense any longer, he said, but felt that he was being accused of 'unworthy and interested interference in literary quarrels now going on in St Petersburg', and he could not continue in his post as tutor unless 'reassured of your Majesty's trust in my fitness to educate your son'.[7] What had happened was that a third-rate novelist, Bulgarin, liked by the Tsar as he never gave the censors any trouble, had many friends at the court of St Petersburg. One of his novels had been mocked in an epigram by the radical poet Pushkin, a close friend of Zhukovsky, and subsequent gossip led to unsubstantiated allegations of disloyalty against Zhukovsky. However his letter cleared the air and the Tsar readily forgave him, telling him that the incident should be forgotten.

It was not the last time that there would be disagreement between the Tsar and his son's tutors. Two years later Zhukovsky left for Baden to undergo a cure for his bronchial trouble. Before doing so he recommended two further tutors for the Tsarevich, Peter Pletnev for Russian literature, and Professor Constantine Arseniev for history. The former was readily accepted, but not so Arseniev, who had been dismissed from his chair at the university a few years earlier for speaking against corruption in the judicial system and on behalf of free labour. Zhukovsky stood his ground against the Tsar's wrath, emphasizing the professor's merits as a historian and tutor, and insisting that nobody else in Russia was more suited to give His Imperial Highness a thorough course in the science of government. As for his rebellious past, Zhukovsky answered that loyalty and flattery were not synonymous; there were countless grave defects in their judicial system, and the Grand Duke was reaching an age when the truth could no longer be concealed from him. The Tsar gave in, but made his point after Zhukovsky had gone abroad by dismissing Father Pavsky, a favourite religious teacher known for his outspoken liberal beliefs, for an isolated comment of sympathy with Russian dissenters. Merder interceded on Pavsky's behalf, to be told by the Tsar that he found the dismissal necessary; his son showed too little interest in military matters, and he was still determined that the boy should be a soldier at heart. Yet the Tsarevich took it badly, misbehaving in class, quarrelling and disobeying his tutors, fighting with his companions, and showing a tendency to arrogance.

When Merder suffered a mild heart attack in the summer of 1832 after a particularly trying week in which Alexander had been more unruly than ever, Arseniev unkindly told him that he was responsible. He promptly broke down in tears, promising to behave better in future, and kept his word. When Merder was better the Tsarevich visited him regularly at home, and when he went abroad on medical advice, wrote to him once a week.

In 1834 the Tsarevich celebrated his sixteenth birthday, and the coming of age ceremonies included taking an oath of allegiance and solemn obedience to his father and to the laws of the empire. The ceremony took place in the Winter Palace before a congregation of courtiers, government representatives, foreign guests and clergy. At the same time he was granted a special inheritance, and asked for generous gifts to be made to his mother, sisters, tutors and school companions, and to the governors-general of St Petersburg and Moscow for the benefit of the poor and sick of each city. The coming of age festivities ended with a great ball at the Palace.

There was one notable absentee from the celebrations. In Rome Professor Merder had suffered a second heart attack a few days earlier, and died with his pupil's name on his lips. The Tsarevich was back in the schoolroom the day after the ball, and during his mid-morning break he received a summons from the Tsarina. When he came back to the room tears were falling down his cheeks, and he threw himself on his knees by the nearest chair as he sobbed to the master on duty. Once the shock had passed he threw himself harder than ever into his studies, knowing that was what Merder would have wished.

Three years remained of Zhukovsky's educational plan. The Tsarevich's final examination results were good, and by the spring of 1837 his formal schooling was considered to be complete. He had a natural aptitude for languages, acquiring a satisfactory knowledge of French, German, Polish and English as well as Russian. His history was strong, mathematics and natural sciences less so. By no means could he be considered an intellectual; literature, music and art meant nothing to him.

Nevertheless he often attended the theatre and opera, and Russian society took every opportunity to observe the tall graceful-looking young man who would soon rule over them. He enjoyed dancing, though this passion probably owed much to a young ballerina with whom he was said to be having an affair. Zhukovsky, regarded by his contemporaries as excessively puritan in such matters, wrote to warn him that while men were not angels, 'too much pleasure may be as dangerous as too little knowledge', and 'preserve your moral integrity if you wish to win the ultimate good'.[8] Yet he would have known better than to discourage his young pupil from the occasional fling, and the Tsarevich conducted his affairs with due discretion.

The next stage of his preparation for life, in accordance with a schedule devised by his father, was to be a seven month tour of Russia, on which he was accompanied by Zhukovsky and General Kavelin, who had replaced Merder. As the only Russian railway of the time ran from Tsarskoe-Selo to St Petersburg, a distance of less than twenty miles, the entire journey was made by coach. At almost every town on their route they attended civic receptions and reviews, church services, banquets and balls, and were conducted around countless schools, hospitals, factories, charitable institutions and churches. Local officials and dignitaries queued to meet their future Tsar, while peasants who had heard of his imminent appearance walked several miles just to catch a glimpse of the carriage.

Alexander soon had enough of this over-regimented programme with its perpetual red carpet treatment. He knew there was much that his father and guardians would rather keep out of sight, and began insisting on unscheduled stops in some of the dirtiest, most neglected villages where he would brush aside the protests of his retinue who warned him that if the programme was disrupted, some civic functions and receptions might have to be cancelled. Taking understandable pleasure in upsetting their schedule, he would leave his carriage and walk, entering peasant huts incognito as a guest. He knew this was the only way to find out how the other half lived.

A visit to Siberia – the first ever by a Romanov – had been planned, but it was at his request that they explored convict settlements and talked to prisoners in chain gangs. When told that many of the men in chains were guilty of murder, he asked why they should be condemned to a living death; 'Capital punishment could not be more cruel.' At Tobolsk he asked to meet some of the exiled Decembrists. Their living conditions shocked him, and when he and Zhukovsky put their case in an impassioned plea to the Tsar, improvements in the conditions of their exile were soon sanctioned. Ironically, in view of events some eighty years later, a warm welcome awaited him at the town of Ekaterinburg where he was shown the Mint, the goldfields, and a mineral store where he was presented with examples of jasper, malachite, and gifts including a lapis lazuli inkstand.

In Viatka, north-eastern Russia, he met the exiled revolutionary writer Alexander Herzen. At Zhukovsky's instigation, he asked his father to allow him to return to St Petersburg. The Tsar replied that this would be unfair to the other exiles, but instead allowed him to settle in a town nearer Moscow. A duly grateful Herzen observed his young benefactor at close range. The young Grand Duke, he noted, lacked his father's stern expression, as well as 'the hoarse, abrupt, utterance of his uncle Constantine', and seemed more friendly than both.

After seeing much of 'our mother Russia', visiting thirty provinces in only seven months, he felt he had learnt to love and respect it even more; 'we may be proud that we belong to Russia and call her our motherland'.[9] The next stage of his education was a tour of Europe to see other royal courts and, no less importantly, eligible princesses. Visiting Copenhagen in the summer of 1838, he caught a cold which rapidly turned to bronchitis, and was confined to bed for several days. For three months he was unable to throw off his racking cough and fever. Throughout the summer he stayed in Ems, with Zhukovsky anxiously watching by his bedside until he recovered. Once up and about he was twice observed by the perceptive Marquis de Custine, who noted at first the gentle, well-meaning expression on his face, but a disturbing contrast between youthful smiling eyes and a constant contraction of the mouth, suggesting a lack of frankness and perhaps concealed sadness as well. A second meeting produced a less favourable impression; of a complexion no longer fresh, the eyes betraying a melancholy beyond his tender years, a power of dissimulation frightening in one so young, and above all an appearance of suffering. If he should ever come to the throne, de Custine remarked cautiously, 'he will obtain obedience through the constraint of a gracious character rather than by terror'.[10] Others thought him charming and good-natured but weak and colourless, without his father's strength of purpose, possessed of a retiring spirit which either reflected tact or a disinclination to quarrel.

After the doctors advised that he should spend the winter in southern Europe, the Tsar reluctantly allowed him to convalesce in Italy, and then only on the strict understanding that they should resume their travels in January 1839, despite Zhukovsky's protests that the Tsarevich was not fully recovered and that to leave warm sunny Italy for the treacherous January and February climate of northern Europe would be unwise. At his age a recurrence of bronchial trouble 'might well lead to dangerous consequences'. The Tsar's answer was only to be expected; bad weather should not be allowed to interfere with a soldier's journey. Zhukovsky's fears were soon justified, for his young charge was left with persistent bronchial trouble which developed into a painful and chronic asthmatic complaint from which he suffered throughout his life.

After they resumed their journey north, Zhukovsky wrote to the Tsarina with thinly veiled sarcasm that 'we do not really travel: we gallop. Nothing else is to be done at this time of the year. . . . In all cities and town the few allotted hours are crowded with presentations, balls and banquets, in brief, everything that can be seen in St Petersburg.'[11]

Nevertheless the Tsarevich would soon accomplish one of the main purposes of his travels. Within fifteen months he would proudly lead his bride to the altar. Tsar Nicholas I had tentatively made up his mind as to who should be the next Empress of Russia. Princess Alexandrine of Baden, he thought, would be suitable for his son, but when the two young people met she made no impression on him. Even so the Tsar was prepared to let his son choose for himself, as long as his bride-to-be was neither Roman Catholic nor commoner. In March General Kavelin suggested to the heir that they should make an unplanned stop in Darmstadt. Maybe it was because the entourage was suffering subsequent exhaustion from too much travel in too little time and needed a rest, as Zhukovsky suggested; maybe he had other motives. The Tsarevich had no intention of spending what the poet called 'a possibly dull evening' with their host Louis II, Grand Duke of Hesse, but reluctantly agreed to stop at the quiet German town. The Grand Duke invited them all to the theatre and supper at the palace afterwards.

If he had intended the imperial heir to fall under the spell of his daughter Princess Marie of Hesse, his plan could not have worked better. At fourteen Marie was still a child but tall for her age, intelligent and self-possessed without appearing too precocious. Early maturity had owed something, perhaps, to the unhappiness of her childhood; her parents had been estranged for some years before her mother's death from consumption, when Marie was eleven. It was said that not only had she been born several years after her parents ceased to live together, but also that the Grand Duke's master of the horse was her father, and that the Grand Duke had only acknowledged her as his daughter in order to avoid scandal. Such gossip made no difference to the smitten Tsarevich, who probably suspected that it was a ploy to try and put him off her. To Zhukovsky it was evident that the future Tsar had become a changed man, passionately in love with the girl. With or without his parents' consent he was determined to consider himself betrothed to her, even declaring at one point that he would sooner abandon the succession than give her up. Before he left Darmstadt she gave him a locket containing a piece of her hair.

When he reached The Hague a few days later to stay with his aunt Anna, Princess of Orange, and her family, to celebrate Easter and his twenty-first birthday, she was impressed with his 'tact, grace and dignity, with a naturalness which charms'. Most importantly she wrote to the Tsar assuring him that 'I am certain that the differences of places and objects have not distracted him from the principal goal which was to occupy him'.[12] Though the Tsar and Tsarina were less than wholehearted in their approval of their son's choice and initially refused their consent, they gave permission after he proved obdurate. Rumours of her uncertain parentage disturbed them less than reports that her health might be unequal to such a calling. The last princess from Darmstadt to marry into the Romanovs, Grand Duchess Natalie, first wife of Tsar Paul I, had died in childbirth after a labour lasting five days, and a post-mortem revealed a curious bone malformation which would have made it impossible for her to produce a living child. Moreover it was feared – and time would prove them right – that Marie might have inherited her mother's consumption. In addition the Tsarina, a daughter of Queen Louise of Prussia, considered the Hesse family grossly inferior to the Hohenzollerns and Romanovs.

Whether unofficially betrothed or not, the Tsarevich had to continue his itinerary. Next on the schedule was England, where he was to spend a few days as the guest of Queen Victoria. Not quite twenty years of age herself and still unmarried, she found him charming although not a perfect Adonis; 'he is tall with a fine figure, a pleasing open countenance without being handsome, fine blue eyes, a short nose and a pretty mouth with a sweet smile'.[13] While she acknowledged that Tsar Nicholas I 'was not a person to be trusted or encouraged', she admitted that she found his son 'certainly irresistible', and after a ball at Buckingham Palace on the evening of 10 May, which lasted until 3.15 the next morning, she decided that they were 'great friends already and get on very well'. According to Zhukovsky the Tsarevich himself was suitably impressed with England, and after a three day stay at Windsor, as well as visits to Westminster, the British Museum, Woolwich, Ascot and Oxford, he was full of praise for the English; 'he liked the way they work and what he called "the neatness and greenness" of their countryside'.[14]

At the end of May he returned to The Hague, and with his parents' permission he made his way to Darmstadt where plans for his betrothal had just begun. Yet Marie was not yet fifteen, and he would have to bide his time. Soon after he returned to Russia, his father began to introduce him to the business of state, encouraging him to study official documents and become more closely acquainted with his ministers.

Towards the closing weeks of 1839 the Tsarevich returned to

Darmstadt, and in April 1840 his engagement to Princess Marie was officially announced. A few weeks after her sixteenth birthday in August, the party set out for Russia. In December she was received into the Orthodox Church and was given the names Marie Alexandrovna. On 16/28 April 1841, the eve of the groom's twenty-third birthday, they were married in the Chapel of the Winter Palace.

The young couple were given apartments in the Anichkov Palace, and for a while they were blissfully happy in the company of each other. The Tsarevna had wide-ranging intellectual interests, and she soon persuaded her husband to take a more intelligent and well-informed interest in literature, philosophy, music and poetry. Though he could never become a wholehearted patron of the arts, their court still became the focus for a group of intellectually minded friends who spent their evenings in conversation or dancing, listening to music, and reading aloud. Despite state censorship in Russia that forbade newspapers and journals to publish any information about or criticism of government affairs, the reign of Tsar Nicholas I witnessed a golden age of literature, with the publication of work by Pushkin, Dostoevsky, Turgenev, Gogol and Leomontov. Paradoxically they were critical of the repressive regime, and censors who attempted to prohibit or interfere with the publication of their writings had limited success. In spite of his negative historical reputation, the Tsar was no philistine. He had been an admirer of the novels of Sir Walter Scott since meeting him while on a visit to Britain in 1816, and he attended the first performance of Gogol's *The Government Inspector* at the Alevandrinsky Theatre. His sister-in-law Helen, wife of Tsar Alexander I's youngest son Michael, was renowned for her *soirées* at which the Tsarevich and Tsarevna were regular guests mingling with musicians, men of letters and patrons of the arts. The Tsar gave her *carte blanche* to invite whom she wished, even writers whose work was officially banned, and who probably did not hesitate to criticize the regime, albeit diplomatically, in her presence. Such meetings influenced the Tsarevich in his resolve to change matters and allow greater freedom from a climate of admittedly ineffectual censorship once he ascended the imperial throne.

The Tsarevna's relations with her parents-in-law left much to be desired. A shy and retiring girl of only sixteen with a sheltered upbringing, it was only to be expected that she found the towering figure of the Tsar imposing, not to say alarming. Although he could be genial towards his family, she never overcame her shyness in his presence. Her manner was inclined to be stiff, and smart members of St Petersburg society complained that she seemed cold and distant, lacked charm, had no conversation and no taste in dress. Behind her back they called her '*la petite bourgeoise allemande*', making fun of her religious fervour and fondness for music and poetry. The bitter damp Russian climate did not agree with her delicate health. As feared she had indeed inherited her mother's frailty of physique, and the climate brought on a racking cough and intermittent recurring fever in winter, which became worse with age.

Her first years in her adopted country were brightened by the presence of her elder brother Prince Alexander, who was initially treated with great favour at court. On his arrival in Russia he was promoted to first lieutenant in the *Chevaliers Gardes*, and two months later became a colonel. His military career went from strength to strength, culminating in his appointment in 1850 as commander of the guards cuirassiers. However he disgraced himself by spurning the Tsar's wish to marry his niece, Grand Duchess Catherine Michaelovna, and falling in love instead with Countess Julie of Hauke, one of the Tsarevna's ladies-in-waiting. As such a marriage would never meet with imperial sanction they slipped out of the empire and married in secret at Breslau, Germany, in October 1851. For his sins the Tsar dismissed Prince Alexander from the Russian army and stripped him of his rank of general, so he volunteered for service in the imperial Austrian army instead. The Tsarevich pleaded successfully for the restoration of his Russian military status, and Emperor Francis Joseph created him a general in the Austrian army. By the time he retired in 1862 he had seen service in two more wars and received the rare accolade of being awarded the highest decorations of valour from four countries.*

* On their marriage Countess Julie Hauke was created Countess of Battenberg by the Grand Duke of Hesse. Their eldest son Prince Louis of Battenberg saw the family name anglicized to Mountbatten in 1917 during the First World War.

Within a year of their marriage the Tsarevich and Tsarevna had become parents. Their first child, a daughter Alexandra, was born at Tsarskoe-Selo in August 1842, and a son Nicholas thirteen months later. Six more children followed in due course: Alexander (1845), Vladimir (1847), Alexis (1850), another daughter Marie (1853), Serge (1857) and finally Paul (1860). These regular pregnancies took their toll on the mother's strength, and after the birth of the last she withdrew increasingly from court life as her health declined.

Alexander was a devoted father. He hung portraits of Marie and the children on the walls of his study at Tsarskoe-Selo, his desk was covered with miniatures of them, and while the youngsters were small he liked to let them play on the floor of his study beside him while he worked. At the suggestion of his wife English nannies, already employed at some of the German courts, were engaged to look after them.

Sadly Alexandra, the only child who never reached maturity, succumbed to infant meningitis on 16/28 June 1849 at the age of six. 'We have lost our little angel this morning,' the Tsarina's lady-in-waiting Marianne von Grancy wrote to Prince Charles of Hesse. 'God willing He will support [the mother] in this trial, for in the state in which she finds herself strong emotions can prove fatal. She has been admirable in her soul throughout this long and cruel illness . . .'[15] The child's equally grief-stricken father treasured her blue silk dress for the rest of his life.

In addition to new parental responsibilities, the Tsarevich became ever more closely involved with the work of his father's government. He respected his wife's judgment and regularly sought her opinion, taking state papers home for them to read together, as well as blunt reports on the condition of the country and people which officials thought were too hard-hitting for the eyes of the Tsar, accustomed to believing that all was well with his empire and subjects and reluctant to acknowledge otherwise. As the Tsarina's health deteriorated she went more frequently to the German spas, the Tsar accompanying her and leaving his eldest son to act as unofficial regent in his absence. Becoming familiar with the personnel of the higher civil and military administration in Russia, he became the best-prepared heir apparent ever to succeed to the Russian throne.

If he lacked confidence in his own judgment where matters of statecraft were concerned, Zhukovsky was always there to offer words of warning and much needed encouragement. 'Far from being an unlimited privilege, autocracy is a fearful responsibility,' he advised the Tsar-in-waiting. 'You must train your will to join your vision, and the acceptance of any measure – once you know it to be good – must at once be followed by action, no matter what opposition you find.'[16] Opposition was to be found everywhere; adverse economic conditions in the Russian empire, illiteracy and oppression, and obstructive or inept ministers. When the Tsarevich came close to being overwhelmed by despair, as had so often been the case when he was a boy in the schoolroom, confronted by seemingly insoluble mathematical questions, Zhukovsky gently asked him if the Grand Duchess, his wife, had found it easy to study and learn Russian. It had been a hard struggle, Alexander confirmed. The analogy was self-evident, the poet told him; 'Her Imperial Highness is a good exemplar.'

So were some of the writings that came his way in spite of the occasionally strong but often erratic arm of official censorship. In 1847 he received a copy of the *Contemporary Review*, the first periodical to publish the work of Turgenev. The stark portrayal of Russian peasant life in *Sovreménnik* (*Sportsman's Sketches*), particularly in the short story *Khor and Kalinich*, made a deep impression on him and his wife when he read it aloud to her – and on many others. Among the Russian intelligentsia the mood was changing. Intellectuals were starting to look around themselves and appreciate that the peasantry were flesh and blood, not representatives of an inferior species. Turgenev's writings did more than anything else to bring home to them awareness of the terrible living conditions, squalor and sheer misery of those who had the misfortune to be born into a way of life (if not living death) which condemned them to a pitiless existence in a climate which comprised three parts winter gloom and one part searing summer heat, crammed into rotting, leaking wooden huts where they perished from cold, malnutrition or hunger when harvest failed. Under such circumstances, short life expectancy could only be a blessing. As a young man the Tsarevich had seen much of this with his own eyes, and Turgenev's powerful writings, it was said, 'illuminate[d] for him the unquenchable humanity which somehow managed to survive that degradation'.[17]

At the same time it stiffened his resolve to do more for them than pay mere lip-service once he was in a position to do so. He chaired a committee which his father had called, to study and change the conditions of serfdom, although bureaucracy put paid to the implementation of its recommendations. Despite Tsar Nicholas I's time-honoured reactionary image he was an advocate of reform, albeit at a cautious pace, and described serfdom as a 'flagrant evil', though taking steps to eradicate it was probably not high on his list of priorities. Even if it was, subsequent history would show that a combination of inertia and obstruction from vested interests were a match for any sovereign intent on altering the status quo.

Certain matters were beyond the reach of the Tsarevich and sometime regent. In 1846 Zhukovsky appealed passionately for clemency or remission of sentences on behalf of the Decembrist mutineers exiled to Siberia for life at the beginning of the reign some twenty years earlier. Reminding Tsar Nicholas of the happiness he had found with his family, could he not 'think what the return to the light of their homes will mean to him'. Yet the sovereign remained deaf to their entreaties. Where he was concerned, from a sentence of 'penal servitude for life' there could be no remission.

Yet the enlightened views of pupil and tutor were not proof against the shadow of revolution which shook much of Europe in 1848. From Baden, where he was nursing his sick wife, Zhukovsky evidently believed that the forces of radicalism had gone too far. Surveying events in Berlin with alarm, he wrote to the Tsarevich in March that it was sad 'to think that the Prussian monarchy should have been vested by such brigands'. The only hope for them lay in Russia; 'let her turn away from the West and stand firmly behind her stout high wall'. It was certainly a very different arch-conservative Zhukovsky who could write scathingly that anarchy was everywhere, thanks to the activities of 'brigands in tatters, drunkards, escaped prisoners, and Jews'.[18]

Such letters convinced the Tsarevich that the forces of radicalism, and any thoughts of emancipation, had to be resisted, for a time at least. The fears of his mother for her relatives in Berlin, and of his wife for her family at Darmstadt, added to his distress and his conviction that revolution and reform were to be feared. When one of the army regiments under his nominal command was despatched to Hungary to help the Habsburgs put down insurrection, he bid the officers Godspeed in their determination to help save the crown of an imperial ally from 'the impious clutch of the criminals'.

In Russia censors tightened their grip, banning the works of liberal writers such as Turgenev, Gogol and Pushkin. Universities and schools were put under close supervision, foreign travel was forbidden altogether, public meetings were banned, and police were given full powers to enter any private house or flat on suspicion of 'untoward activities'. Only the salon of Grand Duchess Helen remained an inviolate forum for the exchange of radical ideas and championship of the writings of suppressed men of letters, many of whom had long been and still remained her close personal friends. While the Tsarevich remained uneasy about some of her opinions he was still on close terms with her, and despite his dread of revolution he could not bring himself to condemn her views as did many other members of the family.

Tsar Nicholas I celebrated the twenty-fifth year of his reign in December 1850. Among the congratulatory messages he received from deputations sent by government officials and servants were several gilded reports from his ministers on the state of Russia during the last twenty-five years, naturally laying much (and thoroughly exaggerated) stress on the glory of his reign. Suitably flattered, he passed them to the Tsarevich to read, writing on one particularly favourable script: 'God grant that I succeed in handing Russia over to you as I have tried to make her: strong, independent, and beneficent; the best for all of us at no-one's expense.'[19]

He was well aware of his son's faults, notably over-sensitivity and lack of resolve, and once exclaimed in a moment of exasperation that the young man was 'an old woman', adding that 'there will be nothing great done in his time'. All the same he was impressed with what the once unpromising boy had become, above all with his dedication to duty, in the active and interested part he had taken in the work of committees studying serfdom. Even though the Tsarevich had shown a somewhat unseemly interest in liberal politics and ready adherence to the court of

Grand Duchess Helen, the Tsar hoped that the events of 1848 had given him a timely warning of the dangers of unfettered liberalism. Perhaps he could be trusted to restrict his reforming zeal to social issues.

Yet the reign of Tsar Nicholas was not destined to end on a note of triumph. By now foreign diplomats in St Petersburg sensed an increasing arrogance in the bearing of the Tsar, who appeared to regard himself as omnipotent. To him true glory meant an expansion in Russian territory, and he saw himself imbued with a mission to fulfil his grandmother Catherine the Great's dream, namely the acquisition of Constantinople and the Straits. If the other Great Powers of Europe could be persuaded to agree, why should Britain and Russia not divide the European possessions of Turkey, 'the sick man of Europe'? He was unaware of the resentment his high-handedness had provoked among other European sovereigns. Even when his ministers made it clear to him that Britain and France were not prepared to accept such a strategy, he felt he could still count on the support of Austria, in return for Russia's part in helping the Habsburg empire suppress the revolutions of 1848.

In July 1853 he sent troops into the Danubian principalities of Moldavia and Wallachia, technically part of the Turkish Empire but nominally under Russian protection. When the Sultan of Turkey demanded immediate withdrawal and received a firm refusal, he declared war on Russia. Britain and France jointly insisted on Russian evacuation, and as the Tsar held firm they declared war in March 1854, with Emperor Francis Joseph of Austria promising diplomatic support.

Never a soldier at heart, the Tsarevich hated the very idea of war, but to oppose his father's policies was unthinkable. While there was mass inefficiency, corruption and an astonishing lack of medical supplies on both sides, with massive casualties from disease as much as fighting, no amount of courage on the part of Russian forces could make up for bad organization. The Tsar had to face the fact that his empire's system had failed. One military reverse followed another, and he gradually lost heart. With frustration and distress the Tsarevich watched the commander-in-chief, Prince Menshikov, make one blunder after another, and in February 1855 he replaced him with the more able Michael Gorchakov.

Tsar Nicholas I was already seriously ill. It was not in his nature to contemplate anything other than a quick, easy victory for Russia. Cold reality and bitter disappointment shattered him; a severe cold that developed into pneumonia, and a suspected collapsed lung, did the rest. His declining health had been kept secret until the last moment, and only two days after Menshikov's dismissal, Russia learnt that His Imperial Majesty was dead. It was rumoured that he had taken his own life in despair after recognizing the inevitability of Russian defeat. Shortly before his death on 18 February/2 March, so official accounts and biographies of both monarchs read, he called his family around the rough camp bed on which he had always slept and on which he would go to join his forefathers, and told his son that he was handing over his command, but not in the good order which he would have wished. The loyal weeping son told his dying father how it was his earnest wish that in Heaven he would pray faithfully for their Russia and that he himself would receive divine assistance, while with his last breath the Tsar exhorted him to 'hold on to everything'.

Such a scene, depicted by sentimental engravings of the Tsar lying on his bed with a hand on the head of his kneeling son, reinforced the picture of Russian Majesty, the weary old warrior bequeathing his inheritance to a faithful son. It would never have done for Tsarist Russia to admit that the Romanovs were not immune to the widespread pattern in eighteenth and nineteenth-century Europe of crowned heads and heirs being in violent disagreement with one another, most marked in the Hohenzollerns of Prussia and the Hanoverians in England. The truth about Tsar Nicholas I's death was very different from the official version. Father and son's arguments over conduct of the war had come to a head with the Tsarevich's appointment of Gorchakov, made without the consent of the Tsar, who was already unwell. Never a man who could accept anything but blind obedience to his will, the enraged sovereign promptly suffered a stroke or heart attack which proved fatal within a few days. The end came so suddenly, according to some, that only servants on duty were present when he breathed his last.

2

'Well disposed to and desirous of reform'

At the age of thirty-six, Alexander Nicolaievich was Tsar of Russia. He had inherited an empire on the point of collapse, and many of his father's generation lacked confidence in his ability to deal with the magnitude of the task ahead of him. When he received a deputation of the St Petersburg nobility at the Winter Palace a few days after his accession, they found 'a man who saw in the very obstacles of the future so many pledges of a final success'.[1] Yet there were still high hopes for the future at the start of his reign. Others looked ahead with optimism, if not unmixed with trepidation, to a new age, echoing the view of the liberal censor Nikitenko who considered that 'a long and, I must say, joyless page in the history of the Russian empire has come to an end'.[2]

In outlook and personality Alexander was very different from Tsar Nicholas I, though he sought to emulate him in many ways. He copied his father's habits such as sleeping on a hard camp bed, and adopted a look of imperious majesty though it did not come easily to him. Some thought that he 'affected the manner of a grand seigneur', and was but a pale imitation of his father, his face 'a mask and a caricature of a mask at that, stripping his face of its pleasant, natural expression, often giving him a repellent rather than a majestic look'.[3] If this was the case, it concealed his determination to be his own man. One of his biographers, Stephen Graham, maintained that he was the only Tsar who believed in freedom, perhaps 'due to a rebellion of his spirit against the military authority assumed by his father and his father's subordinates over and above everyone and everything in the realm'.[4]

Lacking his more ebullient father's capacity as a natural leader of men, he could still inspire affection and fear. Accession to the throne had not changed his mind about the horror and futility of war, or led him to agree with his father that military training held the key to life. On the other hand he was convinced in his mission to alleviate the well-being of his people. History, Zhukovsky had warned him, would pass judgment on him before the whole world, and it would remain 'long after you and I have left the earth'.

Through these dark days when he was coming to terms with his inheritance he had the unremitting support of his family. His eldest brother, Grand Duke Constantine, who had inherited their father's drive for action without his narrow outlook, could be relied on to encourage any efforts on behalf of emancipation, economic growth, and modernization of the armed forces and government structures. If the new Tsar was sensitive, patient and unsure of himself, Constantine was quick-tempered, impatient to make decisions, and intolerant of those who feared or wished to impede change. The new Tsarina and his enlightened aunt Grand Duchess Helen also shared his modern-thinking outlook.

Yet before he could devote serious attention to reform, the war had to be won, or if defeat was inevitable, at least concluded with as much dignity as a vanquished government and army could muster. On hearing of the death of Tsar Nicholas I the British Prime Minister, Lord Palmerston, had advised Queen Victoria that it was 'possible that the new Emperor may revert to the peaceful policy which he was understood to advocate in the beginning of these transactions, but it is possible on the other hand that he may feel bound to follow out the policy of his father'.[5]

While the new sovereign was reluctant to dishonour Russia's good name by admitting the inevitability of failure, their cause looked increasingly desperate. Just before his death Tsar Nicholas I had agreed to a conference in neutral Vienna to discuss peace terms. His successor felt nothing but bitterness towards Emperor Francis Joseph, whose refusal to assist the Russian cause as a quid pro quo for services rendered in putting down revolution in the Habsburg dominions six years earlier had broken the heart of Tsar Nicholas, and replied in angry terms to a letter of condolence from Vienna. Instead of finding in the Austrian Emperor a faithful friend and ally, wrote Alexander, the late Tsar 'saw you follow a political course which brought you ever closer to our enemies and which will still bring us inevitably, if that course does not change, to a fratricidal war, for which you will be accountable to God'.[6]

Nevertheless the Tsar declared that he was ready to agree to conditions accepted by his father, and offer his hand in reconciliation; but if talks at Vienna should lead to unacceptable conditions and no prospect of honourable peace, he felt there was no alternative to continuing the war. A conference opened in Vienna in March, with Prince Alexis Orlov representing the Tsar. Four proposals required immediate attention. The Russian protectorate over Moldavia, Wallachia and Serbia was to be replaced by a joint guarantee of the four Powers; all territories should be permitted to navigate the Danube; the Dardanelles were to be closed to men-of-war from all nations; and finally Russia should be forbidden to maintain any ships in the Black Sea. Russia's time-honoured right to protect the Sultan's Christian subjects would be surrendered subject to Turkey's acceptance of a pledge from the Great Powers to confirm and observe the inviolability of all privileges and rights already granted to the Christians.

When Orlov suggested that the Black Sea should be closed to the warships of all nations, the other representatives objected at once. He had raised the issue on behalf of Grand Duke Constantine, who had foreseen the threat posed by a strong Turkish fleet to the undefended southern shore of Russia, and the Tsar supported his brother's reasoning. However Russia was in a minority of one at the conference table, and failed to win any support. The other delegates had assumed that the new Tsar would be just as obstinate as his father. It was not an unreasonable demand, for the Black Sea fleet lay at the bottom of Sebastopol Harbour and Russia, in no financial position to build another for some time, would be defenceless in the face of attacks in the near future. However, her bullying attitude to Turkey in recent years had not been forgotten, and the conference dispersed without reaching any agreement.

The Tsar therefore decided to stake everything on the defence of Sebastopol. When Gorchakov requested permission to evacuate the fortress, he was encouraged to stay. Offensive operations cost the Russian army several thousand casualties, and the allies opened a fierce bombardment in preparation for a general assault. In September Gorchakov evacuated the town, and it fell to Anglo-

French forces after a siege of almost a year and losses of more than 100,000 killed and wounded. The Tsar decided to go south to do what he could to encourage his defeated troops, their failure mitigated slightly by successful occupation of the strategic fortified Turkish city of Kars a few weeks later. Hardly bothering to eat or rest, he travelled about on horseback, accompanied by a few equerries, meeting survivors of the siege, including children who had dug the trenches and endured hunger and grief; he talked to mothers of soldiers killed in battle, and widows who had taken the place of their husbands at the front. Such desperate courage in the face of overwhelming odds, chaotic organization and lack of supplies, hollowed faces, and tattered uniforms all told their own story.

Returning to St Petersburg he immediately summoned a council of war to discuss the allies' peace conditions. Almost without exception, the verdict was unanimous that war must come to an end. To fight on without allies, no money in the treasury and no credit, and above all without the support of the people, was courting disaster. Moreover international opinion was hardening. Emperor Francis Joseph of Austria and King Frederick William IV of Prussia warned that they would seriously consider declaring war unless Russia returned to the negotiating table, and even Sweden had just signed a treaty of alignment with the western powers.

In December an Austrian envoy presented terms agreed with England and France, and in February 1856 the peace congress met at Paris. Russia had to cede the mouth of the Danube and part of Bessarabia, and to undertake not to maintain naval forces on the Black Sea or interfere in Turkish affairs. Sebastopol was restored to Russia in return for Kars, which reverted to Turkey, and the Great Powers agreed to take a responsible interest in future in protecting the rights of Turkish Christians.

The Tsar found these conditions dishonourable. Led by Prince Alexander Gorchakov, cousin of the commander-in-chief, his advisers submitted counter-proposals, but the Austrian government remained firm; if the original terms were not accepted unconditionally she would break off diplomatic relations. Faced with stalemate, the Tsar reconvened his council. His foreign minister Count Carl Nesselrode warned him that unless they made peace, within a year Russia might be faced by a general European coalition, effectively blockaded, and forced to make peace on conditions far more humiliating than those offered at present. Other members warned that southern territories, perhaps even Finland and Poland, might be lost to Russia. Unconditional acceptance of Austria's demands, no matter how unpalatable, would leave Russia in a strong position to recover her pre-war power and prosperity within a few years. There was no alternative, and in March 1856 a settlement was agreed at the treaty of Paris.

While this defeat seemed little short of humiliation at the time, the Tsar was determined to put the past behind him. The shock to Russia's system spurred her ruler and government into picking up the gauntlet, seizing the challenge the empire needed to bring her into the nineteenth century. As Gorchakov had told his sovereign on returning from Paris, peace would allow him to devote himself to home affairs. Some of his earliest appointments, following soon after publication of peace terms, assured people of his determination to make a new start. The arch-conservative Count Peter Kleinmichel, who had protested against easier means of travelling on the grounds that it 'unsettled morality', was dismissed from his post as minister of communications, as he had failed to provide for the upkeep of roads needed for military supplies to the Crimea. He was succeeded by General Constantine Chevkin, who was charged with beginning work at once on plans for new railways. There had been only six hundred miles of track throughout Russia, and none in the Crimea, a major shortcoming which the war had highlighted.

Another crucial appointment was the replacement of Count Orlov, chief of the Third Section, associated with repressive controls of the post-1848 period, with the more liberal Prince Vassili Dolgorukov. Restrictions on universities were lifted and books and journals published abroad and smuggled into Russia, but stigmatized as revolutionary or seditious, notably Herzen's paper *Kolokol* (*'The Bell'*), no longer risked confiscation or suppression. Its chief demands, namely emancipation of the serfs, abolition of corporal punishment, and curtailment of censorship, reflected the Tsar's views, and he was known to read it with approval. Permission was granted for the translation of the Bible into Russian, press controls barring the re-publication of Pushkin, Gogol and other circumscribed authors were removed, and discrimination against certain religious sects ceased.

Further measures were announced at the coronation in August 1856. Moscow was richly decorated for the occasion, with all houses and mansions repainted, churches and abbeys within the Kremlin regilded, providing a dazzling picturesque backcloth for the coronation procession which entered the Kremlin and stretched for over a mile, a cavalcade of high-stepping horses, glittering breastplates and marching feet, lasting two hours. Of the imperial family the Dowager Empress Alexandra passed first, her carriage lined in velvet, her horses sporting plumes of white ostrich feathers. The Empress Marie followed in a more modest carriage of silver and blue, preceded by four Cossacks of the Household, followed by a hundred nobles attired in ancient boyar dress. Then came the Tsar himself, seated alone with bared head in a glass and silver coach drawn by eight greys. As he drew towards the cathedral eight thousand bells began to toll from Moscow's sixteen hundred churches, and onlookers fell to their knees, partly in an act of homage, partly in a sudden impulse of thanksgiving. The sight of the two elder children, Grand Dukes Nicholas and Alexander, also on horseback, brought further cheering.

The coronation ceremony itself lasted five hours, although lack of rehearsal was evident. Count Blodov and Prince Shakovsky allowed the cushion bearing the Order of St Andrew to fall as they were about to hand it to the Tsar; when the four court ladies tried to fix the crown on the Empress's head it nearly clattered on the floor, saved from falling only by the folds of her cloak.

After the ceremony the Tsar gave an outdoor banquet attended by three hundred thousand of his subjects. The sky was illuminated by fireworks, fountains flowed with wine, and three regiments of infantry served the food, while thousands of scarves and commemorative medals were distributed.

A coronation manifesto had promised a new beginning, with pardons to survivors of the Decembrist conspiracy thirty years earlier, and some members of the Petrashevsky Circle, a group of revolutionaries exiled during the revolutions of 1848. Thirty clauses of amnesties were read out, remissions of fines and taxes were granted on a sweeping scale, and regions which had suffered most from the war were awarded substantial tax exemptions. Though the Tsar's poorest subjects benefited most, the nobles were pleased at the removal of a punishing passport fee imposed by

Tsar Nicholas I, who had inveighed against 'purposeless travel' and tried his best to discourage it on the grounds that it fostered 'the restless spirit of our age'.

The Tsar had made a good start with his people, but some foreign observers at the ceremonies tempered their enthusiasm. Earl Granville, representing Queen Victoria at the coronation, reported at length on the new ruler:

> His usual manner is singularly gentle and pleasing. He does not give the idea of having much strength either of intellect or of character, but looks intelligent and amiable. Although the education of a Cesarwitch must be subject to pernicious influences, the present Emperor has had advantages which those in his position have not usually had. The Emperor Nicholas came to the throne without having had the confidences of his predecessor. He initiated his son into everything that was going on, while others who knew the good-nature of the Grand Duke Alexander's character, told him that which they did not tell his father. He was supposed to have different tastes from the late Emperor, but, since the death of the latter, he has liked the late Emperor's favourite residence which he himself had formerly disliked, he has taken to all the military pursuits of his father, and is said to have shown undignified haste in issuing regulations about, and in appearing in, new uniforms. He is liked by those who surround him, but is blamed for not having those habits of punctuality and of quick decision in business which characterised the late Emperor.[7]

Meanwhile, back at Balmoral, the Queen's husband Prince Albert was writing to his mentor Baron Stockmar with mixed feelings about the sovereign and his empire. The coronation he called 'an apotheosis and homage paid to the vanquished, and which cannot fail to inspire both worshipper and worshipped with dangerous illusions in regard to the real state of things'. He was suspicious of efforts being made by Russia to win French support in an anti-English coalition of Powers, and maintained that Russian financial resources were not exhausted, 'but, on the other hand, that her force in men is very much so', while conceding 'that the Emperor is well disposed to and desirous of reform'.[8]

Count Achille Murat, the French ambassador, was less critical. While the Tsar was reluctant to commit himself to a closer relationship with France, despite the hopes of Gorchakov who felt that forging a link with France might lay sure foundations for the future of Russian foreign policy, Murat informed Emperor Napoleon III that he was impressed with the new sovereign, about whom there was 'something of the spirit of old chivalry'. He struck 'none of the attitudes so beloved of his father. . . . I am convinced that he will do more good to his country within a few years than his father did throughout his whole reign.'[9]

The coronation over, Tsar Alexander II could proceed with the cause long dear to his heart – emancipation of the serfs. Both Tsars Alexander I and Nicholas I had been opposed in principle to serfdom and had made half-hearted efforts to initiate the process, but the combined opposition of officials and gentry had frustrated them at once. From his experience as president of secret committees appointed to examine the problem, he was well aware of the difficulties. At a meeting of the Moscow nobility he had declared solemnly that 'the present practice of owning souls cannot continue unchanged', and in the words of a memorandum prepared by one of his father's special committees about ten years earlier, it was better to abolish serfdom from above than to wait until the serfs began to liberate themselves from below. To seek the nobles' cooperation as widely as possible he visited the grand duchy of Finland, the kingdom of Poland and the Baltic provinces, to tell them of his intentions. Most landowners were determined to block any moves towards emancipation, on the grounds that it would be a recipe for anarchy and bankrupt the empire. Conservatives at court told him that catastrophe would surely follow liberation. His minister of the interior, Serge Lanskoy, shared his sovereign's ideals, while warning him at the end of 1856 that the landowners would not make a start, as they complained that they were 'being kept in the dark about the intentions of the government and that they are unable to formulate any independent plan of their own'.[10]

A committee set up in January 1857, comprising landowning nobles opposed to the issue under the chairmanship of Count Orlov, and pro-emancipators including Lanskoy, Count Blodov and Rostovtzev, made no progress. When Grand Duchess Helen told the Tsar that men like Prince Orlov would be the ruin of it, he replied confidently that they all knew his will and they would be too loyal to work against it. He was too optimistic, for the diehards were experienced committee members who marked time by reading reports sent from the ministry of the interior and wasting session after session in discussing trivial details, accusing the progressives of irrelevance when they attempted to focus on the matter in hand. To endow freed serfs with land, they claimed, would be premature, perilous and make a mockery of every sacred Russian tradition. Their prevaricating tactics were self-evident; at length, they opined, the Tsar would follow his predecessors' example and follow the path of least resistance.

However he was not to be underestimated, and nor were his allies on the committee. Lanskoy produced a report describing a method already adopted in the Baltic provinces where land remained the property of the gentry but the peasants' right to work it was safeguarded by legislation. He did not recommend indemnity to the owners of serfs, partly on financial grounds, partly as a matter of principle. Indemnity would be unnecessary, as the peasants would discharge their liability by payments spread over ten or fifteen years. These financial transactions might be considered as a means of enabling them to attain some self-respect. The Tsar read the report, made notes of approval in the margin, and had it sent to the secret committee. It infuriated the diehards, who felt that the principle of inculcating self-respect in the peasants and the concept of introducing 'ideas' into their minds smacked of republicanism. The Tsar received Prince Orlov's private objections with a polite but firm refusal, reminding him that the committee had sat for nine months and achieved nothing. All fruitless discussions must cease, and if Lanskoy's proposals were at odds with their own ideas, they should draft a report stating their reasons.

On his return from manoeuvres in the south of Russia in September 1857, the Tsar asked his brother Grand Duke Constantine to join the committee. Where the Tsar was unsure of himself, his younger brother was more forceful, quick-tempered, and cared not what others might think of him. Service in the army against the Hungarian rebels in 1849 and in the Crimean campaign had given him a loathing of army life and the futility of war. From then on he was a man of peace, despite his keen interest in the navy, and in political terms a progressive. Diehards on the committee knew better than to argue with the Grand Duke, but continued to use every means possible to provoke him by acting as a brake on progress. In November the Tsar decided the time had come for decisive action, and after receiving Rostovtzev, then Grand Duke Constantine, in private audience, he asked Lanskoy to have a special 'Rescript' ready in three days. The draft of the Rescript dealt with arrangements for the peasants to own their land and property by stages within a set number of years. Lanskoy was asked to have printed copies sent to the governors-general and the marshals of nobility in every province. Other committee members were furious, and Orlov made an abortive last-minute attempt to prevent copies from leaving the printers. As the Tsar had intended, the Rescript's contents were soon widely discussed in the press. Now that the more positive findings of the committee were widely known, there could be no turning back.

On New Year's Day 1858 the committee was replaced by a central group for emancipation which included only the more progressive members, namely the Grand Duke, Lanskoy, Rostovtzev, Milyutin and their allies. Even so progress was still slow, particularly as several members objected to the Grand Duke's brusque manner. Although his brother never ceased to support him, at length he decided he had had enough of 'the ignoble nobility'. Frustrated and disheartened, he departed for a relaxing cruise abroad, to return refreshed by his absence, and the brothers' joint determination for results paid off. A general plan of procedure was soon produced. The Tsar reminded the governors and provincial nobility that he deplored inaction, at the same time permitting the press to carry articles on the inevitability of emancipation. Once the serfs were assured that it was no mere fantasy, he felt – or at least hoped – that the nobles would see the wisdom of cooperation. Governors were ordered to see that the nobility within their provinces were organizing committees for preparing and submitting emancipation plans; and a central committee was created to oversee the coordination of plans and the preparation of legislation.

Now the more enlightened sections of opinion in the empire, as well as the serfs themselves, could look forward to a new era of progress. Ioann Solokov, rector of Kazan Theological Academy, declared that Russia was striving to be born again, and that the church must be prepared 'to summon all sons of the fatherland to take part and cooperate in this great undertaking of rebirth in the name of Christian truth and love'.[11] Even so many still hoped that emancipation might simply be talked out as impractical. In December 1858 Empress Marie wrote gloomily to her brother Prince Alexander that matters proceeded 'very slowly on account of the passive resistance of those in high places, and of the great prevailing ignorance. . . . The situation is very serious, and the Tsar's position very difficult, since people show little or no sympathy with him. But thank God he is not losing courage.'[12] Neither side had a monopoly on ignorance. The peasants thought that emancipation would mean living a life of ease with no financial obligations, while the nobility and landowners prophesied chaos and disorder.

The framing of the act, which took almost five years, made considerable demands on the patience and determination of the Tsar and his advisers. If it was to bring stability to Russia through a secure peasantry and a satisfied nobility, certain conditions naturally had to be met. Freed serfs needed sufficient land to sustain them, and they would be required to compensate their former landlords for land received, but not for their personal liberty. To respect the landlords' feelings, the serfs would have to work for a specified period following emancipation. They would receive their land allotments not as individuals but as members of a village commune, a conservative and stabilizing institution without whose influence liberated serfs would be totally lost in a new world way beyond the limits of their experience.

By autumn 1860 draft legislation was ready for the chief committee, and another four months had to elapse for final study and revision by the state council. It was with relief that the Tsar saw his efforts being brought to a successful conclusion, as the year had brought him much sadness. In February the faithful Rostovtzev, whose health had given way after years of hard work and anxiety at intrigues and a perpetual whispering campaign against him, took to his bed and died with his sovereign keeping vigil beside him. To the dismay of reformers the Tsar appointed in his place Count Panin, a thorough reactionary who had once publicly declared that whoever had put the idea of emancipation into his sovereign's head deserved the gallows. When Grand Duchess Helen objected, she was told that she did not really know Panin; 'his principles consist in obeying my orders'.

That same autumn the Tsar was at Warsaw for a meeting with Emperor Francis Joseph of Austria and Prince William, Regent of Prussia, in place of his brother the incapacitated King Frederick William IV, whom he would succeed on the throne within three months. The Tsar's mother, Dowager Empress Alexandra, had been in failing health for some time, when he was brought news that she had taken a turn for the worse. He hurried back to Tsarskoe-Selo and was with her when she passed away, aged sixty-two.

Progress on emancipation was aided by the illness and resignation of Prince Orlov, to be succeeded as chairman by Grand Duke Constantine. The central committee sat for the last time on 14/26 January 1861, and the Tsar publicly thanked his brother for his efforts in helping to complete the work. Two days later the Bill was sent to the council of state, and the Tsar opened the session. Although he looked tired and pale, he spoke with a firm and clear ringing voice as he voiced his intentions that the council should settle the matter within a fortnight so that it could be made public as soon as possible; 'It has aroused anxiety as well as expectations among landowners and peasants. All further procrastination will do great harm to the country.'[13]

The act was ready for the Tsar's signature on 19 February/3 March 1861, the sixth anniversary of his accession. While not prepared to accept the nobility's worst fears that the liberated serfs would celebrate with a riotous display of drunkenness and violence against their former masters, he thought it politic to withhold the news that emancipation was a *fait accompli* until after Butter Week, the Orthodox pre-Lent carnival, when Russian consumption of alcohol was generally at its greatest. At the same time he dispatched high-ranking officers from his personal suite to the provincial capitals to oversee the publicizing of the act as well as the imperial manifesto and, if there were any disorders, to take any action necessary to quell unrest.

Two days later the Emancipation Manifesto was published in Moscow and St Petersburg, and in the provinces two days later. At the same time came the first announcement of new laws under which the appanage peasants would be given tenure of the buildings they occupied, with a time limit of forty-nine years to pay for what they received.

In retrospect emancipation would be seen as the most far-reaching act of Russian legislation to take place in the nineteenth century, but at the time its reception was muted. Some Russian liberals were already generous enough to hail their sovereign as the Tsar Liberator, while others thought the pace of reform had been too slow and had granted too little. Such aspirations were echoed by a leading article in *The Times*, which remarked perceptively that emancipation was 'the first and greatest, but it cannot be the last of Russian reforms', and that an autocrat responsible for such organic change 'must expect to see it followed by a free criticism of bureaucratic abuses, and perhaps by a firm demand for a liberal Constitution'.[14]

Many of the nobles felt it was a case of too much too soon; Russia and her peoples, they said, were not ready for such a cataclysmic move. Enthusiasm was most marked at the Michael Riding School, where the Tsar read out in person the manifesto to a crowd gathered at St Petersburg to watch the changing of the guard, while elsewhere that same Sunday the proclamation was read out in all churches of the empire. When he came back to the Palace, he was greeted with ecstatic cheers from the crowds who had waited to see him. Inside the palace, he emotionally told the family that it was the happiest day of his life. However, where the manifesto was read and the act explained to provincial assemblies during the next few weeks, the mood was subdued.

The difficulties resulting from emancipation became apparent all too soon. Most of the peasants did not understand the responsibilities that ownership had conferred on them, but believed that the Tsar, their 'Little Father', had made them a gift of their land. To their dismay they were now liable for the poll tax; since the wealth of the country lay in the soil, those who worked the soil and were thus in a position to feed themselves should pay their way towards the treasury. They had not expected this, any more than they had envisaged annual payments to redeem the land, which proved to be well in excess of their former rents. To them, liberty surely meant the end of their communal commitments. Although technically free men, ironically they now found themselves in greater poverty than before. Once liberated they lost their time-honoured entitlement to timber and firewood from manorial forests, and were now denied the use of meadows and pastures which the landowners often retained in their possession. Some of the more imaginative told their peers that the real manifesto providing proper freedom was being kept from them, others believed that the true liberation would follow after another two years.

While some meekly accepted their lot, others accused government clerks of trying to rob them; riots broke out throughout the empire; peasants murdered officials and landowners alike in the belief that they were trying to steal the Tsar's gift of land from them. They were ever loyal to their *'Tsar Osvoboditel'* (Liberator), imagining that in resorting to violence they were protecting him against his enemies, the ministers, clerks and clergy who wielded power in his name and abused it. Arrests were made, and early rejoicing or eager anticipation gave way to sullen disenchantment. The worst unrest broke out at Bezdna in the province of Kazan where peasants, refusing to be pacified by the squire and priest, launched themselves on an orgy of violence, destruction and arson. When the governor-general sent forces to quell them, they offered resistance with pitchforks and scythes, which was brought to an end when the commanding officer panicked and gave orders for the soldiers to fire into the crowd. Over fifty were killed and about a hundred wounded.

As for the nobility, some of their worst fears were confirmed by an estimate that in general they had lost about one third of their land. A few were moved to speak bitterly of emancipation as an act of bureaucratic ineptitude at least, state robbery at worst. Landowners had lost their serfs and much of their lands; many whose land was heavily mortgaged were hit severely, and they found state compensation inadequate. Used to spending without a thought for the morrow, they often spent what they had and then suddenly faced ruin. Only a few had the forethought to sell up quickly and enrol in the ranks of the state bureaucracy or other professions.

Worse were the outbreaks of student unrest. At the time there were eight universities in Russia, enrolling about five thousand students between them. Moscow, with nearly one thousand, was the largest, followed by St Petersburg with seven hundred. Most students were sons of petty bureaucrats and impoverished landowners, and were of limited means. The disappointment that emancipation did not after all herald the start of a new golden age was the probable catalyst for discontent, and encouraged students to campaign for a change in the system. When riots at Kazan University had to be quelled by the police, charters were handed out to the peasants, and flysheets attacking the monarchy were distributed, the Tsar was unnerved. Despite the protests of the Empress he dismissed the liberal Evgraf Kovalevsky as minister of education and replaced him with Admiral Putiatin, a reactionary who prohibited student gatherings without the authorities' permission, and rescinded the rule that enabled poor students to enrol and study at university free of charge. Riots in autumn 1861 in St Petersburg and Moscow were put down savagely by the police, with several dozen seriously wounded. In desperation the Tsar dismissed Putiatin and replaced him with the more liberal-minded Golovnin who repealed his predecessor's measures.

The subsequent dissatisfaction and strain told on the Tsar. For five years he had fought inertia and obstruction in order to bring freedom to the peasants. That his efforts should have been so misinterpreted and produced such violence and misery in its wake embittered him. He had achieved all this, and it was being widely rejected. His health suffered, his asthma worsened, and he suffered sleepless nights broken by severe coughing. When his doctors advised a rest, he insisted on keeping to his accustomed daily routine. Every morning he took a short walk along the St Petersburg river, and those who recognized him always cheered him with enthusiasm. It was a comfort to him to see that they were glad of him, and to visitors at the Winter Palace he retained his customary geniality and courtesy, but some of those who had audiences with him found him prone to impatience, stubbornness and occasionally outbursts of sudden anger. Uneasy, indeed, lay the head that wore a crown.

3

'Majestic yet gentle authority'

The decade that brought emancipation to Russia would also see the coming of a shadow which would darken the Russian skies during the reign of Tsar Alexander II, and ultimately claim his life. In 1862 the publication of Ivan Turgenev's novel *Fathers and Sons* gave the Russian vocabulary a new word – nihilist – 'a person who does not take any principle for granted, however much that principle may be revered'. Turgenev's fictional hero Bazarov was derided by the right, who thought his creator was making him a hero and thus encouraging revolution, and by the left, who felt he was ridiculing their cause by portraying him as a caricature.

Nevertheless the name 'nihilist' soon entered everyday Russian language, especially after fires throughout St Petersburg in May 1862 laid waste to several streets of wooden tenements and squares. Turgenev visited the city one day when a market was ablaze, and a friend verbally reproached him; 'Look what *your* nihilists are doing! There is arson all over St Petersburg.' Fires lasted for more than a week, destroying timber yards and shopping arcades, threatening poorer quarters of the city where few buildings were built of stone, as well as the imperial library and Anichkov Palace. The Tsar had left for Tsarskoe-Selo, but when he learnt of the destruction he and his second son, Grand Duke Alexander, returned to the city where they spent a day helping the firemen, unrecognized by the crowds. Only towards dusk did they return to the Winter Palace, their faces, arms and uniforms blackened with soot and sweat. That evening the Tsar summoned the governor-general and ordered that all looters and those responsible for the arson were to be court-martialled. The city authorities and police, he felt, had failed in their duty, and a full inquiry into the cause of the disaster would be launched forthwith.

Thousands had been made homeless and lost everything they owned. The Semenov Palace and two other squares were turned into refugee camps on the Tsar's orders and the Empress arrived from Tsarskoe-Selo to visit them, distributing gifts to those who had suffered most. Grand Duchess Helen turned half of her palace into an improvised canteen, and several of the nobility followed her example. The Tsar transferred substantial funds from his private purse into the relief fund, and stayed in the city until everything was calm again, riding and walking about the worst stricken areas where people crowded around him.

Several tales passed from mouth to mouth about his acts of kindness. One day, walking along the Catherine Canal, he watched a boy in a tattered smock stand by a stall piled high with clothing sent by the Empress and Grand Duchesses. He stretched out his hand, turned away, slipped on the cobbles and bruised himself. The Tsar stopped to help him up and leaned him against the iron railings of the quay, wiped the blood off his knee, and asked him why he had not waited for a new shirt to be given him. Nervously the boy stammered that he knew the clothes were for the *'pogoréltzy'*, or victims of the fire, and as his house had not burnt down he would be a thief if he had taken one. Muttering a few words to his equerry, the Tsar pulled off the boy's tattered garment, put a new shirt on him, then told him gently to run home and make sure he did not fall again. 'Who are you?' the child asked. People laughed and the Tsar frowned at them as he replied, 'Your Tsar and father.'

Stung into action by their sovereign's criticism, the police made many arrests on little or no evidence, determined to find scapegoats, and seized thousands of 'subversive' pamphlets, but the inquiry established nothing. To those who advised him to introduce firmer censorship, the Tsar said he did not want any panic measures to be taken. Nevertheless he was not always dissuaded from taking action. When students at Kazan University had a requiem sung for peasants killed at the riots in Bezdna, the Tsar ordered the arrest of a professor who had made a speech after the service, and the officiating monks were sent into exile.

Unrest also broke out beyond Russian frontiers, particularly in Poland, one of the Tsar of Russia's kingdoms. Polish nationalism had flared into insurrection in 1830, but the army of Nicholas I had vanquished the rebels and ruled the country with a rod of iron. After his coronation as king at Warsaw Alexander II granted a general amnesty to Polish prisoners, and about 9,000 exiles returned to their native land from Siberia between 1857 and 1860, all with their minds set on national independence. Prince Michael Gorchakov, former commander-in-chief at the Crimea, served five years as viceroy of Poland until his death in May 1861. While he had relieved much of the pressure of Tsar Nicholas I's most oppressive Russification measures in the state, except its right to have a Polish national army and to summon a diet, nationalism had continued to thrive. After his death there was further unrest, and the appointment of General Lüders as his successor made matters worse.

The following year the Tsar replaced him with his faithful brother Grand Duke Constantine. The country was partitioned and placed under martial law, and the Tsar needed somebody whom he could trust implicitly. Only the day after his arrival in Warsaw Constantine was shot and wounded in the shoulder by a tailor's apprentice. Although the Tsar sent him a telegram ordering him to return to St Petersburg at once his brother preferred to stay, and his wife, Grand Duchess Alexandra, supported him. After his recovery the Grand Duke publicly appealed to the citizens of Warsaw to desist from violence, while his assailant was tried and hanged. 'Let there be no other execution in Warsaw,' the Grand Duke said afterwards. Even so he and the Grand Duchess were in future always escorted by Cossacks.

In July 1862 Grand Duchess Alexandra gave birth to a son in Warsaw. To please the Poles they named the boy Vacslav, but the Russians insisted that the true Russified form, Viatcheslav, should be used – a compromise which pleased neither nation.

The Tsar's second son, Grand Duke Alexander, was sent to Warsaw to stand as godfather to the child. A large, clumsy youth of seventeen, gauche, shy and ill at ease in society, he had a habit of looking at people with an embarrassed expression on his face, pulling at the collar of his uniform. Lacking in social graces, he was less inclined to stop and talk to the adults his family wanted him to meet, preferring instead to indulge in rough and tumble with his cousins. Inclined to knock things over, he was nicknamed *Kossolapy Sachka* ('clumsy Sasha'), or 'Sasha with the bear's paws'.

Constantine had a rather abrupt manner with children, and was unimpressed with him. When Alexander spilt a decanter of red wine at the dinner table his uncle scolded him, remarking 'See what a pig they have sent us from Petersburg'.[1] Overshadowed by his brilliant, much-admired elder brother Nicholas, Alexander sorely lacked self-confidence, and such teasing did nothing to help. He never forgot this insult, and for the rest of his life he bore a grudge against his uncle, who was not to know that this clumsy adolescent would be his sovereign one day, and would not hesitate to make life uncomfortable for him.

Constantine's recommendations of 're-Polonization' – more liberal state administration and local government, regulations governing the use of the Polish language, and Polish educational institutions – were well meant. However, they did not go far enough for the Polish nationalists who wanted nothing short of independence, by force if necessary. In January 1863 they slaughtered Russian soldiers asleep in their Warsaw barracks, and national resistance turned to general uprising. This spread through the kingdom into the nine formerly Polish provinces known as Russia's Western region, where powerful landlords and Catholic clergy were ready to give vent to their hatred of Russian domination. For a while it looked as if England, France and Austria might join in on the side of Warsaw after giving their tacit blessing to the rebels, but Russia put down the unrest at no little cost to the Poles, with horrifying brutalities on both sides. While the Poles butchered scores of Russian peasants including women and children, the Russians erected gibbets in the streets where rebels and civilians were hanged in their hundreds, with thousands more sent to Siberia. The insurrection was finally quelled in May 1864, when the more conservative Count Theodore Berg was sent to replace Constantine as viceroy.

Such savage reprisals were not enough to tarnish the name of the Tsar Liberator. A new education act, with measures to improve primary and secondary education, was extended to include children of the lower classes, and autonomy was restored to the universities. In January 1864 the Tsar gave the empire local self-government in the form of *zemstvos*, an undertaking estimated in importance second only to emancipation. *Zemstvos* were new provincial and district administrative bodies, their functions confined largely to local economic needs with responsibility for matters such as the building and maintenance of primary schools, roads, hospitals and clinics, welfare work, and agricultural aid. Many of the liberals optimistically saw them as a first step towards representative government, while the Tsar shared the more prosaic opinion of Peter Valuev, his minister of the interior who had overseen relevant legislation, that these bodies would be unable to undermine crown prerogatives as they would have neither legal power nor police authority. To some extent they would be merely cosmetic, a useful outlet for the ambitions and energies of people who longed for something to do, and thus help to prevent or at least reduce the growth of political discontent and agitation.

When the law received imperial approval, radical liberals were disappointed to find that there would be little democracy in the *zemstvos*, and they would be of negligible political significance, as the election of members was based on indirect and unequal suffrage, and left very much in the hands of landowners and local gentry. Others wisely recognized that any step which extended political rights, no matter how small, was better than none and that too much progress too soon would engender political instability.

Next for reform were the country's laws and judicial system, which had been subject to review since Tsar Nicholas I had appointed a committee to do so in 1850. Tsar Alexander II reconvened it in 1861 and it completed its work within three years, a decisive step towards fulfilling the Tsar's promise to provide 'the protection of law equally just to all'. Ancient courts and codes were replaced by new ones based on the institutions and principles of Anglo-Saxon and continental systems; namely, that all were equal before the law and that punishment should only be meted out for violation of existing law. Trial by jury, an independent judiciary, tenure for competent and principled judges, and an organized and self-governing bar were all introduced. A wide-reaching reform, it prompted the suggestion that at first very few, probably not even the Tsar himself, completely understood its provisions. When reminded a few years later that he could not dismiss a certain judge on grounds of personal dislike since he had signed a law making judges irremovable except on the grounds of misconduct, he asked in astonishment whether he had really signed 'such nonsense'.

Corporal punishment was abolished for civilians – peasants could no longer be flogged by landowners or police officers – and in both armed services. General Dmitri Milyutin, appointed war minister in 1862, was given responsibility for army reform, as was Grand Duke Constantine in the navy.

Censorship regulations were relaxed in 1865 without surrendering government control over what was written and read. Foreign publications were allowed into Russia, but their sale made subject to political approval, while publishers and editors were granted more freedom of judgment in choosing or rejecting materials, with provision for more judicial consideration and less arbitrary suppression of politically questionable material. Though censorship was ostensibly to be controlled by the ministry of the interior, the law did not alter the likelihood that in practice it would remain a haphazard practice implemented without much consistency. Experienced Russian publishers, editors, authors, importers and salesmen were long accustomed to the obstacle of state censorship and had found their own ways of circumventing the issue without incurring ministerial wrath. Freedom of expression, which encouraged the development of a Russian intelligentsia and a renaissance in literature, music and painting, allowed the empire to reassert her prestige and take her place alongside other countries in Europe where the fine arts were encouraged. More importantly, perhaps, the enlightened autocrat in Tsar Alexander II saw it less as a means of supporting reform for its own sake and more a way of undermining opposition to the tsarist system. Like emancipation, it was all part and parcel of permitting reform from above in order to prevent revolution from below.

Army reforms, a high priority since the end of the Crimean War, were delayed partly as the peace-loving Tsar had intended emancipation to be enacted first, partly as he wanted to keep his country out of foreign strife, and partly as reform would strain the treasury's slender means. However, progressive voices considered that change in such an unwieldy, ill-equipped, ill-trained and very expensive organization, made up mainly of men drawn from the lower classes and subjected to tyrannical discipline, was long overdue. Among these reforms was the adoption of new improved weapons and different training methods for the fighting units; developing a new system of recruitment now that serfdom, the main source of conscripts a few years earlier, was a thing of the past; and a programme of economic development to support modern military services. Milyutin's ideas, largely if sometimes reluctantly supported by the Tsar, included reorganization of personnel from the war ministry downwards; allowing privates to rise to officer rank on grounds of merit alone; training officers to exercise more humane discipline, with severe penalties for fraudulent quartermasters who attempted to sell rations and pocket the proceeds; improvement of services including engineering, provisioning, medical and military justice; a programme of education, to improve literacy in the ranks; modernization of equipment, such as replacing muskets with rifles and cast-iron cannon with steel ones; and adoption of universal conscription, making 'defence of the Fatherland' by military service the duty of all classes. Not all veteran officers agreed with him, and the Tsar occasionally took exception to some of his ideas, such as abolishing St Petersburg regiments on the grounds that their picturesque uniforms were a needless expense, but opposition generally gave way to allow the promise of effective change.

The Russian economy was stimulated by a new budget. Plans for several thousand miles of new railway track were approved; at the Tsar's accession the Russian empire's total railway mileage had comprised some 660 miles, much of it the Polish section of the line linking Warsaw and Vienna. By the time of his death, this had increased to about 14,000 miles. Permission was granted for the opening of private banks. Autonomous administration of the grand duchy of Finland was organized; assimilation of Jews was encouraged, and some anti-Jewish legislation was repealed. The arts were encouraged, by the founding in 1862 of the St Petersburg Conservatory of Music, and a similar body in Moscow later.

The Tsar was also concerned about Russia's low standing among the other Powers, caused largely by his father's arrogance and subsequent ostracism by his brother sovereigns. Only Prussia could be counted as a friend, if not a dependable ally. Prusso–Russian ties, always strong, had been strengthened by the accession of the Tsar's uncle as King William I of Prussia in January 1861, as well as the appointment of the former Prussian ambassador to St Petersburg, Otto von Bismarck, to the post of minister-president in Berlin. Relations with Austria had not improved since the Crimean War, and France was a maverick, with Emperor Napoleon prepared to give Russia support or at least pledge neutrality only when it suited him. In England Queen Victoria and her ministers distrusted Russian expansion in central Asia, a persistent threat to India and eastern trade routes.

The Tsar was gratified by Prussia's moral support during the Polish insurrection, but his gratitude was tempered somewhat by Bismarck's declaration of war on Denmark in 1864 over the duchies of Schleswig and Holstein. To him it looked like Prussia was declaring war on a comparatively powerless neighbour on the weakest of pretexts. When he asked Gorchakov to contact Berlin and ask the Russian *chargé d'affaires* to approach Bismarck, Gorchakov backed him by asserting that Russian interests in the Baltic were not best served by a partition of Denmark, leading to a united and strong Scandinavian country, and Russia would oppose it. Berlin answered evasively, and Gorchakov announced that the Tsar intended to work for a truce and conference in London. The Tsar was also disturbed as he was head of the house of Holstein-Gottorp, and announced that he was reclaiming his hereditary rights over the duchies and ceding them to the Grand Duke of Oldenburg.

In May 1864 the Tsar stopped in Berlin on his way to Kissingen and told Bismarck it was time to make peace, but Bismarck maintained that no German could be insensible to the misery of so many fellow countrymen compelled to live under the Danish yoke. Still smarting as his claims to the title had not been recognized, the Tsar said he would oppose the union of the duchies with Prussia. Yet there was nothing he could do, and when Denmark was overwhelmingly defeated a few weeks later, peace was inevitable. A partition of the duchies led to war with Austria, and the Tsar maintained to King William I of Prussia that peace terms should be submitted to a European congress. Bismarck countered this by answering that to submit the future of Prussia to the uncertainty of a European congress might provoke revolution in Berlin. The spectre of 'revolution' in a friendly capital was enough to deter the Tsar from pressing his case any further.

Notwithstanding the uncertain state of affairs at home and abroad, under Tsar Alexander II court life at St Petersburg was magnificent. The Tsar regularly hosted *Les Bals de Palmiers*, special occasions for which a hundred palm trees, specially grown at Tsarskoe-Selo, were brought to the Winter Palace in horse-drawn boxes. A supper table was laid out around every palm, to seat fifteen people, and when guests were ready the Tsar made the rounds of all. The occupants rose as he approached; he would say a few words to some of them, then pick up a piece of bread or fruit and lift a glass of champagne to his lips, so they could say that the Tsar had done them the honour of eating and drinking with them.

Observers were impressed by his demeanour and elegance on such occasions. At a court ball in 1865 the French writer Théophile Gautier described him wearing 'a white tunic reaching half way down his thighs, frogged with gold and trimmed at the neck, wrists and hem with blue Siberian fox, the breast being plastered with orders. Clinging sky-blue trousers sheathed his legs, and ended in close-fitting top-boots . . . his expression is of majestic yet gentle authority, lit up from time to time by a smile that is full of charm.'[2] Others tempered their praise with awe. The diplomat Lord Frederick Hamilton would later recall 'a wonderfully handsome man even in his old age, with a most commanding manner, and an air of freezing hauteur. When addressing junior members of the Diplomatic Body there was something in his voice and a look in his eye reminiscent of the Great Mogul addressing an earthworm.'[3] Less critically, the Prussian commander Field-Marshal Helmuth von Moltke noted: 'He has not the statuesque beauty or the marble rigidity of his father, but is an extremely handsome, majestic man. He appeared worn, and I could perceive that events had impressed a gravity upon his noble features which contrast strongly with the kind expression of his large eyes.'[4]

Within a few years of his accession, those close to the Tsar began to voice concern for his health. On his return from Warsaw in 1860 he had appeared in a state of virtual prostration, and foreign diplomats feared he might be suffering from tuberculosis. Two years later he wrote to Grand Duke Constantine that he was often seized by internal trembling when particularly stirred by anything, 'but one must control oneself, and I find prayer the best means to this end'.

In the summer of 1864 he and the family enjoyed a brief respite from cares of state, with visits to other royal courts in Germany, namely Prussia, Darmstadt and Württemberg. The Romanovs were related to most of the ruling German Kings and Grand Dukes. At Berlin the hosts were his uncle King William I and Queen Augusta of Prussia, and he was treated to the customary round of military inspections and parades. The King's daughter-in-law, Crown Princess Frederick William, thought the Tsar 'was stiff and made a far less pleasing impression on me than his wife at which I was surprised as I had expected the reverse', while she found the Empress 'kind and amiable to me; she looks delicate, is not good looking but pleasing'.[5]

In September they went to Darmstadt, the court of the recently widowed Grand Duke Louis III, elder brother of the Tsarina. His nephew's wife, Queen Victoria's second daughter Princess Alice, wrote proudly to the Queen of seven-year-old Grand Duke Serge as having 'such a passion' for her infant daughter Victoria, then seventeen months old. Alice, destined to die of diphtheria at the early age of thirty-five, would not live to see Serge become betrothed to the child which she was carrying at the time, or to see Grand Duke Alexander become godfather and eventually father-in-law to the daughter to whom she would give birth some seven years later.

Yet the first marriage to be made by a son of Tsar Alexander II would not ally them with any of the German houses, but instead the Danish. In fact the royal Danish house of Glucksburg was German through and through, although after defeat at the hands of Prussia early in 1864 Denmark would henceforth become ever more virulently anti-German.

Grand Duke Nicholas Alexandrovich, the Tsarevich, was a tall if delicate and slightly built good-looking young man. He had much of his father's temperament, with the enquiring mind of his mother. As children he and his younger brother Alexander had created their fantasy world 'Mopsopolis', portrayed in their pen and ink drawings, a city inhabited by 'Mopses', or pug dogs. During the Crimean war the English had naturally been detested at the Russian court, but the boys were wise enough not to make their satire too obvious by portraying their enemies as bulldogs instead.

As heir to the throne Nicholas was sometimes treated with severity by his father, who rather surprisingly did not show him the same understanding shown to him by his own father. Nicholas, a sensitive youth who resembled his father in adolescence in many ways, was sometimes impatiently regarded as effeminate. Perhaps the Tsar wanted to prepare him adequately for a harsh life ahead, but if this was the case, he had a rather brusque way of showing it. His mother, who saw in him a similar intellect to her own, so devoted herself to his needs that at times it seemed she might almost forget the younger children. A precocious child, his intelligence developed quickly and he asked serious questions which impressed if not disquieted his tutors. His governor Count Stroganov remarked that his maturity of thought and expression seemed almost unhealthy in one so young.

In September 1864 the Tsarevich celebrated his twenty-first birthday. The precocious youth had developed into a well-read adult with his father's liberal leanings, marked artistic interests, and a graceful manner. Altogether he had little in common with his more boisterous brothers. A certain frailty of physique only too accurately reflected his delicate health. During adolescence, according to some accounts, he had challenged one of his cousins, Prince Nicholas of Leuchtenberg, to a friendly wrestling match, in the course of which he was thrown and could not move for several minutes. According to another, he fractured his spine after falling from his horse in the riding school at Tsarskoe-Selo. Whatever the truth of the matter, his injuries came back to plague him only a few years later.*

In the summer King Christian IX of Denmark had been officially approached with a proposal for his eldest unmarried daughter, Princess Dagmar, to become engaged to the Tsarevich.

* At the time it was believed that they were responsible for the cerebro-spinal meningitis which killed him. More recent research and theories suggest that they merely aggravated the tubercular tendency which, as the *Lancet* pointed out at the time, already existed in the Romanovs. Grand Duke Alexis Michaelovich (1875–95) and Grand Duke George Alexandrovich (1871–99) were both sickly young men who died from tuberculosis in San Remo and in the Caucasus respectively where they had been sent to take advantage of the milder climate.

He gave his assent on condition that his daughter was allowed to make up her own mind after meeting him. The Tsarevich was given a photograph of her, and he kept it with him all the time. If she was less pretty than her elder sister Alexandra, who had married the Prince of Wales the previous year, Dagmar had more personality, a sharper wit and wider interests, as well as the same sense of style and love of fine clothes. Accompanied by Count Stroganov and a large suite, the Tsarevich left Russia in June 1864, and met the Danish royal family at Fredensborg, where the Princess 'shone with the freshness of her sixteen years'. The two young people were urged to wait a little longer; meanwhile the Tsarevich went to Berlin to attend manoeuvres with his father. On the previous night he suffered from severe pain in his back, and though obviously unwell he insisted on taking part in attending proceedings, but eleven hours on horseback that day left him exhausted. Hoping it did not portend anything worse, he returned to Copenhagen to propose to Princess Dagmar. Amid lavish family celebrations it was announced that they would marry in the following spring, after he had undertaken an extensive programme of cultural visits throughout the rest of Europe.

In Italy he broke his itinerary to visit his mother, who had left the fierce winter of St Petersburg and was staying on the Riviera. She had brought the younger children with her, and a childish letter from eleven-year-old Grand Duchess Marie to the Tsar still survives:

> Today the weather was fine and we walked and drove with Mama. Yesterday was cold and Mama only walked on foot, we were on the hill by our house. Mama went by road and I went on the narrow path with Sergei, and we were much faster on the higher path than Mama. . . . I hope that Nixa [the Tsarevich] will soon come to us and will stay for a long time. I think that the Winter Palace is very empty, and will be terribly dull for Christmas and Easter, and I'm also very upset that I won't be with you on Sunday, walking and driving in a stately carriage, this time we will pick violets and other flowers.[6]

The Tsarevich's back pain had returned with a vengeance, and he was confined to bed for several weeks while being treated for an abscess. Officially he had nothing more than rheumatism and perhaps a touch of malaria, but with his increasing headaches and sickness the family began to fear the worst. He was too weak to return home, and already disagreements between doctors and specialists as to the exact nature of his illness were giving cause for alarm.

By the new year of 1865 he was evidently losing ground. At the Villa Diesbach, Nice, he was examined by two physicians who saw nothing dangerous in his condition, but in March he complained that the terrible noise of waves on the shore made it impossible for him to sleep. As the sea was merely lapping on the beach, this acute sensitivity to sound was a bad sign. He was moved further inland to the Villa Bermond, but by Easter it was clear that nothing could save him. Many sorrowing relations, including Princess Dagmar and members of her family, flocked to his bedside. The Tsarina would not leave him, and her ladies-in-waiting were so overwrought that Count Stroganov ordered brusquely that those who could not control themselves were to leave forthwith. Among them was Princess Marie Meshchersky, who was romantically linked with the Tsarevich's brother, Grand Duke Alexander. If she had entertained hopes of becoming Grand Duchess Alexander, or leading him in the footsteps of the Tsarina's wayward brother Prince Alexander of Hesse, now she foresaw that unless medical science could perform a miracle, such hopes would surely come to nothing.

When the Tsar arrived at the villa, the Tsarina woke Nicholas to tell him. He kissed her hand, taking each finger in turn, and asked her what she would do without him. As it was the first time he had spoken of death, his father knelt by the bed, weeping silently. The next day Dagmar hardly left his bedside, arranging his pillows and stroking his hand, talking softly all the time. One of the ladies of the imperial household in attendance described how the Tsarevich took communion with her, and while reading his prayers he took the communion cloth and pressed it close to his heart. After the improvised service, 'his poor dying face was filled with tears and so lit up with joy that the priest said he had never seen a dying person so radiantly happy.'[7]

On the evening of 12/24 April, as Russian sailors and French infantry and cavalry mounted a silent vigil outside the villa, family, suites and doctors filled the room. A group of clergymen chanted prayers for the dying as the thin, wasted twenty-one-year-old heir slipped away. To the sorrowing relatives, his death from cerebro-spinal meningitis was surely a relief after 'eight days of agony constantly fluctuating between hope and despair'. Another lady of the household present wrote of the parents' 'long and heartrending goodbye to their child . . . I was envious of everything, of them and him, and to have had a child whom they had loved so much, and who had loved them so much, to be so loved in death . . . they are to be envied even in these moments of supreme grief, and that it is sorrowful to see the coffin and feel that death is not the greatest loss that awaits us.'[8]

For some years, since (if not before) the birth of their youngest child Paul in 1860, the Tsar and Tsarina had been growing apart from each other. Mutual devotion to their delicate eldest son had helped to keep them together. The Tsarina was distraught at his death, perhaps feeling a sense of guilt for having passed her weak constitution on to the son who had been educated to succeed to the imperial throne. That her younger sons were tough, healthy and for the most part heavily built strapping young men could not console her.

Her husband was so grief-stricken that for a while he seemed almost a stranger to those about him. A girl watching the family funeral procession from a ground floor window of the Marble Palace observed his 'erect shoulders, firmly set mouth and sad eyes', and was shocked at the contrast with his appearance a few days later when he left Kazan Cathedral after a requiem. 'His shoulders were bent, and he walked so slowly that we all felt as though his loss had robbed him of all his strength.'[9]

Legend has it that on his deathbed the Tsarevich had taken his brother Alexander's hand and that of his betrothed, and joined them together to signify his last wish. This sentimental tale owes its existence to a mistranslation of the memoirs of Prince Vladimir Petrovich Meshchersky, an official companion to the Tsarevich who had accompanied him on his travels throughout Russia and Europe. Translated into English, his prose states that as he was dying the young man 'transferred trust and love to the new heir of the crown'. This has been misconstrued to suggest that he had transferred his 'beloved' to the new heir.*

There is more truth in the prosaic explanation that Dagmar, knowing what was expected of her, dutifully transferred her affection to the new Tsarevich. Though the two young people may not have been in love with each other yet, Alexander's willingness to fall in with family plans may have owed as much to natural inclination as duty. Perhaps he had been slightly jealous of the ease with which this charming young princess had come to his brother. At the time of her sister Alexandra's engagement, in England Queen Victoria had looked with concern on the Prince of Wales's brother Alfred, whom she felt was too taken with 'Alix' for their liking and had let it be known that if her brother had refused this jewel he would be more than happy to marry her himself. If Alexander was in love with Princess Meshcherschky, he was also sensible enough to appreciate that even as a second son of the sovereign, he would never be allowed to make such a marriage. Now he was the eldest surviving son and heir, he needed no prompting as to the path of duty.

Countess Alexandrine Tolstoy wrote of his misery, and of the general expectation that he would marry the princess who had almost become a widow before she was a wife: 'He speaks of his brother, of his last memories of him, of his illness, of mistakes which have been made in the treatment of the illness, in such a heartrending manner. . . . With a heart so profoundly and loyally loving, a nature so upright, he has nothing to fear from the hereafter. God willing, he will marry this enchanting little Princess Dagmar.'[10]

Dagmar herself obviously felt that events were beyond her control. With hindsight Grand Duke Alexander Michaelovitch, who was not born until the following year, felt that fate had dealt her a heavy blow. The gods, he wrote, from his rather jaundiced viewpoint as a post-Revolution exile in the early 1930s who had been glad to

* A broadly similar case occurred in 1892 in England when Albert Victor, Duke of Clarence, died a few weeks after his betrothal to Princess May of Teck. Muttered allusions to the coincidence by some of her elder relatives proved self-fulfilling when she became engaged to the Duke's far more satisfactory brother Prince George, later King George V.

shake off his imperial past, 'went out of their way to warn Marie [the name she subsequently took]'. After the death of Grand Duke Nicholas, 'a superstitious person would have rushed back home and tried to marry one of the fifty available heel-clicking German reigning Princes', but for the dynastic ambitions of her father who looked to his daughters to add to the family's prestige, to say nothing of 'a friendly Fleet and a friendly Army'.[11] Be that as it may, it was destined to become one of the most successful Romanov marriages of all, in which mutual respect and a determination to do their dynastic duty ripened into genuine devotion.

Even as the Tsarevich Nicholas was dying, a rumour went round Moscow and St Petersburg that the Tsar thought his second son unworthy to take his brother's place and intended to nominate his third son Vladimir as successor instead. Such a course of action, it was said rather unconvincingly, had its precedent in the choice of Grand Duke Nicholas, later Tsar Nicholas I, in preference to his elder brother Constantine. The Tsar soon dispelled any doubt on the subject by confirming that his eldest surviving son was to be his heir. Soon after returning to his capital he called upon his subjects to take an oath of allegiance to the new Tsarevich, Grand Duke Alexander. He also received a deputation of Polish nobles who had come to convey their condolences on the death of his eldest son. After delivering them a stern address on the political sins of their compatriots who had agitated for independence, he presented the new Tsarevich to them, saying that he bore the name of the Tsar who had formerly established the kingdom of Poland; 'I hope he will know how to govern his inheritance worthily, and that he will not endure that which I myself have not tolerated.'[12] Whether the Tsar seriously considered the possibility of excluding him from the succession is questionable.

Brought up as a soldier, observed one anonymous contemporary, 'without any political education, with a poor knowledge of languages for a man in his position, and with a disposition more given to self-indulgence than to work, the new heir-apparent found that time was above all things necessary to adapt himself to the altered state of things'.[13]

Little attention had been paid to his education so far; as he was not heir to the throne his tutors had made no special effort to groom him as a future sovereign. They had regarded him as unpromising material, sluggish and ponderous beside his quick-witted brother. The Tsarevich had always been painstaking and desperate to please, but mentally he was slow and tended to take life too seriously. Uncomely, uncouth, and bad-tempered, he was spoken of as the ugly duckling of the family, lacking in manners, all too keen to fight, clumsy, knocking against everything, upsetting chairs or anything else unfortunate enough to be in the way. Court officials had always slighted or ignored him, and it must have given him satisfaction to consider that now he would be treated with more respect. Even Constantine Pobedonostsev, later to become a trusted friend and counsellor, had always praised the natural gifts of the late Tsarevich, while lamenting that his brother Alexander 'had been so badly misused by Nature, who sent him into the world with the shabbiest of intellectual outfits'.[14]

In order to groom him as his successor, Tsar Alexander II introduced him as an observer into meetings with his ministers and councillors, while the tutors redoubled their efforts. None made greater efforts or exerted more influence than Pobedonostsev, who took it upon himself to convince him of his duty to respect and defend the Tsarist autocracy.

Another influence on the Tsarevich – again, not perhaps for the best – was that of Meshchersky, six years his senior. Having made the acquaintance of Tsar Alexander II and his family at the Crimea in 1861, he had become one of the select circle around the Grand Dukes. Between him and the late heir there had always been a certain tension, and Grand Duke Nicholas had once called Meshchersky's attitude towards him 'the feeling of unhappy love for a woman who responds to it with indifference'.[15] He had chosen his words perceptively, for the man's homosexuality was later to cause the imperial court problems. Nevertheless the bonds of friendship between him and the new heir to the throne became ever tighter, and a few months later Alexander could write to him assuring him of his friendship 'for all the torments and troubles you have suffered for my sake'. Between them they produced a hardworking, conscientious Tsar-in-waiting, though it would ultimately be a misfortune for the Romanov dynasty that there was no Zhukovsky of his generation to inculcate something of his father's liberalism in the young man.

4

'Deep in his soul he is a despot'

In the private life of Tsar Alexander II 1865 was a crucial year. Not only did he lose his eldest son and heir; he also began an extra-marital affair which would in time alienate him from most of his family.

Some years earlier he had befriended Michael Dolgorouky, a courtier and landowner, who had put his house at his disposal in the summer of 1857 when he was in southern Russia on manoeuvres and attacks of asthma prevented him from sleeping under canvas. A notorious spendthrift, Dolgorouky died soon afterwards, leaving his family almost penniless. The Tsar undertook to become the children's official guardian and to provide for their education, sending the sons to military academies and the daughters to the Smolny Institute, a finishing school founded by Catherine the Great. Before long people began to notice that the Tsar was visiting the Smolny more and more frequently, and that the reason was the presence of the Dolgorouky sisters – or more particularly Catherine, the elder and prettier.

When they left they went to live with their eldest brother Michael and his wife. The younger sister, Marie, was soon married. Catherine, who celebrated her eighteenth birthday in 1865, was often invited to balls and receptions in the capital, and the Tsar always seemed to be paying her attention. Like his father and indeed most previous Tsars of Russia, he had had casual shortlived affairs, but mistresses came and went. It was taken for granted that Catherine Dolgorouky, nearly thirty years his junior, would be the next. Although he made his feelings clear to her she was careful enough to behave with circumspection at first, and sufficiently level-headed to refrain from leading him on. The last thing she wanted was to be the target of a brief infatuation and then discarded.

Almost unnoticed the Tsar and Tsarina were drifting apart. Contrary to Romanov tradition he had married for love, and to some extent it had been a match of opposites. His leisure activities hardly went beyond hunting, riding and, despite his abhorrence of war, military manoeuvres. She was a well-educated German princess who was not content to abandon her own preferences and prejudices at court, her intellectual interests, love of poetry evenings in her apartments, liberal views and suspicion of her father-in-law's reactionary ministers, and her insistence on engaging English nurses for the children. Never popular in Russia, she became less so over the years. Her failing health, her inability to bear the rigours of a northern winter and subsequent visits to her homeland at Darmstadt, a rather schoolmistress-like insistence that the obstacles which her husband met in his moods of black depression were there to be overcome, and above all a vaguely perceptible air of martyrdom, drove a wedge between them. Despite her Protestant birth she had become more ardently Orthodox, ready to fall under the influence of her father-confessor, Bashanov, bearing her humiliation with fortitude, finding compensation in her devotion to the Russian Church. She still worshipped her husband, but without understanding him. The once attractive, lively young princess had become a sickly, pious, sentimental, querulous woman, often confined to her apartments for weeks.

While there was no question of a public split, it left the Tsar open to temptation from a mistress, especially one intelligent and sympathetic enough to be something of a soulmate as well as one who could satisfy the desires of the flesh. Even so, any such affair might be no shortlived fling, but develop into a liaison which could only result in embarrassment and scandal. Some saw a connection between the death of the son on whom the Tsar had pinned his hopes and the beginning of his extra-marital relations, looking at the 'shining void between his working office and the cell-like bedroom with its camp bed', filled by the docile, beautiful, yet determined figure of Catherine Dolgorouky, who 'alone could give him new life'.[1]

This golden age of Tsar Alexander II, as some historians have dubbed it, was drawing to a close. After he had reigned for ten years, a decade which had seen several far-reaching and overdue if often contentious reforms, he was losing his enthusiasm for progress. Grand Duke Constantine, whose liberal policies had been discredited by the Polish revolt, found it increasingly hard to obtain an audience with his brother. Grand Duchess Helen was likewise tainted by her sympathy for the Poles, and by the assertions of a fanatic official that she kept up a clandestine correspondence with Alexander Herzen, the exiled propagandist who had lived in London since 1851. The social consciousness of the Tsarina, once an enthusiast for reforms and a steady influence on her husband, had given way to increasing preoccupation with her children, her religious devotion, and her failing health.

That he was charting a dangerous course between pressure from the right and the left became clear in 1865, when delegates to the Moscow provincial assembly of the nobility voted overwhelmingly to present an address congratulating him on the creation of the *zemstvos* and formally petitioning him to complete the task by summoning a general assembly of elected representatives from throughout Russia to discuss the common needs of the entire state. This assembly, which the nobility would choose from the most capable people available, would be the logical culmination of governmental reforms undertaken since His Majesty's accession to the throne.

In reply he declared that he did not refuse to give up any of his powers from motives of petty ambition, and that he would sign any constitution they liked, if he felt it was for the good of Russia, but to take such action in haste would run the risk of Russia falling apart at once. The right to consider and initiate reforms, he reminded them, was his exclusive prerogative, as an autocrat whose power was derived solely from God. No group of persons was entitled to speak on behalf of others. As Tsar of all the Russias he and he alone, through his ministers, could order matters for the common good. This firm reply did not prevent the assemblies of the nobility from continuing to ask for a representative imperial body, and other *zemstva* which came into being followed their lead. Several ministers and other politicians came to his defence, arguing that he had already relaxed controls too much and that to yield any more would invite chaos and anarchy. As an example they pointed to Poland where, they said, a policy of granting concessions had failed, and the same would surely happen elsewhere throughout the empire.

The arch-conservatives soon had their chance. On 4/16 April 1866 Dmitri Karakozov, a member of a self-styled terrorist cell within a student revolutionary organization, made an attempt on the life of the Tsar. He was returning to his carriage after a walk in the gardens of the Winter Palace when Karakozov pushed his way through a group of sightseers, produced a revolver and fired a single shot. One of the bystanders, Ossip Ivanovich Komissarov, a hatter's apprentice, struck at the man's hand and the bullet embedded itself in the pavement. Karakozov made no effort to escape, and was handed over to the police. The apprentice was rewarded personally by the Tsar with a diamond ring and a generous pension.

This assassination attempt resulted in warm demonstrations of loyalty. Crowds lined the streets to the Winter Palace, and people wept as the Tsar rode past to acknowledge his thanks, or crowded into churches to give thanks for their sovereign's deliverance. The government of the United States of America, which had lost its own president by the hand of an assassin but twelve months earlier, sent a message to express joy that danger to the ruler's life had been 'averted by Providence'. His attacker was interrogated for several weeks but gave no hint of a conspiracy, insisting that he had acted alone in order to try and draw attention to the plight of the peasants, and went to the gallows.

It was enough to convince the Tsar, or at least his advisers, that something must be wrong with the educational system. The reformers and his more progressive-minded allies, among them Grand Duke Constantine and General Milyutin, argued that there was no need for alarm. To attempt to stifle public opinion, curtail reforms, or tighten state control because of one incident would be a sign of panic. However, the more outspoken reactionaries, including Count Dmitri Tolstoy, former over-procurator of the Holy Synod, and Prince Paul Gagarin, chairman of the committee of ministers, saw in the assassination attempt proof of their conviction that reforms had gone too far and the government, even the state, was threatened by anarchy. The Tsar, they said, must strengthen the police, tighten censorship, overhaul the educational system, and intensify Russification, free from the taint of western theories of personal liberty.

Some of the peasants thought Karakozov's action was the result of a conspiracy of dissatisfied landlords intent on killing the sovereign and then rescinding his emancipation measures. Reactionaries began intriguing against so-called 'peasant lovers' in high places whom they declared were inciting the peasants against the nobility. The Tsar, some sensed, was not the enlightened soul he had wished to appear. At the time of emancipation General Alexander Timashev, the chief of staff of gendarmes, spoke with sadness of the personal devotion he had had for Tsar Nicholas I, and which he could not extend to his eldest son. 'For his principles, yes; for his person, no. The Emperor deludes himself about what is happening. Deep in his soul he is a despot.'[2]

The Tsar privately confessed as much only a few months later. Otto von Bismarck, then Prussian minister in St Petersburg, reported a long conversation with him in a despatch to Berlin in November 1861 in which he said with conviction that 'to abdicate the absolute power with which his crown was invested would be to undermine the aura of that authority which has dominion over the nation. The deep respect, based on an innate sentiment, with which right up to now the Russian people surrounds the throne of its Emperor cannot be parcelled out. I would diminish without any compensation the authority of the government if I wanted to allow representatives of the nobility or the nation to participate in it.' What, he ended by asking, would become of relations between the peasants and the lords if his authority 'was not still sufficiently intact to exercise the dominating influence'?[3]

He was increasingly weary of criticism from all sides. A report submitted to him at this time drew attention to the fact that many members of revolutionary circles were students, implying that the responsibility for this was Russian education. The new middle-class intelligentsia, it was claimed, had no roots in the land; if atheism, materialism and socialism did not come naturally to them, they were corrupted by unreliable teachers and the radical press. Shortly afterwards he dismissed the liberal Count Alexander Golovnin as minister of education, after accepting that his laxity had allowed students to develop seditious ideas. His successor was Count Tolstoy, who issued a rescript requiring alterations in the school and university curricula. Education, he declared, must be directed 'to respect the spirit of religious truth, the right of property, the fundamental principles of public order; and that in all schools the open and secret teaching of those destructive conceptions which are hostile to the moral and material well-being of the people will be forbidden'.[4] The materialistic approach of nihilism and other revolutionary creeds was thought to come from the popularization of natural science, and greater emphasis should be placed on the classics. Subjects which stimulated independent thought, like history, science, modern languages and even Russian, were curtailed, and students were encouraged to learn Latin, Greek, pure mathematics and Church Slavonic instead. At the same time a few extreme left publications were closed down. Many frustrated undergraduates soon moved to Geneva or Zurich, where they could study a wider curriculum and also listen freely to professional agitators and anarchists.

In the autumn of 1866 Princess Dagmar of Denmark arrived at St Petersburg to prepare for her new role as wife of the heir to the imperial throne. One of her first appearances in public was a visit to the cathedral in the fortress of St Peter and St Paul to lay a wreath on the white marble tomb of the man to whom she had been betrothed but briefly. On being received into the Orthodox Church soon afterwards, she took the name and title of Grand Duchess Marie Feodorovna.

The wedding took place on 28 October/9 November 1866 in the Winter Palace chapel, with the bride in a dress of silver tissue, a train of silver brocade lined with ermine, sparkling with jewels, and the Tsarina placed the special diamond nuptial crown on her head. As a 21-gun salute thundered out over the city the Tsarevich, attired in the blue and silver uniform of his Cossack regiment, led her through a succession of crowded galleries to the Palace church for the marriage ceremony.

The splendour of the imperial court into which Princess Dagmar of Denmark married was a revelation for the bride, who was leaving one of the poorest countries of Europe for one of the richest. Her parents, King Christian IX and Queen Louise of Denmark, may have been sovereigns, but expense kept them from making the journey to St Petersburg to be with her on this special day, and they sent their eldest son Frederick, the Crown Prince, instead. Denmark's treasury, never full at the best of times, had been further depleted by defeat during the war with Prussia of 1864. Also present was the bride's brother-in-law the Prince of

Wales, on his own, as the Princess of Wales was expecting a third child and unable to travel herself. Queen Victoria had to be persuaded to let her eldest son travel to St Petersburg for the occasion, and she only assented with extreme reluctance, telling her ministers that the government greatly overrated the political importance of his presence. Having conceded, she stood firm on a suggestion from the Tsar's ambassador at the court of St James, Baron Brunnow, that His Majesty would be 'greatly flattered and pleased' to receive the Order of the Garter, as such a gesture would surely help to renew cordial relations with Russia which had been interrupted by the Crimean War. She refused on the grounds that she had never given the Garter to any other sovereigns except on their visits to England, or 'in very exceptional circumstances'. The Prince of Wales's genial manner made him popular at St Petersburg, but Queen Victoria's attitude cast something of a shadow over his presence.

The composer Tchaikovsky was commissioned to write a Festival Overture based on the Danish national anthem dedicated to the Tsarevich and Tsarevna on the occasion of their marriage. It was given its premiere in January 1867, thus beginning a career of imperial patronage which would last until Tchaikovsky's death nearly thirty years later. For his work he was presented with a pair of jewelled cufflinks, which he sold almost at once to pay off some of his debts.

After his son's marriage the Tsar showed less interest in ensuring that the young man was given appropriate experience in government and an understanding of his future responsibilities. This was partly the result of family divisions following the estrangement of the Tsar and Tsarina. The heir had always been closer to his mother, and resenting Catherine Dolgorouky's presence, he treated his father with increasing coldness. Never the most original of thinkers himself, the heir was easily influenced by his mother's confessor Father Bashanov and the ambitious arch-conservative Pobedonostsev, who impressed on him that reform was a dangerous thing and that the autocracy must be preserved at all costs.

The Tsarevich was also easily drawn into the prevalent anti-German movement, which found sympathy and encouragement from the Tsarevna. What the Germans had done with the Elbe duchies of Schleswig and Holstein, it was feared, they could do to the Baltic provinces. A story was told that, soon after assuming command of the Preobrajensky regiment, a list of its officers was read out to him. His face grew longer and longer with the recital of one German name after another, until his reader reached the letter W – and read out 'Woronzov'. 'Thank God for Woronzov!' he exclaimed.

Catherine Dolgorouky had resisted the Tsar's amorous advances for over a year, but her distress after the attempt on his life in 1866 brought home to her just how much he really meant to her. In January 1867 the affair became widely known. Rumours that she had a miscarriage at the palace, with the Tsar acting as nurse or even midwife and sending panic-stricken for a doctor, can be discounted; the more likely catalyst was an indiscreet rendezvous in St Petersburg. A few of the Tsar's ministers, who knew but agreed to maintain discretion, disliked or suspected her manner and her increasing influence over him. Any ministers who might be dismissed immediately remembered that she had been 'cold' to them. When the news leaked out Princess Michael Dolgorouky, determined to have no part of it, told her sister-in-law that her presence in St Petersburg was doing family and country great harm and she would have to leave. She submitted meekly, writing a farewell letter to the Tsar as she left for Naples. The Tsar respected her decision to go, knowing that if she felt strongly enough for him she would return. In fact she could never stay away for long, and she would send him anguished telegrams signed 'Hoffman' from the Polish border assuring him not only of her safe arrival, but that she still loved him devotedly; 'my heart flees to you.'

When he accepted an invitation from Emperor Napoleon III to attend the International Exhibition in Paris in the spring of 1867, he wrote to her at Naples asking her to meet him there. Although his sons Grand Dukes Alexander and Vladimir were accompanying him, he considered that discretion could be upheld. Napoleon had despatched invitations to eighty sovereigns, rulers and leading royalties, and only Queen Victoria and the Pope declined. Where Russia was concerned, he hoped for an entente in order to contain the German threat to his uncertain empire. His hopes of courting the Tsar were not helped at a review at Longchamps, when 30,000 French troops paraded before the Tsar and King William of Prussia, and a Polish *emigré* aimed a shot at their carriage. The bullet missed the Tsar, though nobody doubted that it was intended for him; the leader of the escort dashed forward in time and the bullet wounded his horse. While the Tsar and his sons remained calm, the Emperor almost fainted. Recovering his composure, he embraced the Tsar, telling him that they had been under fire together, but the Tsar was not impressed. Only the entreaties of Empress Eugénie, pale and shaking, dissuaded him and the Grand Dukes from leaving forthwith.

The French took the Romanovs to their hearts, impressed with their great height, good looks, their impeccable French, calling them excellent riders and dancers, and well accomplished in the art of *'petites politesses'*. Catherine Dolgorouky was staying at an hotel and the Tsar met her secretly, persuading her to return to Russia. While there was some knowing gossip about *'la belle Princesse Russe'*, open comment and scandal there was none, as she was careful not to be seen in public. As one observer of society life, Hermione Poltoratzky, put it in a letter to her brother Albert in London, 'She appears nowhere and there has been very little talk'.[5] Regrettably, there had been enough to render the Tsar *persona non grata* for the time being at the court of St James in London. The Prince of Wales was anxious to make some tangible expression of gratitude for his friendly reception at St Petersburg the previous winter, and thought it would be politic to stretch forth the hand of friendship to Russia. The prime minister, the Earl of Derby, wrote respectfully to Queen Victoria that he agreed with the Prince of Wales's regret that it had not been possible to invite the Tsar, if only for two or three days; 'a very unfavourable impression may be produced on his Imperial Majesty's mind by the contrast between the flattering reception which he will undoubtedly meet with at Paris, and the total absence of any recognition from this country'.[6] Officially the reason was that the Queen was in Scotland, but those in the know suspected that she had taken offence at the fact that Catherine Dolgorouky had also been in Paris at the same time.

Soon after his return to Russia the Tsar established her in her own residence in St Petersburg, where neither his family nor the public could ignore their liaison any longer. The Tsarina knew that she no longer had his undivided affection, but she attached no importance to what she thought (or hoped) was mere infatuation. Tsars had generally been unfaithful to their wives, and she probably expected him to tire of Catherine before long. She was the soul of discretion, shunning society and refusing to associate with those who would gladly have used her as an intermediary to gain favours from the Tsar.

During the Franco–Prussian War, the sympathies of Tsar Alexander II were firmly on the side of Germany, as were those of the court and ministers, while those of his heir – who had never regarded himself as bound by family ties to the Hohenzollerns – lay with France. In June 1870, as the clouds of war were gathering, the Tsar was taking the waters at Ems. He and his suite occupied a fashionable hotel, while Princess Catherine Dolgorouky was installed in a neighbouring villa. The Tsar freely confided in her, telling her, as the diplomat Maurice Paléologue would later write, 'secrets which the French government would have paid heavily to know'. When ministers in Paris allowed themselves to be provoked by Prussian chicanery, he triumphantly told her that he had been right all along; 'in this business all the blame lies with France'.[7]

Like the heir, many sections of Russian opinion supported France. The newspapers were mostly hostile to Prussia, and some Russians volunteered to fight for France; large sums of money were subscribed; Red Cross workers and field ambulances went out to help the French wounded. On hearing of French capitulation at Sedan the Tsar gave a grand banquet at Moscow in celebration, and subsequently awarded the Cross of St George to the victorious Moltke. Even so, the speed of the Prussian victory and subsequent hegemony of Bismarck's Berlin gave him food for thought. But when the war ended with the establishment of the Commune, the Tsarevich considered himself vindicated, muttering wearily, 'It is to this, then, that all these ideas lead?'[8]

In May 1872 Princess Dolgorouky gave birth to a son, whom they named George. At around the same time the Tsarina's doctors confirmed that her recurring indisposition was tuberculosis, and she did not have long to live. While the Tsar was solicitous towards her he no longer confided in her as he did before. He seldom went to her apartments in the Winter Palace except to fetch her to dinner. She adored him still and was bitterly hurt by his infidelity; she said she could forgive the insult to the Empress, but not the cruelty to the wife. Always religious, now she became more deeply concerned with mysticism and embraced the Church with fervour, attending mass two or even three times a day. She spent increasing amounts of time abroad, at Nice, or in her native Germany, at Karlsruhe, Darmstadt or Kissingen or at Livadia in the south. Serge and Paul remained with her much of the time to comfort her.

In November 1873 Catherine gave birth to a daughter, Olga. Eight months later the Tsar signed a secret *ukaz* to the Senate, by which his children by Catherine were raised to the rank of Prince and Princess with the title of Highness and given the patronymic of Alexandrovich, which amounted to official recognition of his paternity.

The Tsar lived mostly in his large study below the Tsarina's apartments. He slept on a camp bed, when he slept at all; asthma often prevented him from doing so, and he preferred to work at his desk through several nights at a time, rather than lying down. Though he had previously been a very light drinker, now it was rumoured that he drank heavily.

The family was fiercely divided. His brothers, bred in the tradition of Nicholas I, would not permit the least criticism of their sovereign, even in the most intimate family circle, but their wives considered themselves unbound by any such restraint. As for his sons, they were devoted to their mother and deeply resented the wound that the affair caused her. Apart from Alexis, who was very much under the influence of his uncle Constantine and evidently shared the same relaxed moral code, saying he did not see why a mistress should create a gulf between father and son, and Paul, too young to understand but young enough to be shielded by the others from the unhappy state of their parents' marriage, they did not accept the situation. If the Tsarina had to recognize that this was no ordinary liaison, her sons were furious with this callous violation of their father's marriage vows, and the intense misery he was causing her. They refused to conceal their disapproval, and became increasingly aloof towards him.

Only their sister Marie, who had always been especially close to her father, avoided taking sides. Though she was devoted to both her parents, as yet she could not find it in her heart to blame him for anything, believing that as their father and Sovereign he should be beyond criticism.

Meanwhile the fourth of the young Grand Dukes, Alexis, seemed equally prepared to flout convention. As a youth he had been considered the best-looking of his brothers, 'the Beau Brummell of the family', until the life of a *bon vivant* wrought havoc with his waistline. His elder brothers had likewise become portly in their love of the good things of life, though the two youngest, the more ascetic Serge and Paul, remained slender to their dying days. Alexis fell in love with Alexandra Zhukovsky, daughter of his father's former tutor. Matrimony between them was out of the question, at least on Russian soil, although it was rumoured that they married in Italy in 1870 when he was aged twenty, and that the marriage was never recognized in Russia and later annulled. A son, Alexis, was born in November 1871, given the name Baron Seggiano, and in March 1884 became Count Alexis Alexeievich Belevsky-Zhukovsky.

Ostensibly to broaden his experience in the navy as a young lieutenant, but in fact to keep him away from unsuitable liaisons, Grand Duke Alexis was sent to undertake a tour of America. Serving on the warship *Svetlana*, he arrived in New York in 1871 to an enthusiastic reception including a procession up Broadway with bands and national guardsmen, the bells of Trinity Church chiming *God save the Tsar*, and a sign on the Astor House hotel welcoming the 'Son of a noble father, representative of this nation's dearly cherished ally'. The Russian Baltic Fleet had visited America in 1863, showing Russian solidarity with the American Union at a time when Britain and France were inclined to recognize the Confederacy instead. The pilot who guided the *Svetlana* into North River was disappointed to see an ordinary-looking young lieutenant standing watch, exclaiming that he was 'no more royal than I am', until it was pointed out to him that the Grand Duke had to take his turn on watch like all the other officers.

Although Alexis was taken aback by the Americans' overwhelming enthusiasm for European royalty, he enjoyed himself on visits to major cities including Washington, Philadelphia, Boston and Chicago, with invitations to grand receptions, factories and local landmarks. Most exciting of all was the wild west, where he shared a bottle of whisky with Buffalo Bill Cody, went buffalo hunting with General Custer, and was almost charged by an angry bull in Colorado which sidestepped six bullets from his revolver.

Returning across America eastwards via Memphis and New Orleans, he rejoined the *Svetlana* at Florida, circumnavigated the Horn, and sailed round Japan and the coast of China.

Between 1868 and 1882 the Tsarevich and Tsarevna had four sons and two daughters. The eldest, Nicholas, destined to succeed his father on the throne, was born on 6/18 May 1868. Next came two sickly brothers, Alexander and George. According to their cousin, Grand Duke Alexander Michaelovitch, 'an ignorant nurse and a negligent physician were responsible for Nicholas II wearing the crown, having overlooked the illness that attacked his elder brother, a lusty infant'.[9]* Alexander, born on 26 May/7 June 1869, developed a severe cold and cough which developed into pneumonia, and he died on 20 April/2 May 1870.

George, born on 27 April/9 May 1871, developed consumption in adolescence, but survived to the age of twenty-eight. Fortunately the remaining three children, Xenia, Michael and Olga, all enjoyed the best of health and survived to maturity.

To outside observers the Tsar and Tsarina could still keep up a façade of closeness and informality. The family regularly visited Livadia, their 'garden of Eden', a summer palace in the Crimea which the Tsar had purchased in 1860 on medical advice as the mild climate would be better for the tubercular Tsarina than St Petersburg. An American traveller in 1867 noted his reception at the palace, where 'we assembled in the handsome garden, for there was no room in the house able to accommodate our three score persons comfortably. The Imperial family came out bowing and smiling and stood in our midst. With every bow His Majesty said a word of welcome. All took off their hats and the Consul inflicted an address on him. He thanked us and said that he was very much pleased to see us. . . . Everybody talks English. The Emperor wore a cap, frock coat and pantaloons, all of some kind of plain white drilling, and wore no jewellery or any insignia whatever of rank. No costume could be less ostentatious.'[10]

The Tsar had always been deeply attached to his daughter Marie, who had filled the gap left by the death of the sister whom

*This error, that of stating that Alexander was the firstborn, has been perpetuated by several biographers since.

she had never known. In fact she had almost gone the same way at the age of seven at Tsarskoe-Selo from a disease of the pharynx, probably acute angina laryngea. He dreaded the thought of her leaving Russia, even when Queen Victoria's second son Alfred, Duke of Edinburgh ('Affie'), asked him for her hand in marriage. He had first met Marie on a family visit to Jugenheim, Germany, in the summer of 1868; though she was only fifteen at the time, she made a tremendous impression on him and soon afterwards he told the Queen that he intended to marry her. The Queen had reservations about accepting a Romanov Grand Duchess into her family, partly on religious grounds and partly as she thought the family were 'false and arrogant'. Moreover Britain and Russia had traditionally been enemies since the Crimean war and before, and she was still suspicious of St Petersburg's intentions over the Black Sea and Central Asia. The Tsar would not commit himself, writing to Queen Victoria in August 1871 after the Duke's visit that 'while not in any way opposing a union between our two families, we have made it a principle never to impose our will upon our children as regards their marriages'.[11]

However, the choice of suitable brides for Alfred was dwindling. He was a shy taciturn man of twenty-nine, a hard-working naval officer and an enthusiastic amateur violinist who shared the piano-playing Marie's love of music, but lacked the geniality of his more popular elder brother the Prince of Wales. The Tsarina had decided views on the match as well. Although she was impressed with English nurses for her children, she did not care for England, and although she had never been there, she felt her daughter would never be happy in the country.

By coincidence, in June 1873, the Tsarevich and Tsarevna were about to visit England, taking their two sons, on what would be the Tsarevich's only journey there. At the same time the Shah of Persia, who had just paid an official visit to St Petersburg, was doing likewise. Having invited himself, he was expected to stay longer than the customary three days allotted to such occasions. However, society was determined to exceed the magnificence of his Russian reception in London, and some feared that the Russian guests would be paid less attention. In Russia there would be jealousy at anything done for the Shah. As the St Petersburg press put it, 'proud Albion' would do all she could to astonish the eastern potentate by the pomp and luxury of his reception in order to outdo Russia.

The Prince and Princess of Wales shared this general dismay, and went out of their way to treat the imperial heir and his wife with every attention possible, entertaining them at their London home, Marlborough House. Queen Victoria met them briefly at Windsor when the Prince and Princess brought them over, as she noted in her journal for 21 June; 'Bertie & Alix arrived with the Cesarevitch & Minny (Dagmar) looking very dear & nice, quite unaltered, & as simple as ever. He is very tall & big, good natured & unaffected.'[12] At Spithead the Tsarevich was honoured with a naval review, and military reviews at Windsor, Woolwich and Aldershot. In London they visited art galleries, hospitals, racecourses, and the Tower, and the Tsarevich even spent an afternoon in the Court of the Lord Chief Justice, listening to the trial of the Tichborne case. Towards the end of their visit, the Tsarevich dined with the Duke of Edinburgh and the Elder Brethren of Trinity House, and delivered a graceful speech of thanks for his reception in French, expressing the hope 'that our cordial and affectionate relationship may continue to the end of our lives'.[13]

Even so, the fact that the Shah of Persia had upstaged the Romanov guests made it an uncomfortable time for the latter. Their hosts were equally disturbed, and a rather embarrassed Queen Victoria wrote to the German Crown Princess of the 'intense disgust of the Russians who cannot disguise their annoyance (excepting dear, gentle, sweet Minnie whose unassumingness and simplicity are very striking) – and it is very unfortunate and *genânt* that they should be here at the same time for no one takes any notice of them hardly'.[14]

Though the Tsar and Tsarina were reluctant to part with their daughter, they had to accept the inevitable. After a short period of courtship Marie and Alfred were betrothed in July 1873. Queen Victoria demanded that one of her parents would have to bring her to England to meet her before the wedding took place. The Tsar denounced the Queen privately as a 'silly old fool', ungallantly forgetting that she was thirteen months younger than him, while the Tsarina offered to meet her halfway at Cologne, a suggestion the robust Queen dismissed as 'simply impertinent'.

Having originally opposed the betrothal, the Tsar now accepted it with good grace. He showered some of the finest Romanov jewellery on her, including sapphires left to him by his mother, as well as a collection comprising the necklace, earrings, bracelets and brooches once owned by Catherine the Great and bequeathed to her daughter-in-law. The Duke of Edinburgh was appointed honorary chief of a Russian guards regiment, and the Tsar offered the Prince of Wales the same honour. However, Queen Victoria forbade him to accept, on the grounds that there was no precedent for such a gift, and that it would be unpopular in England. The disappointed Prince tried to make her change her mind by stressing that an English prince marrying a Russian Grand Duchess for the first time was in itself a great change, 'so I cannot conceive that the alteration of any old-established custom here could be unpopular in England'. She would not be moved; it was in order for 'Affie' to accept a foreign regiment, as he would be the Tsar's son-in-law 'and will live often in Russia'.[15] The bride's brothers, particularly Vladimir, were incensed, seeing the Queen's attitude as a reflection on her.

Marie and Alfred were married in the chapel of the Winter Palace on 11/23 January 1874 at a double ceremony. The first service was performed by the Metropolitans of St Petersburg, Moscow and Kiev, according to the rites of the Greek Orthodox Church. Grand Dukes Vladimir, Alexis and Serge, and the groom's brother Prince Arthur, relieved each other in turn in holding the golden crowns over the heads of bride and groom. Lord Augustus Loftus, British ambassador to St Petersburg, was greatly impressed by 'the deep tone of the choir, the thrilling force of the chants mingled with the grand voices of the clergy, the magnificent dress and jewelled ornaments of the priesthood, and the impressive forms of the Greek service, gave an imposing and solemn effect to the ceremony'.[16] The second ceremony was conducted according to the rites of the church of England. Queen Victoria was not present, but she sent the Prince and Princess of Wales to represent her, and she chose Arthur Stanley, Dean of Westminster, to perform the English ceremony. She also sent the bride a sprig of myrtle and a prayer book with illuminated hymns, and a plain prayer book for the groom.

It was a bitter wrench for the bride's parents. The Tsar, who looked pale and appeared deeply moved throughout the ceremonies, told Lady Augusta Stanley that his daughter had 'never caused us anything but joy. We lost our eldest girl and we had so ardently wished for another – her birth was a joy and a delight, not to be described, and her whole life has been a continuation. When she was in the school room, our hours did not suit and I could very seldom have her to walk with me, but then on Sundays she was mine and we always walked together.'[17] The Tsarina, Lady Stanley found, was more reticent and 'evidently did not trust Herself to talk much of what is nearest to Her heart and I believe has never allowed Herself to break down – Poor thing, I believe she is as much comforted and upheld as possible by the sight of Her Daughter's happiness, but it is simply *agony* to Her, – to them both.'[18]

It would have been a mournful occasion had it not been for the presence of the Danish-born sisters, the Tsarevna and the Princess of Wales who, Loftus noted, were 'beaming with beauty and delight at being together'.[19]

The traditional round of wedding celebrations, receptions and entertain-ments took place on a scale which could not but impress the English guests. Prince Arthur's governor, Major-General Sir Howard Elphinstone, found everything done 'on a scale of magnitude and magnificence which it is impossible to surpass and which could not be equalled in any but such huge palaces', with evergreen trees and shrubs used indoors for decoration; in one supper room prepared for five hundred people at fifty different tables, 'palms and exotics have been used to so large an extent that it gives the place the appearance of a conservatory'. He added that the heat of the rooms was 'almost unbearable, and several ladies left the ballroom almost in a fainting state'.[20]

After a short honeymoon the bride and groom left Russia and arrived at Windsor early in March. Queen Victoria called her new daughter-in-law 'most pleasingly natural, unaffected and civil', even if she was not pretty or graceful and held herself badly, but these good impressions did not last long. The Tsar and Tsarina had informed Queen Victoria that they wished their daughter to be known as Her Imperial Highness, 'as in all civilised countries'. Thoroughly offended as she was not yet imperial herself (and would not be until her proclamation as Empress of India in 1877), the Queen retorted that she did not mind whether she was known as Imperial or not, as long as Royal came first.

An equally trivial dispute about her official title followed. Which came first, Duchess of Edinburgh or Grand Duchess of Russia? Out of her depth, the Queen asked her private secretary Sir Henry Ponsonby, who was amused by the fuss and quoted Dr Johnson to his wife; 'Who comes first, a louse or a flea?' Marie sought revenge in mischievously flaunting the magnificent jewellery from her father at her first drawing-room in England. The Queen, whose own jewels were comparatively modest, looked at them coldly, 'shrugging her shoulders like a bird whose plumage has been ruffled, her mouth drawn down at the corners',[21] while her daughters could hardly conceal their jealousy.

Marie was very disappointed with England, where she found the food abominable, late hours very tiring, London 'an impossible place, people are mad of pleasure', and visits to Windsor and Osborne unutterably tedious. In her eyes Buckingham Palace and Windsor Castle could never compete with the splendours of the Winter Palace. Though she spoke perfect English she disliked it intensely, preferring to converse in French, traditionally the second language at the Russian court. If most people in England thought the Duchess of Edinburgh extremely brusque and masculine in her manner, she made it equally plain that she did not care what people thought of her. An imperious manner with servants, and defiance of English convention by smoking cigarettes in public, made her deeply unpopular. At the time of her wedding Lady Stanley noted that she thought 'herself quite determined to be a thorough Englishwoman and her Mother's example in Russia has taught her how to adopt her Husband's country'.[22] Such noble intentions evidently did not long survive her arrival in her husband's country.

In spring 1874 the Tsar went to Berlin for the betrothal of his second surviving son Vladimir to Princess Marie of Mecklenburg-Schwerin. Vladimir was a cultured, intelligent young man who looked and acted like a more refined version of the Tsarevich.

After the engagement the Tsar went to England, accompanied by his son Alexis. Though it was intended as a purely family affair, not a state visit, the Tsar of Russia could hardly come to London without his arrival being turned into an event of major importance. *Punch* welcomed him with a full-page cartoon and a short list of 'Things the Czar Won't Do', including 'Burst into tears at the sight of the Crimean Memorial in Waterloo Place, and renew the Treaty of Paris on the spot, out of consideration for the feeling of the neighbourhood', and 'Understand what an "immense draw" he will be at the Crystal Palace on the 16th [May], along with the fireworks'.[23]

The visit began inauspiciously as plans for the first day, 13 May, were thrown into confusion when the yacht, expected at Gravesend at 11.30 a.m, ran aground off Dover. Queen Victoria and her family were waiting with a luncheon party at Windsor, when word came that they would not arrive until late afternoon. Luncheon was put off and a dinner hastily organized instead, only to be cancelled when it transpired that he would arrive sometime in the evening. In the end he reached Windsor by train at 10.00 p.m.

Once in England he was delighted to see his daughter again, and for the next week she was reluctant to leave his side. He rode on horseback in Windsor Park, dined with the Prince of Wales at Marlborough House, attended the Russian chapel in Welbeck Street, and was guest of honour at a Guildhall banquet with the Lord Mayor of London and Corporation, where speeches were made extolling peace and Anglo–Russian friendship. A grand review was held at Aldershot and the Tsar on horseback saluted troops just back from the Ashanti war. He also visited the Royal Arsenal, Woolwich, to undertake an inspection of the Royal Artillery and lunch at the Mess afterwards.

Among statesmen he met were the prime minister, Benjamin Disraeli, at a reception at Buckingham Palace, and William Ewart Gladstone, leader of the opposition, at Marlborough House. Disraeli wrote afterwards: 'There I had an audience, which was an audience rather of phrases, but nothing but friendliness and hopes that my Government would cherish and confirm those feelings. His mien and manners are gracious and graceful, but the expression of his countenance, which I now could very closely examine, is sad. Whether it is satiety, or the loneliness of despotism, or the fear of violent death, I know not, but it was a visage of, I should think, habitual mournfulness.'[24] 'He thanked me for my conduct to Russia while I was minister,' Gladstone noted in his diary. 'I assured His Majesty I had watched with profound interest the transactions of his reign, and the great benefits he had conferred upon his people. He hoped the relations of the two countries would always be good.'[25]

Between public engagements he found time to visit the recently widowed Eugénie, former Empress of the French, at Chislehurst. She had been very kind and attentive to him after the attempt on his life in Paris seven years earlier, and now she had fallen on hard times he was eager to repay the compliment. Knowing that any such meeting, no matter how private, would inevitably give rise to comment in the European press, he had taken care to warn the new republican French government of his intention to pay her '*une visite de courtoisie*'.

A state concert was staged at the Royal Albert Hall, with a programme chosen by the Duke of Edinburgh containing suitable selections from Russian Church Orthodox polyphony in honour of his father-in-law. Many of the audience attended less to listen to the performers than to come and gape at His Imperial Majesty, and the Albert Hall Committee had accordingly raised their prices that evening, thus ensuring a substantial profit. In one of her first letters home, Marie had written scathingly of the Albert Hall, 'all ecclesiastical and for me quite boring. You will also have to go to concerts there, and I urge you to leave early. Every concert goes on for several hours.'[26] He evidently took her advice and did not attend the first half of the programme, largely comprising extracts from various Handel oratorios. Some of the audience, eager for glimpses of royalty, must have been very disappointed.

To his suite he expressed himself satisfied with the visit, not least by the vast, curious, good-humoured crowds kept in order by unarmed police. It would perhaps not have surprised him to be the victim of another assassination attempt, yet his eight days in England were relatively free of anti-Russian demonstrations. However, the Queen was disturbed by the change in the dashing young imperial heir whom she had welcomed thirty-five years earlier; he was 'very kind but is terribly altered, so thin, and his face looks so old, sad, and careworn'. Grand Duke Alexis she thought 'enormous, and has a very handsome face'.[27]

For both sovereigns the meeting brought back bittersweet memories. At a state banquet in St George's Hall, Windsor, the Tsar recalled his visit many years before, and that of his father in 1844. Tsar Nicholas I, he told her, had been very attached to England, but '*tout a malheureusement changé*' when the war took place. She had been poorly served, he went on, alluding to the bellicose Lord Palmerston. When she regretted that there had been misunderstandings, he added that he saw no reason why their countries should not be on the best of terms. After that his emotions got the better of him, as tears came to his eyes and he thanked her for her kindness to his daughter. The Queen gently put her hand out across the Tsar and took that of the Duchess of Edinburgh, 'she herself being nearly upset'.

Writing to him from Windsor after bidding him farewell, the Queen wrote (20 May) of her great pleasure in seeing him again after so many years, and how

> You have been able to see how much we appreciate in England, all that you have done for your people, and allow me to tell you that nobody more than me has admired the great Act of the Emancipation of the Serfs! You have given me personally great pleasure by the assurance of your wish that our two countries will remain not only on friendly but on cordial terms. You cannot desire this more earnestly than I do both on account of the great national interests involved and for the sake of the daughter whom I have learnt to consider as my own.[28]

Before he left English soil the Tsar replied graciously by telegraph that he was 'enchanted' with everything he had seen; 'I shall leave London tomorrow profoundly touched by your so kind reception & persuaded that my beloved daughter will always find a second mother in you. I thank you again from the bottom of my heart for all the proofs of friendship with which you have not ceased to overwhelm me.'[29]

Such formal expressions of gratitude could do no more than temporarily bridge the gulf between two powerful nations which, notwithstanding one recent solitary dynastic marriage alliance, still had good reason to distrust one another. Within three years they would come close to war.

Moreover the campaign of whispers against Catherine Dolgorouky was approaching a new level. While a Tsar of All the Russias could turn a deaf ear to court gossip if he wanted, or if his advisers chose to put sufficient distance between him and trouble, Count Adlerberg and other well-meaning individuals had felt themselves duty bound to warn him about it. In particular there was a rumour that women from the house of Dolgorouky had always brought the Romanovs bad luck, ever since Tsar Peter II had been engaged to one but succumbed to smallpox shortly before what would have been his wedding day in 1730. Those observers in England were evidently unaware that there were more reasons for His Majesty's careworn face than the regular burdens of state.

In August the Tsar attended the marriage of Vladimir and Marie at the Winter Palace. The bride insisted on retaining her Lutheran faith, much to the delight of other German princesses, but to the displeasure of her in-laws. Significantly the wedding took place at the height of summer; as Lord Loftus commented, 'this town is a desert and therefore only those came who were obliged to come'. However he praised the new Grand Duchess, whom he called 'a superior person, not actually pretty but very intellectual and with a graceful and dignified deportment'. He added that the matter of a foreign Princess marrying a Grand Duke yet retaining her own religion was something to which the Russians would have to accustom themselves 'or they will find no wives for the Russian Grand Dukes. I think it a healthy practice and it will do them good.'[30]

As a bachelor Vladimir had sown his wild oats thoroughly, but wedded bliss transformed him, and the marriage proved a happy one. They installed themselves in the Vladimir Palace on the Neva embankment, a luxurious building with all the newest equipment and fittings money could buy. Within a matter of weeks, at Marie's suggestion, elaborate new scarlet summer uniforms were ordered for their servants. When it came to style and elegance, nothing but the best was good enough for the host and hostess at the Vladimir Palace.

5

'You cannot but love him as a man'

Beyond the frontiers of Russia, a mood of restlessness was sweeping the continent. The Panslav movement, encouraged largely by Bismarck's unification of Germany in 1871 and Prussia's forging of the German states and their peoples into one Empire, inspired many similarly minded souls in Russia to see the liberation of all Slavs in European Turkey and the Balkans, and establish them in a Russian dominated federation. Some, particularly the ailing Tsarina, saw it as a religious crusade. The status of the Balkan Christians, still subject to the oppressive rule of infidel Turkey, would be improved; the Church of Santa Sophia could be returned to its rightful Orthodoxy; and Constantinople could once more assume its historic role as the greatest city in Christendom. To the Tsarevich, taking his cue from his mother, it would mean the realization of Russia's age-old dream to open the Straits of the Dardanelles to Russian ships, and the acquisition of several thousand square miles of new territory. None of this, however, meant anything to Tsar Alexander II himself, who thought the Panslavs troublesome dreamers and visionaries who sought the impossible.

The spark to the flame was a rebellion by Slavs in the Turkish provinces of Bosnia and Herzegovina against Turkish rule in the summer of 1875. The Tsar saw no reason to intervene, either on this occasion or subsequently a few months later when the Bulgars precipitated a crisis with the Turks and were beaten into submission, or when the Slavs of Serbia and Montenegro declared war on Turkey. The Russian General, Michael Chernyaev, accepted command of the Serbian forces, Count Nicholas Ignatev, Russian Ambassador to Constantinople, persistently pleaded the Slav cause, and thousands of Russian volunteers poured into Belgrade.

The Tsar was appalled by the strength of feeling among the nobility. In his fervent desire for non-intervention and peace he had the support of his minister of finance, the liberal minded Michael Reutern, who pointed out that the Russian economy was already strained by industrial expansion, and that war would spell disaster for the treasury. They had an ally in Prince Alexander Gorchakov, minister of foreign affairs, who insisted that to disturb the peace by reviving the Eastern question would unleash international tension with consequences which they would be powerless to control. Unless the Panslav movement was checked it would certainly result in war – an undertaking which Russia could ill afford, for political as well as economic considerations.

To his disappointment he was unable to restrain his family's enthusiasm. The Tsarina accepted the Presidency of the Red Cross and, aided by Pobedonostsev, eagerly set herself to relief work organizing and equipping hospital trains at her own expense, while the Tsarevich openly encouraged soldiers in the Guards Regiments to volunteer by granting them extended leave and assuring them of places on their return. Court ladies stood at street corners jingling money boxes, and in Moscow the Slav red, white and blue flag fluttered proudly from public buildings. The press advocated intervention, deploring governmental inaction in the face of the 'infidel Turks' and their intention of destroying the Russians' brother Slavs.

Throughout Europe public opinion was affronted by reports of a Bulgarian rebellion that had been put down by terrible Turkish reprisals. A British diplomat sent to investigate called the Turks' retaliation 'the most heinous crime of the century', with up to 12,000 slaughtered and sixty villages destroyed. In England Gladstone called on Europe to rise up and expel the Turks from Bulgaria. This was encouraging news to Russia, as Britain had traditionally been the only country they needed to fear in their march to Constantinople.

The Tsar harboured no illusions as to the state of opinion in England. While still anxious for a friendly understanding with the country, as he told Lord Loftus, he asked if it was likely that he should 'entertain views hostile to my daughter's adopted country, which might produce a rupture between the two countries?'[1] He emphasized that Russia harboured no intention of acquiring

Constantinople. All that he and his government had proposed to Britain, and by which he still stood, was for the occupation of Bosnia by Austria, of Bulgaria by Russia as a temporary measure until the peace and safety of the Christian population could be guaranteed, and for a naval demonstration at Constantinople where the British fleet would be the dominant power. This, he said, ought to be sufficient proof that the Russians had no intention of occupying the city. As both their countries had a common object – namely the maintenance of peace and the amelioration of the Christian population – and when he had given every proof possible that he had no personal desire for conquest or aggrandizement, he could not understand why there could not be 'a perfect and cordial understanding between Russia and England', based on a policy of peace, which would benefit the mutual interests of each, as well as those of Europe at large.

'Intentions are attributed to Russia of a future conquest of India, and the possession of Constantinople,' he said in conclusion. 'Can anything be more absurd?'[2] The former, he insisted, was an impossibility, and he neither wished nor intended the latter.

Only those close to the Tsar could appreciate the difficulties of his position. His son-in-law Alfred, Duke of Edinburgh, informed Queen Victoria in July 1876 that he [the Tsar] was 'a man of the most sensitive feelings, (who) is deeply hurt at all the unpleasant (to say the least of them) and untrue things said of him in the English press'.[3] Yet it did nothing to lessen the Queen's feelings about the family connection, as she wrote to the Prince of Wales in January 1878; 'I can't say *how* very unfortunate I think it that Affie sh[oul]d have married a Russian.'[4] When the Queen's private secretary Sir Henry Ponsonby asked Lord Odo Russell, British ambassador in Berlin, why the Tsar stirred the German Emperor William up against the English, Russell answered that the Tsar had no cause to like them; 'we have thwarted him on every occasion', and that it was only natural that he 'should feel hurt at his schemes for peace being upset and himself and his Ministers distrusted'.[5]

At length the Tsar was persuaded that only a more direct approach would have any chance of bringing the conflict to a just conclusion. Livadia was a hotbed of Panslav talk, with the Tsarina and her ladies speaking endlessly of Russia's holy mission. Her father-confessor, Bashanov, was an enthusiastic Russian nationalist and Slavophile. He and the Tsarina's ladies all believed that Russia could only be saved by the Orthodox Church, and Poles, Protestants and heathens must be hated by all true Russians. Meanwhile the Tsarevich and Grand Duke Nicholas, the Tsar's brother, spoke of Constantinople as Russia's rightful capital.

By now the Tsar was weakening in his resolve to stand apart from the escalating conflict. Russian volunteers had been fighting beside the Balkan peoples while he and other European heads of state had tried to reach an acceptable settlement with Turkey, and failed. After the Serbs were routed by the Turks in November 1876, and the Six Powers agreed to a conference in Constantinople, Disraeli spoke in London of the 'inviolability of Turkish possessions'.

While the Tsar ordered partial mobilization, he still hoped that the Constantinople conference would provide a peaceful solution. In the autumn of 1876 he authorized Count Ignatev to issue an ultimatum to Turkey demanding a ceasefire or diplomatic relations with Russia would be broken off. Grand Dukes were appointed to the important commands, namely his brothers Nicholas Nicolaievich on the Balkan–Danube front, and Michael Nicolaievich for the second front at Transcaucasia; for a strategically important wing of two corps, the Tsarevich; for a single corps, Vladimir; and for crucial naval operations on the Danube, Alexis.

The conference achieved nothing. In April 1877 the Powers delivered a Protocol to the Sultan of Turkey demanding autonomy for Bosnia, Herzegovina and Bulgaria; but this was rejected, and when Turkey rejected Russia's proposal for simultaneous demobilization and a plan for peace with guarantees for the liberty of the Balkan peoples, the Tsar reluctantly accepted that war was inevitable. After coming to a mutually satisfactory agreement regarding future arrangements in the Balkan area with Emperor Francis Joseph of Austria, keen to add Bosnia and Herzegovina to the Habsburg dominions, he received Germany's ambivalent approval, and accepted the inevitability of England's opposition.

On 12/24 April 1877, his patience exhausted, he declared war on Turkey, which he hoped could remain an isolated affair. In his address to the army he was unfailingly honest; 'most profoundly do I regret having to send you on such a business. As you may know, I kept trying to avoid it until the very last hope had gone. Now I can but wish you success. God bless you.'[6] He was prepared to let himself be guided by popular opinion. Now aged fifty-nine, the same age at which his father had been when he died, he did not have his father's steely resolve. Years of responsibility, insomnia and indifferent health had left him tired, aged and increasingly indifferent. He had given over twenty years of service to his country as Imperial Majesty. While he would never neglect his duties as sovereign, in his later years he looked forward more and more to his whist in the afternoons and, above all, the company of Princess Catherine Dolgorouky. If others wished to guide the destiny of Russia, he would let them have their own way. When they craved war and the laurels of victory, he felt powerless to swim against the tide. While he deplored his empire's bellicosity, the mood of his people, his family and most of his ministers was considerably less sombre.

Amid general rejoicing, the troops proceeded south. The Tsar went with them, travelling with his sons Alexander, Vladimir and Serge. For the first three months Russian operations proved successful, particularly as Roumania allowed free passage to Russian troops when Prince Carol of Roumania, irritated by Turkey's attitude, declared independence and offered aid to Russia. A difficult crossing of the Danube was completed at the end of June, though with great loss of life. The Russian command aimed to control the Shipka pass in the Balkan mountains and the crossroads at Plevna, and then proceed across the Balkans, heading for Constantinople. Coastal advance was not feasible because of the superior Turkish naval presence on the Black Sea.

The Tsar took up his quarters near the front, at Sysov in Bulgaria, while Russian engineers worked quickly to complete bridges across the Danube. The Tsarevich and his forces were holding a 50-mile line along the river Lom, to protect the army's left flank and threaten Turkish forts at Rustchuk, Shumla, Varna and Silistra. Though no military genius, and though his aversion to horses led some to suspect him of cowardice, he commanded his troops courageously against a numerically superior army. Yet this baptism of fire was enough to leave him with a hatred of war. Thereafter he spoke of it as 'an infamy', saying that 'it should be possible for all nations to settle their differences without a single shot being fired'.[7] He wrote every day to his wife, Grand Duchess Marie Feodorovna, who was involved in looking after the wounded and soldiers' families at

St Petersburg and, so it was said, at the war front – having left the city disguised as a nurse to come and visit him.

The Tsar was also writing daily from the front, to Princess Dolgorouky. His wife's enthusiasm for the war had deepened the already wide gulf between them, and the young woman whom he regarded as his wife in all but name was the only person in whom he could confide. 'You will understand better than anyone else what I feel at the beginning of a war I so much wanted and hoped to avoid,'[8] he told her. Adding to his unhappiness was anxiety over the attitudes of foreign governments, particularly Britain, still officially neutral but openly pro-Turkish and anti-Russian in tone. That his daughter was married to the second son of Queen Victoria increased his discomfort further.

Moreover it was humiliating not being permitted to fight himself, for security reasons and because of ill-health. Insomnia and asthma continually plagued him, and his physician-in-ordinary Dr Botkin begged him in vain to return to the north, if not back to Russia. He insisted on sharing the privations of a soldier's life, refusing all pomp and ceremony, living in a cottage with a table, a few hard chairs and a cubicle containing a military camp bed. To alleviate rheumatism, he had a hot brick placed in his bed on cold nights.

After initial successes, with the army capturing Tyrnovo and Plevna, the war soon revealed serious weaknesses in the Russian high command, still dominated by officers whose military abilities were unequal to their titles. Their arms were inferior to those of the Turks, who were equipped with new Krupp artillery and English and American rifles, and transport services were inadequate to bring up forces quickly enough. As the ancient capital of Bulgaria, Tyrnovo had great symbolic importance for Russia, but Russian commanders overlooked the significance of Plevna which stood on a vital strategic crossroad. Left with insufficient defences the town soon fell to the Turks, and after a number of military reverses the Tsar had to move his headquarters to Gorny Studen, west of Tyrnovo.

In the stiflingly hot midsummer he spared himself almost nothing. Living in a small, rough timber house, he rose at 8 a.m. for a short walk, ending up with a visit to a hospital, before breakfast. The rest of the morning was spent working at reports, with lunch at midday in a tent. His household joined him for the meal, which was to take no more than half an hour. After that he continued to work at reports, receive audiences, and visit the men at the front. Only at 4 p.m. did he grant a concession to his doctors by taking a short rest, though he insisted that important messages should be brought to him at once. Next he went visiting hospitals again, returning for dinner at 7 p.m. and more audiences. When told of any victory, he remained calm and remarked solemnly that it was no excuse for undue celebration. The household left him at 10 p.m., when he returned to his room, ordering the batman to leave him enough candles and go to bed. If necessary he continued working on reports until after midnight.

Prince Vladimir Cherkassky, a former member of the emancipation committee and later mayor of Moscow, who had frequently disagreed and argued with his sovereign, visited Gorny Studen as commandant of the Red Cross. While the incompetence of most of the military staff dismayed him, he could not speak highly enough of the Tsar, 'who maintains his calm in spite of his deep mental anguish, who alone of all the people here seems capable of grasping matters of real moment. When you see him, tired and unwell as he is, visiting hospitals, entering into the men's interests and needs, bearing himself with a sovereign's dignity and a friend's compassion . . . you cannot but love him as a man.'[9]

The Russians attempted to retake Plevna, but a first assault in July was repulsed with the loss of several thousand men. Ten days later a second attempt failed, and as his safety at Gorny Studen could no longer be guaranteed, the Tsar was advised to move again. His sons urged him to leave Bulgaria, but he would not turn his back on his troops at the theatre of war. A third assault in September resulted in the loss of 25,000 men, closely following a heavy defeat for Grand Duke Michael's army by the Turks at Tizil Kepe.

Morale was low at home in Russia, where the Tsar was criticized bitterly by some for not taking part in the fighting, and by others for neglecting his duty in not returning to St Petersburg. A council of war was held at his headquarters on 13/25 September at which Grand Duke Nicholas urged retreat across the Danube to Roumania, and his commanders agreed. Only Milyutin, minister of war, opposed them on the grounds that Russia could not afford to abandon a foothold which had already cost them 60,000 lives. They had no alternative, he argued, but to take

Plevna. The Tsar supported him, declaring that there must be no retreat. As in the Crimean War, he ordered that the effort must be continued at all costs.

Totleben took over the siege of Plevna, and instead of a frontal attack he cut off every supply road to the town. In November General Loris-Melikov, Grand Duke Michael's chief of staff, took the town of Kars. Plevna fell to the Russians in December, and the Tsar attended a *Te Deum* in the captured town a fortnight later before finally giving in to the entreaties of Dr Botkin and returning to St Petersburg for a much needed rest. On his return his general appearance caused much dismay. His hair had turned completely grey, it seemed to be an effort for him to maintain his upright military bearing, and he was unable to stand for long. When giving audiences he had to sit down, as his strength was failing him.

With the capture of Plevna the Turkish resistance collapsed. Early in the new year of 1878 Shipka and Adrianople, sixty miles from Constantinople, were captured. The presence of the British navy, six ironclads stationed in Besika Bay ordered through the Straits to Constantinople in January, alarmed Grand Duke Nicholas, as he knew the army was in no condition to fight a war with England. Russian opinion clamoured for Constantinople, but he refused to occupy the city unless ordered to do so by the Tsar. General Skobelev led his force into Adrianople, and Grand Duke Nicholas established his headquarters there.

The Sultan of Turkey sued for peace and the Tsar offered an armistice. By the treaty of San Stefano, negotiated by the Tsar's emissary, Count Ignatev, an agreement was signed with terms which proved particularly advantageous for Russia. It created a large state of Bulgaria, theoretically autonomous but in principle under Russian control, and would surely become a centre for Russian control in the Balkans; full independence from Turkey for Serbia, Montenegro and Roumania, and a large indemnity to be paid to Russia by Turkey, mainly in territory along the Black Sea coast and in Transcaucasia.

The treaty was at once criticized by foreign powers. Still assuming the mantle of Turkey's protector, Great Britain regarded it with grave suspicion, while Austria maintained that it violated a pre-war agreement, and the Balkan countries were equally uneasy if not downright hostile. The Tsar knew that Russia would be hard put to defend it, while at home the Panslavs were dissatisfied, still seeking the liberation and organized association of all Slavs. Although Constantinople still lay open to the Russian armies, many in the ranks were suffering from typhus and in no condition to continue fighting. When the British cabinet sent a naval force into the Black Sea the Tsar had to order immediate withdrawal. Ignatev retired, and the Tsar relied on Ambassador Shuvalov's efforts to ease the tension in London. By June all parties were willing to accept Bismarck's offer of Berlin's hospitality to a congress of the powers to reconsider the treaty of San Stefano.

At the congress Russia recovered parts of Bessarabia lost after the Crimean War, was granted continued possession of territories in Transcaucasia, and allowed indirect control of half of Bulgaria, the rest being set up as an independent state. Yet she was left in the ignominious position of a victor whose spoils of war had largely been shared out by others; she was denied access to the Mediterranean which she had hoped to reach through the back door of Bulgaria. That, Disraeli told Queen Victoria, had been the real object of the war, a view shared by all Panslavs in Russia. Though the war had brought Russia some territorially valuable acquisitions, it had also left her in dire financial straits. Reutern, minister of finance, resigned after sixteen years in the post, having warned that the war would undo his work of having put the economy on a firm footing. Nevertheless Russia had succeeded in freeing the Balkan countries from Turkish rule and establishing the new state of Bulgaria. The sovereign prince of the new state, recommended personally by the Tsar, was his nephew Prince Alexander of Battenberg.

Yet Tsar Alexander II was blamed by his people for national humiliation. The Panslavs accused him of weakness and indecision, for not dismissing Grand Duke Nicholas as commander-in-chief, for not seizing Constantinople from under the nose of the British, for not sending sufficiently shrewd diplomats to the Congress of Berlin. Years of anxiety and declining health had aged him beyond his time. Princess Dolgorouky, the gossips whispered, had sapped her lover of his vitality, and with her jealous possessive character she was a bad influence on him. She never read a book or magazine, they said, and was ignorant, intellectually and socially. However she and the children were now his only real comfort. Olga, their first daughter, had been followed by a son, Boris, who died within a few days of birth in March 1876. In September 1878 a second daughter, Catherine, was born.

The Tsarevich returned from the battlefield much embittered by his experiences. Russia, he also felt, had enemies worse than the Turks, namely corrupt commanders on the Russian side. He was appointed to preside over a Commission after the war, and was disgusted by the political corruption, especially of his uncle, Grand Duke Nicholas. The results of the treaty of Berlin also rekindled his anti-German feelings, and some saw him as the champion of future reform.

On the anniversary of his father's accession he headed a deputation to congratulate His Majesty, and delivered an address expressing the fervent wish of the deputation that the Tsar would 'continue to carry out those wise resolutions which you have hitherto adopted'. The Tsar took this as a personal slight, replying coldly that his endeavour was that his heir would 'find the Empire at the height of its prosperity and power, both internally and externally', and that there were many tasks before them, namely a reduction of expenses, a regulation of the currency, further reconstruction of the army, the imperfections of which had recently been revealed, and the improvement of the sanitary state of the country. 'There are other tasks to be seen after, but they must wait until the existing passions are appeased. If I do not live to see the time, my heir must undertake the improvement.'[10] The Tsarevich retired in silence, and soon afterwards it was rumoured that he had been asked by his father to consider himself under arrest. According to an official account, after a conversation of three-quarters of an hour on 4 March, the Tsarevich left his father's palace in a highly excited state. The Tsar immediately summoned the council of ministers, and informed them that for the safety of the State it was necessary that his son should be kept in custody, and charged him with being in connivance with the most dangerous foes of Russia. Finally, Count Adlerberg was sent to the Tsarevich to inform him that he 'must not leave his palace, and must consider himself a prisoner'.[11]

Before long, however, it would be the sovereign who had to consider himself a prisoner. It was not weariness or ill-health; a far worse threat waited in the shadows.

6

'A liberator's is a dangerous job'

By the time the Congress of Berlin was signed, the Tsar was less concerned with the troublesome Panslavs than with a second coming of the revolutionary movement. Almost undetected by his ministers, it had been growing since before the start of the war. It could in part be attributed to Tolstoy's policy of expelling subversives from the universities, and as part of the Russification, calling Russian students home from abroad. They joined and encouraged the ranks of the disenchanted intelligentsia, socialists, populists and others all aiming to rid Russia of the Tsar.

In January 1878 Bogolubov, an agitator imprisoned for his part in a public demonstration, was flogged by the order of General Fedor Trepov, police chief of St Petersburg – a punishment made illegal some years earlier – for his refusal to salute Trepov during an inspection while he was in prison. When Vera Zasulich, one of a group of emancipated women determined to strike a blow at the heart of Russia for the sake of the masses, walked into the office and shot the police chief at point-blank range, wounding him but not fatally, she made no effort to escape. At her trial public opinion was initially against her, until counsel for the defence drew attention to Trepov's flagrant violation of the law. The mood changed instantly, and when he had finished speaking there was such an outburst of weeping, cheering and clapping that the judge threatened to clear the court. Zasulich was acquitted to enthusiastic applause, especially from generals and high officials who detested Trepov. The police tried to rearrest her as she left court a free woman, but friends and sympathizers surrounded her and a fracas with the police occurred, during which some were wounded and one man who had fired at the police was shot dead himself. She was spirited away and escaped abroad. Several months later General Nicholas Mezentsev, head of the St

Petersburg police, was stabbed to death outside his office by Serge Kravchinsky, a former army officer. His action was justified as a reprisal for deaths of political prisoners in the fortress of St Peter and St Paul, who had died on hunger strike the previous summer. He escaped to London, where he published his memoirs.

To counteract growing terrorism and *kramóla* ('sedition') the Tsar appointed three temporary governors general, namely Joseph Gurko at St Petersburg, Michael Loris-Melikov at Kharkov, and Edward Totleben at Odessa, each of whom had distinguished themselves during the war. Their orders were to ensure that each area within their responsibility would be constantly searched and purged thoroughly in an unrelenting schedule of raids, arrests, expulsions, imprisonments and executions. They were granted full civil and military authority including the right to expel undesirables, send into exile persons considered dangerous, close down subversive publications, use military courts to try civilians accused of terrorism, and powers to arrest on suspicion. Prisoners condemned to death would no longer have the right of appeal, the sale of firearms was prohibited, houses could be searched without warrant, and all university towns were subject to strict regulations. Many of the Tsar's earlier liberalizing reforms were thus reversed, and any action deemed necessary for the preservation of order and eradication of political resistance was permitted.

Early the following year two more senior figures were attacked; Prince Dmitri Kropotkin, hated especially for his brutal treatment of political prisoners, was assassinated, and General Alexander Drenteln, who had succeeded the murdered Mezentsev as chief of the Third Section, was shot and wounded. On the morning of 2/14 April 1879 the Tsar was returning to the Winter Palace after his usual morning walk when Vladimir Soloviev, a schoolmaster, aimed his revolver at him and fired four shots, missing each time. He was seized by an infuriated crowd until the police could apprehend him. On the way to the gendarme headquarters he tried to poison himself, but a policeman stopped him in time. At the trial he refused to answer any questions, and went to the gallows. Although shaken, the Tsar was seen by a fervently loyal crowd defiantly taking the same route next morning.

A small fanatical group calling itself 'Will of the People' was formed by Andrew Zelyabov and Sophia Perovskaya, daughter of a former governor of St Petersburg, who later became Zelyabov's mistress. On 26 August/7 September 1879 they formally condemned 'Alexander Romanov' to death. Their first attempt was on 19 November/1 December as he was in the Crimea on his homeward journey. Contrary to normal procedure the imperial train had been sent ahead of the household carriages containing the luggage, which were delayed because of engine problems. It arrived safely, but the next train was mined and wrecked in an explosion which blew the engine and three coaches off the track, leaving several people injured, but by this time the Tsar was back in the Kremlin. 'Am I such a wild beast that they should hound me to death?' was the Tsar's bitter reaction. In Moscow the public immediately held students responsible, and mounted police had to guard the university until the mood had calmed down. A few days later the paper of the 'People's Will' published an appeal to the Tsar, declaring that it had vowed war against him as the embodiment of reaction and repression; but he would be 'pardoned' if he agreed to call a constituent assembly.

While he had no intention of being coerced into hasty agreements on constitutional issues, he agreed to accept additional precautions. Bullet-proof wadding was sewn into his uniforms, and his sledge and carriage were lined with sheets of steel. On the rare occasions he went outside he was surrounded by a phalanx of officers and agents of the secret police, who were only advised of his itinerary half an hour in advance, and even then sworn to secrecy. He no longer gave audiences in his private apartments in the Winter Palace, and only servants were to open his letters and despatches in future. Much as he enjoyed cigars and cigarettes he was persuaded to give up smoking altogether, for fear that terrorists might turn one into a bomb.

Some months later a far more serious attempt on his life was made at the Winter Palace. Perovskaya learned that repairs were being carried out in the basement, and one of the revolutionary group, a trained carpenter named Stephen Khalturin, known for his pro-republican sympathies and his ability as a workers' union organizer, managed to find employment there. Entering into the spirit of matters in more ways than one, he became friendly with one of the police guards at the palace, spent hours with him in his rooms drinking tea with him, and courting his daughter.

Meanwhile every day he carried a few dynamite charges into the palace in his toolchest or his pockets, placing them in a spot beneath the dining room. According to one account, he was so trusted that he was allowed to sleep at the palace, and concealed the dynamite in his bedding. He was such a hard worker that he was soon appointed foreman. In view of general security, that a workman should have been able to bring explosive substances as a matter of routine on to the premises suggests an extraordinary lack of surveillance. The head of the builders' firm was well known and trusted, and nobody thought to search him or check on the credentials of the team working under him.

A dinner party was planned for the evening of 5/17 February 1880, hosted by the Tsar, Tsarevich and Tsarevna, with the Duchess of Edinburgh (on a visit to her parents at the time) and their special guest Prince Alexander of Bulgaria. Dinner, due to be served at 6 p.m., was delayed by half an hour as Prince Alexander's train was late. The Prince thus saved himself and several of his illustrious relations from falling victim to what would surely have been the most spectacular mass assassination in nineteenth-century Europe. As the Tsar was about to lead the assembled company to the dining room, a deafening explosion shook the Palace, and the room was completely demolished. Eight members of the Finnish Guard were killed, and over forty-five wounded, several dying of their injuries within the next few days. Khalturin had lit a fuse and then hurried out of the palace to meet Zelyabov, who had provided him with the dynamite. They mingled with the gathering crowds and escaped.* The ailing Tsarina, in her nearby apartment, was so heavily sedated that she had slept throughout the noise. She now found breathing so difficult that her rooms had to be artificially impregnated with oxygen from cylinders, but she stayed in the Winter Palace to be near her sons and daughter, who still treated her with the utmost devotion.

Schweinitz, the German ambassador, was astonished by the general reaction. Nicholas Giers, foreign minister, had heard the

* It was said that Khalturin had a nervous breakdown as he was so disappointed at his failure to kill the Tsar. Nevertheless he escaped until two years later he was arrested and hanged for the assassination of the public prosecutor at Kiev.

explosion and told Schweinitz that he had sent a servant to enquire, then calmly drove past the Palace to his dinner. When the man returned with news of what had happened, Schweinitz gave a piece of his mind to an aide who was standing by the fireside sipping his coffee, and left in disgust. A few hours later he presented himself at the Palace and found the Tsar enjoying his usual game of whist, declaring that God had saved him again. The public seemed curiously unmoved, and there was no movement or appearance of panic in the streets although the explosion must have been heard by everyone within several miles. While the middle classes appeared indifferent, society went about pursuing its customary pleasure, the ambassador noted; one could not but 'regard as moribund a social body which fails to react to such a shock'.[1]

If the Tsar appeared outwardly calm, appearances were deceptive. That assassins could penetrate the Winter Palace shocked the family as much as it outraged contemporary opinion. Though the explosion had failed to take any imperial or royal lives, family morale was virtually shattered. Another observer of the evening's events, while agreeing with Schweinitz's statement that the Tsar was content to trust his life to the protecting hand of God, who had recently delivered him twice from the same fate, thought that the monarch was so affected that for a while he almost lost his composure. Grand Duke Constantine wrote in his diary that they were 'reliving the reign of terror [in Paris]' but with the difference that during the revolution the Parisians saw their enemies face to face; 'We neither see them nor do we know them.'[2]

From then on the Tsar lived in daily fear of his life. He attended the mass funeral of the men who had died so hideously, remarking afterwards that it was 'Plevna all over again – here in my capital, but we did break the Turk. We must break this enemy also.'[3] It was revealed that for several weeks he had found a sealed black-bordered letter on his table every morning, always containing the same threat, namely that he would not survive 18 February/2 March, the twenty-fifth anniversary of his accession. When Catherine Dolgorouky received letters threatening her life and that of her children, and news reached her of a terrorist plot to murder them, he ordered her to move into the Winter Palace. A private lift was installed at the palace, joining his apartments on the first floor to a suite of four spacious rooms on the floor above.

He had these decorated and furnished as a bedroom, two nurseries, and a salon. He could only do his work, he said, if he knew they would be safe; and the palace was the most secure place for them.

Nevertheless, that he should instal his mistress and their children in rooms above that occupied by his terminally ill wife, antagonized the rest of the family still further. Police put St Petersburg under a state of siege. Armed guards patrolled streets and a strict curfew was imposed. Yet he was deaf to pleas from his ministers that he should change his daily routine of going for a walk each morning. Some saw it as an act of courage, others as a kind of blind fatalism, which would be seen again in his grandson Nicholas. People would no longer buy tickets for the opera until they had ascertained that he was not likely to be there. However, as he had only gone for the sake of attracting a larger audience for some years past, only staying about half an hour, this was one alteration to his programme which he made without regret. But many residents were so terrified of violence that they moved out of the city.

Aged sixty-one at the time of the explosion, asthma and the fear of assassination made the Tsar seem older still. His eyesight was failing, and despatches had to be printed in larger type. Partly to help his deteriorating vision and partly as a precaution, his advisers suggested that the Winter Palace should be fitted with electric light, but he ruled this out on the grounds that the glare would be excessive. He still worked assiduously, studying state papers and government reports, every day and sometimes well into the night.

As he no longer got on with his eldest son and heir, he felt unable to delegate any duties. Ever the champion of his wronged mother and the silent enemy of Catherine Dolgorouky, the Tsarevich dutifully sat at his father's council table but disagreed with his views on almost everything. He was prepared to offer suggestions himself, even if he had to rely on the inspiration of others. Michael Katkov, editor of the conservative *Moskovskie Vedomosti* ('Moscow Gazette'), recommended to him that he might prevail on the Tsar to appoint a commission with dictatorial power over all government agencies, and entrust it with the task of enforcing a general policy throughout Russia. Though such an idea seemed strange to an autocrat, it would entail delegating authority rather than relinquishing it, and the head of the commission would be responsible directly to him. This body would consist of nine men to be known collectively as the Supreme Executive Commission, given the power to take any action necessary to root out sedition, and to consider ways of improving the government's relationship with the people.

Three weeks after the Winter Palace outrage, the Tsar summoned the regional governors-general to St Petersburg for a meeting with himself, the Tsarevich and Grand Duke Constantine, to draw up new measures for public safety. On the initiative of Loris-Melikov, it was decided to grant a constitution to Russia, though first there had to be an interim period during which details of a constitutional regime could be considered and approved. For this period the Tsar proposed to abrogate the powers of the other governors and make Loris-Melikov dictator in all but name.

A confirmed liberal who numbered radical poets and publishers among his friends, he had proved himself an efficient but even-handed, scrupulously fair temporary governor of Kharkov. His exemplary war record had been followed by courageous humanitarian work in Astrakhan when it was ravaged by plague, during which he had won the confidence and trust to everyone who had worked with or under him. Though he kept his views to himself, he believed that the size and importance of the terrorist movement was being exaggerated for political reasons by those who surrounded the Tsar, and felt that once this phase of terror had been eradicated, they could all return to a more liberal, reforming regime. An attempt on his own life a few days after he took office, by Ippolit Mledecki, a converted Jew connected with the People's Will (and who was arrested, tried and executed within forty-eight hours), did nothing to make him alter his opinion.

Though under great mental strain and suffering even more severely from asthma, the Tsar was determined to hold displays to celebrate the twenty-fifth anniversary of his accession. Parades, concerts and receptions were held to glorify the Tsar Liberator. Yet for the central figure himself, it all seemed hollow. He could take but little pride in his achievements, for the first ten years of his reign had promised much but delivered too little. He was hunted by unseen enemies, and had virtually lost the respect of his family.

Mindful of the need to draw a clear distinction between non-violent liberals and terrorists, Loris-Melikov recruited army intelligence officers of proven ability to serve in the police department, and soon rounded up many members of the People's Will. As the terrorists were few in number, creating a climate of fear out of all proportion to their strength, with careful surveillance it should not be beyond the forces of law and order to round them all up.

He believed subversion was the result of widespread dissatisfaction among the people. The peasants felt that the Emancipation Act had been unfairly enacted, officials of the *zemstvos* were frustrated by administrative interference and a subsequent lack of authority, and students were angered by the regulations and programmes of Count Tolstoy. Morale was as low throughout the empire as it had been in the aftermath of the Crimean War. The Tsar's reforms of the 1860s, he declared, had coincided with the rise of Socialism, thus prompting Russian officials to withdraw the freedoms they had granted. Had liberal concessions been strengthened, not curtailed, 'the coming struggle with Socialism would have presented no danger to the state'.

The solution was a renewal of effort to show that the Tsar paid enough attention to the voice of his people. The unpopular Tolstoy was relegated to the state council, and replaced as minister of education by Andrew Saburov. At the suggestion of Loris-Melikov – a decision he would soon regret – Pobedonostsev was appointed procurator of the holy synod, in order to gain the support of the Tsarevich, and initially he backed the new regime of Loris-Melikov unequivocally. Most others were impressed with the relaxation in censorship, and an end to harassment of the liberals. It was almost like a return to the early 1860s, when Russia had seemed on the verge of a bright new dawn. The Tsar, it was said, would thereby regain the goodwill of his people, and forestall further agitation for an imperial *zemstvo* and a constitution. He was thus convinced that he had been pursuing the wrong path for fourteen years, and declared himself 'almost in agreement' with what his new adviser told him.

In May the imperial court generally went to Gatchina for the summer manoeuvres, while the Tsarevich, Grand Duke Vladimir and their respective families left the capital for their summer residences. Though her strength was ebbing the Tsarina still wanted to spend summer at Gatchina, and her physicians agreed that she should be allowed to do so if she wished. She had been at Cannes during the previous autumn and winter, and evidently felt well enough to travel. In May her daughter, the Duchess of Edinburgh, warned that her mother had little time left, came to be with her. The Duchess had become so disenchanted with life at England under the matriarchal eye of her mother-in-law that she was eager for any excuse to return home. Nevertheless she was aghast at finding Catherine Dolgorouky and her children installed in apartments directly above her mother, and the discovery precipitated a violent row with her father. Shaken by the loss of his last ally in the family, he hurriedly left for Gatchina first to be at the manoeuvres. His daughter had evidently jolted his conscience, for he returned to St Petersburg every morning to enquire after his wife's state of health.

However, in her sleep, early on the morning of 22 May/3 June, she found release from her sufferings. At the funeral at the Cathedral of the Fortress, the Tsar and their sons bore the coffin from the cathedral to the tomb, though the sons must have reflected with some bitterness that their father had contributed to his wife's death. As still officially no more than a maid of honour, Princess Dolgorouky was not obliged to attend.

The widower was now free to make legitimate his relations with the woman whom he had long regarded as his 'wife before God'. A month later he astonished his chamberlain, Count Adlerberg, by telling him that he intended to marry the Princess Dolgorouky the following week at a ceremony in a back room at Elizabeth Palace, Tsarskoe-Selo, under conditions of utmost secrecy. Alderberg asked if it would not be more prudent to wait until the heir to the throne and his wife, who were abroad at the time, had returned, but he insisted that there was no time to lose. In any case, he must have known what the answer from his heir would have been. Forty days was the minimum interval permitted by the Orthodox Church. Every day, he said, he had to take the risk that a new attack on his life would ultimately prove successful, and that he was 'concerned therefore to secure as soon as possible the future of the being who has lived only for me during the past fourteen years', as well as their children.[4]

On 6/18 July they were married in an apartment of the palace at Tsarskoe–Selo. A priest, a deacon and a chorister were waiting for them. The Tsar was attired in the blue uniform of a hussar of the guard, the Princess in her favourite beige walking coat. A field altar had been set up, a table bearing a cross, a gospel, two torches, nuptial rings and crowns, and once the couple arrived the ceremony began, two aides-de-camp holding the wedding crowns over the heads of the kneeling bride and groom. The preparations for the private ceremony had been made with such secrecy that not only had no other guests or foreign representatives from other powers been invited, but no government officials, palace staff or servants had been notified, apart from those involved in the ceremony. On their marriage he conferred on her the title Most Serene Highness Princess Yourievsky, and the children were legitimized by imperial *ukaze*.

When they returned from Denmark he sent for the Tsarevich and Tsarevna and asked them to be eternally kind to her. A few days later he consulted Loris-Melikov and asked for his advice on the matter of title. He admitted that while there was no precedent for a widowed Tsar marrying a second time and having his second bride crowned Empress (Peter the Great had divorced his first wife, married his mistress, and both had been crowned Tsar and Tsarina), precedents could always be created by an autocrat.

Throughout foreign courts the Tsar's move was condemned, though there was some understanding for his position. In Berlin the German Crown Princess Frederick William considered that 'the unbecoming haste with which the Emperor had the marriage rite performed while the mourning for the poor Empress was yet so fresh, I think can be accounted for and to a certain extent be justified by his desire to do his duty as a man of honour by a lady and his children whom he had placed in so painful a position'. While it was impossible not to feel bitterly the want of respect to the late Empress's memory, 'much as the children feel their father's marrying again, yet it must be preferable for them to feeling ashamed of the life he was leading'.[5]

There was nothing the Grand Dukes could do about the Tsar's order that they and their wives should dine with himself and the Princess Yourievsky, but the Grand Duchesses maintained their glacial reserve towards the woman whom they dubbed 'that scheming adventuress'. As the late Tsarina's eldest surviving child, and the one who had felt most bitterly towards their father, the

Tsarevich was particularly incensed. For the sake of good manners, like his brothers he was prepared to be civil if not courteous to her in person, but when she was not around he did not hesitate to denounce 'the outsider', whom he found both 'designing and immature'. Aged thirty-three, she was two years younger than him. He even talked of moving with his wife and children to her home country of Denmark, though as his accession to the throne could come at any time it must have been no more than an idle threat.

Catherine was not officially entitled to be addressed as 'Your Majesty', but her husband intended to crown her his consort at a later date. There was a theory that Loris-Melikov suggested that the marriage should be publicly announced, that she should be declared Empress, and that it should be emphasized that for the first time the imperial house was truly Russian. At the same time a *zemsky sobor*, an executive assembly of delegates from the *zemstvos*, should be summoned to place Tsardom on a new constitutional and national basis. Had this been done, some feared, there might have been a movement to set aside the Tsarevich in favour of George Alexandrovich Yourievsky. While Loris-Melikov might have found such an idea feasible, it was unlikely. In any case the Tsar privately made it clear that, whatever the father and son feelings, the Tsarevich was and would remain his heir.

Among the family, only Grand Dukes Constantine and Michael remained faithful supporters of their brother and young new sister-in-law. Before taking their wives and children to St Petersburg to meet them, they told them firmly that they must be ready to meet their new Empress, brushing aside their wives' protests that 'she' was not an Empress yet by reminding them that as faithful subjects of the Tsar they had no right to criticize his decisions. The Princess would be crowned Empress once the period of state mourning for 'Aunt Marie' had passed, and until then she was to be treated as one. Michael's sons all accepted the matter without question, though the Grand Duke terminated the discussion abruptly when his son Serge started asking awkward questions about their new cousins' ages.

Some of the ministers, notably Loris-Melikov, accepted the marriage as a perfectly reasonable arrangement, and actively sought the friendship and support of Princess Yourievsky. The

Tsar found solace in the company of this 'second family', and after an hour with the eldest child, eight-year-old George ('Gogo'), he always seemed in good spirits.

The Tsar's nephew Grand Duke Alexander Michaelovich described how at a family meal the Tsar, in his sixties, acted more like a besotted youth of eighteen, whispering words of encouragement in his wife's ear, asking how she liked the wine, agreeing with everything she said, and satisfied that the younger members at table had evidently accepted her. After dinner the governess brought the children in so he could lift the little boy on his knee. 'Tell us, Gogo, what is your full name?' his father asked. 'I am Prince George Alexandrovich Yourievsky,' the eight-year-old child announced proudly, as he started to brush his father's sidewhiskers with his small hands. 'Well, we are all very glad to have made your acquaintance, Prince Yourievsky. By the way, prince, would you care to be a Grand Duke?' At this question Princess Yourievsky blushed deeply.[6] It was a display of paternal affection which the rest of his family found little short of nauseating, in particular Grand Duchess Michael, who angrily told her husband that she would 'never recognize that scheming adventuress' who had broken up the family and was 'plotting to ruin the empire'.[7]

In November 1880 the Tsar and Princess Yourievsky left Livadia for the last time and made for the north. At Kolpino, a station to the south-west of St Petersburg, the imperial train halted. On the Tsar's orders the whole of the family had been summoned to the railway room to meet the Princess for the first time. To the Tsarevich had fallen the none too agreeable task of breaking the news of the secret marriage to them. In a striking display of family unity which would have probably deceived casual observers, the Tsar and his son embraced with a great show of affection. The Tsar was anxious to demonstrate that there was no rift between them, and the Tsarevich must have decided out of loyalty to his father and the empire (if not to the memory of his mother) that a house divided against itself could not stand. It was a peculiar place for such a rendezvous, only to be explained by the fact that at a waiting room on a station the morganatic wife would have precedence over every Grand Duchess, which she would not at court at the Winter Palace. The next time she was to meet the whole family, her husband must have hoped, it would be when she was no longer merely his morganatic wife but had been crowned his consort.

At around this time Loris-Melikov informed the Tsar that he felt terrorism had passed its peak. On his advice the Tsar abolished the supreme executive commission, thus signalling the end of the mood of crisis and dictatorship, and named Loris-Melikov his new minister of the interior. He was the most powerful individual in the government, with the Tsar completely dependent on him, other ministers in total sympathy with his views or, if opposed to him, knowing better than to criticize. In order to retain the goodwill of the masses, or at least the intelligentsia, he decided to look at proposals once made by his earlier enlightened minister of the interior Peter Valuev, and Grand Duke Constantine, a new legislative body. Under this scheme, he proposed that the Tsar should invite representatives of such groups as the *zemstva*, assemblies of the nobility, and municipal councils to join in drafting legislation on subjects approved by the ministry of the interior, and that he should enlarge the state council with representatives from the very same groups. The council would consider the legislative drafts and make recommendations to the Tsar. Such an arrangement had been rejected in the past, but Loris-Melikov was confident of success.

In January 1881 he submitted the idea to the Tsar in writing. It had nothing in common with western constitutional reforms, he hastily assured him, and would not limit the autocratic prerogatives at all. To adopt the scheme would be to ensure the cooperation of the educated classes against *krámola*. The Tsar had only one major reservation, the enlargement of the state council. When that was dropped, he approved the remainder of the proposal, and authorized the minister to edit it for publication.

While most ministers agreed with the measure, there were mutterings of discontent. Some of the more conservatively minded began to suspect that Loris-Melikov was attempting to subvert the principles of autocracy and introduce constitutionalism by the back door. None was more dissatisfied than the Tsarevich, whose motives were not entirely political. The minister's ready acceptance of Princess Yourievsky had lowered him in his estimation, as had his apparent willingness to discuss matters of state with her. Influenced by Pobedonostsev, he was increasingly sceptical where moves towards constitutional government were concerned. Pobedonostsev was convinced that Loris-Melikov, whose early reforms he had welcomed, was leading the Tsar into jeopardy. Russia needed a strong, autocratic sovereign. Rumours spread that the Tsarevich's residence, the Anitchkov Palace, was the centre of opposition, and that he was under house arrest because of his attitude towards his father. In fact he was prudently keeping his counsel to himself, perhaps fearing that he would be the autocrat himself sooner than later.

After the long winter of the Tsarina's illness and the uncertainty of Princess Yourievsky's anomalous position at court, the Tsar had resolved to make a new start and begin the year 1881 with a magnificent state ball at the Winter Palace. The arrival of the Tsar and the Princess accompanied by the elder Grand Dukes and court dignitaries gave the signal for the start of proceedings. Following a family procession and an evening of dancing which stopped as the clock struck midnight, the Tsar led his family and guests to the supper tables.

Nothing could hide the Princess's discomfiture. According to Madame de Rynkiewicz, wife of the governor of Warsaw, 'she looked as though, apart from the Emperor, she found herself in an enemy camp'.[8] There had been much discussion as to whether she would sit down at table or follow the tradition of the sovereigns who always remained standing, walking between the tables and talking to the guests in turn. She did indeed accompany the Tsar on his rounds of hospitality, 'but her face was twitching and her lips were tightly drawn'.[9] Meanwhile, Loris-Melikov was seen to leave the room regularly, returning each time to speak a few words to the Tsar, reporting on the security measures surrounding the Palace and reassuring him that so far all was well. Their conversation was drowned by the chorus of the imperial opera, whose programme of dirges did nothing to lift the assembled company's spirits in an already tense atmosphere. The Tsar made every effort to be pleasant and affable to his guests, as he had always done, but Princess Yourievsky's evident discomfort overshadowed his efforts. She was under no illusions as to what the others thought of her and, wrote Grand Duke Alexander with hindsight, 'had no strength left to continue the struggle with the cruel world that would not forgive her success. She wanted to finish it all, no matter what price. She would have consented to the declaration of a republic in order to be left alone with her Sasha and her children.'[10]

The revolutionaries were temporarily quiet, biding their time and perturbed by the new climate of liberalism at the top. Loris-Melikov was doing his work well, and Zelyabov and Perovskaya feared that if he continued to win and hold the Liberals' confidence it would make the revolutionaries' work almost impossible. Yet they were not to be deflected from their mission. They set about mining every street that they thought the Emperor might travel through, as well as theatres and shops that he occasionally visited. The capital was so panic-stricken that when the Tsar attended a gala performance at the opera just before Christmas 1880, the house was almost empty. Only a few weeks earlier, Loris-Melikov had believed that the enemy was disarmed or frightened into inactivity. The increasing incidence of bombs left around in St Petersburg, while not causing explosions or fatalities, and the subsequent arrests, proved that all was not well. He tightened up security, and begged the Tsar to leave St Petersburg for the more secluded Gatchina for a while at least until all was clear. The Tsar refused, claiming that it would only be giving in to the terrorists. Only with reluctance did he agree to a Cossack escort accompanying his carriage whenever he appeared in public.

In January Loris-Melikov presented the Tsar with the final draft of his plans for accommodating a representative system with imperial autocracy, his official manifesto stating that all members of the *zemstva* would be invited to participate in a Council of State – a first step towards parliamentary government for Russia. The Council, or *Gosudarstvenny Soviet*, would be an enlarged deliberative assembly, but would not have executive power or be able to enact legislation. The Tsar appointed a committee under the presidency of the Tsarevich, to supervise a programme for enactment of the reform. It was rumoured that an imperial proclamation on the granting of a constitution would be made in March, on the anniversary of emancipation. In February the draft of the new Act was presented to the Tsar, who kept it to consider a little longer, and asked Loris-Melikov to prepare a manifesto for publication.

Meanwhile Sophia Perovskaya kept vigil outside the Winter Palace, watching the Tsar's routine attentively. She discovered that on Sundays he usually inspected the guards at Michael Palace, and then went to visit his cousin, daughter of Grand Duchess Helen. 'Will of the People' therefore decided to mine one of the streets leading to the Parade Ground, renting a nearby shop and turning it into a dairy, digging a tunnel from the basement to the centre of the thoroughfare. Work was still in progress when Zelyabov was arrested on a different charge altogether. Proudly he told the police that plans for the Tsar's destruction were so advanced that they could be realized without his further cooperation, and his arrest would make no difference. Even more determined to proceed with their plan of assassination, Perovskaya enlisted four collaborators, and told them that as the mining was not completed they would use hand grenades instead. Two other terrorists had been arrested in February. Had Perovskaya been among them, the Tsar might have died peacefully in his bed.

The manifesto was handed to the Tsar on the morning of 28 February/12 March. He read it and promised he would sign it the next day, when it would be published in the press. He also ordered that the council of ministers should meet on the following Wednesday for final consideration, framing and announcement of the project. At the same time Loris-Melikov warned him in the presence of the Tsarevich not to attend the Parade Ground the following day as some terrorists, notably Perovskaya, were still at large. The Tsar solemnly told him that he had only reluctantly accepted a bodyguard, and if he was not safe when surrounded by Cossacks he might as well abdicate. For the last few months, since the end of official mourning for the Tsarina, he felt he could appear in public with the woman whom he soon planned to make Tsarina; he was convinced that society was beginning to accept her as such, if not the children by his first marriage; he was beginning to enjoy court life more. Above all the dreaded Zelyabov had been captured. Slowly but surely he appeared to be regaining something of his old optimism and hope for the future.

There may have been another reason for his unusually relaxed demeanour. Paléologue suggested that he had confided his ultimate plans to nobody except Princess Catherine. When his political reform had been achieved and when she had been crowned Empress, he would have fulfilled his duty to his people and to her. Within six months or a year hence, he would renounce his throne and abdicate in favour of the Tsarevich, retiring with his wife and their children to France to live out the rest of their days as private citizens. How much truth there was in this was a secret which both husband and wife took to their graves.

After discussing business with Loris-Melikov he attended religious services in the Chapel of the Winter Palace, and lunched with the family. Afterwards he walked away for his regular sight of the guards ceremonies at the Michael Riding School. Everyone who saw him there was impressed by his unusually high spirits; he seemed twenty years younger. He called at the residence of his cousin Grand Duchess Catherine, then ordered the coachman to drive him back to the Winter Palace. It was all part of his regular Sunday routine, though mindful of the shadow hanging over him, he had accepted advice to vary his programme for security reasons. He always returned to the Palace by a different way from that which he set out. Nevertheless the terrorists were also ready for him, no matter which route he chose.

On this route Sophia Perovskaya had stationed four people, each carrying a bomb, and had taken her own place at a vantage point from which she could signal to them as the Tsar approached. The four bomb-handlers were all fanatics who knew that whoever threw the fatal device would probably pay with his life at the same time.

The first, thrown by Nicholas Rysakov, a student of mining, damaged the Tsar's carriage and wounded or killed two Cossacks and three horses.* Disregarding pleas for his own safety, the Tsar was unhurt and got out to see if he could help the wounded. Rysakov was seized, and when one of the police officers expressed relief that His Majesty was safe, another of the terrorists, Ignatius Grinevitsky, ran at them to throw another grenade, concealed in a snowball, at the sovereign's feet.

The resulting explosion shook the windows of the Winter Palace. The Tsar's face was streaming with blood, the left eye was torn from

*According to two accounts in *The Times*, 14 March 1881, the first explosion killed a *moujik* standing nearby, wounded one of the six Cossacks forming the escort, and two horses, but another account said that one officer and two Cossacks were killed outright. A cypher telegram from the *chargé d'affaires* at St Petersburg to Paris reported that one Cossack was killed, five injured, and 'there are said to be other victims'.

its socket, and both legs were shattered below the knee. It was probably only the intense cold which prevented him from bleeding to death on the spot. Semi-conscious, he murmured 'Home to the Palace to die'. His attendants moved him on to a stretcher and took him to lie on a couch in his study. Princess Yourievsky arrived to help the surgeons to bind his legs to stop the continuous flow of blood, giving him oxygen and rubbing his temples with ether, but they could do no more than ease his last moments. Also among the horrified group present was Grand Duke Nicholas Alexandrovich, twelve-year-old son of the Tsarevich. Any boy of such an age, watching his grandfather slowly die in such gruesome circumstances, could not fail to be shaken to the core. The effect on young Nicholas, already timid and unsure of himself, yet all too painfully aware that only his father's life stood between him and the office which his grandfather had filled, can scarcely be imagined.

Two hours after the explosion a bulletin was issued from the Palace, stating that there could be 'no hope' for His Imperial Majesty's life. Holy Communion was administered, and a few minutes later the Tsar breathed his last. His eldest son, who now succeeded him as Tsar Alexander III, was temporarily numb with shock. It fell to his brother Vladimir, who had regained his composure more quickly, to announce their father's death to the bewildered, shocked if not surprised crowds. As it was considered ominous for the new reign if the imperial messenger used the words 'death' or 'die', Vladimir called out in a loud voice, '*Godusar Imperator Vam Prikazal Dolga Jit!*' ('The Emperor has bidden you to live long!').[11]

Grinevitsky had been wounded in the attack and also died the same day. He outlived his victim by a few hours, regaining consciousness before he drew his last breath, but refusing to say a word to the police at his hospital bedside.

Maurice Paléologue was not alone in his observation that 'a liberator's is a dangerous job'. Nearly a century after his death, W.E. Mosse maintained that Tsar Alexander II 'proved himself not only a disappointing "liberal" – if indeed that term can be applied to him – but, more seriously, an inefficient autocrat'.[12] Yet he admits that while the Tsar could not be termed a successful ruler, his policy of modernization made him one of Russia's great westernizers, and that during his reign the Russian empire passed from the semi-feudal to the early capitalist stage of its development. What was often criticized as a vacillating policy of attempting to please one side and then the other was not such a failure after all. At worst, it was because he had no alternative; at best, it was an ingenious walk along the tightrope of opinion in a fiercely polarized political climate. This judgment was echoed by another recent historian, Edward Crankshaw, who took issue with the assessment of Tsar Alexander II as 'a reforming monarch who drew back appalled by the radical and revolutionary forces he had unleashed and fell back into reaction', arguing that he displayed a lamentable lack of cutting edge, alternating between enthusiasm and apathy, stubbornness and defeatism, vision and myopia,[13] while admitting that he was the most intelligent and humane of the Romanovs.[14]

Tsar Alexander II had ascended the throne when Russia was at the nadir of her fortunes, shocked by defeat in war on a scale which his father and ministers could never have envisaged. His efforts to assist the emergence of Russia from the past had only met with moderate success, partly because of flaws in his own character, partly as economic, political and intellectual forces in the western world of the mid-nineteenth century were beyond the control of any one individual, even the head of state of what was theoretically the world's most powerful empire. The fact that he died at the hands of revolutionaries who had hounded him for a couple of years, estranged from most of his family, and with the political education of his son and heir in the hands of a dyed-in-the-wool reactionary whose presence was a major factor in the dynasty's eventual downfall, should not be allowed to obscure the achievements of the autocrat who was at the same time justly heralded as 'the Liberator'.

Though some less partial subjects remained unmoved by their sovereign's violent death, others were undoubtedly distressed by the loss of an enlightened well-meaning man who had lacked the ruthlessness, if not the vision, to be a good Emperor. Whatever his failings as the autocrat of an unwieldy semi-medieval nation, he had striven to do his best for them, and many were united by grief. A Danish traveller to St Petersburg some weeks later wrote to her son at Heidelberg of the national mood, saying that the people's grief was 'like a tombstone'; and 'so stony that you cannot move or ease it by your sympathy'.[15] Only a year earlier Tchaikovsky had been invited to write music for the opening of an exhibition of art and industry planned to celebrate the Tsar's silver jubilee, but turned it down, claiming the suggestion filled him with 'extreme revulsion'; he had 'always nourished a pretty fair distaste'[16] for the sovereign. A year later he was in Rome, and had recently spent some time with Grand Dukes Serge and Paul who were also in the city, when a Russian sailor told him of the assassination. He was stunned by the news, as well as distressed at being abroad at such a dreadful moment of national disaster; 'I wanted to rush back home, to find out the details, to be amongst my own people, to take part in the demonstrations of sympathy for the new Emperor, to howl for vengeance along with everybody else.'[17] He had planned to accompany Serge and Paul to Athens and Jerusalem, but now nothing could be further from their minds. Paul, the composer noticed, took the horrifying news particularly badly; he suffered 'a terrible fit' and boarded the train home 'completely ill'.

Meanwhile, in England, the Tsar's old political adversary Disraeli, in failing health and with only six weeks himself to live, used his last appearance in the House of Lords at Westminster to salute the memory of 'the most beneficent prince that ever filled the throne of Russia'.[18] In the judgment of Grand Duke Alexander, 'idyllic Russia' ceased to exist on that day. 'Never again would a Russian Tsar be able to think of his subjects in terms of boundless confidence; never again would he be allowed to give his undisturbed attention to the cares of the state.'[19]

It was ironic that the Tsar should have been assassinated, and the similarly liberal Loris-Melikov threatened, while the Tsarevich was left alone. In the judgment of Stephen Graham, 'they insisted on murdering a liberal intelligent Tsar to make a stupid reactionary Grand Duke Emperor'.[20]

Part II: Tsar Alexander III, 1881–94

7

'A thorough disciplinarian'

The funeral of Tsar Alexander II was held with the strictest security imaginable. Representatives from several foreign courts came to join the horrified family, not without misgivings on their part or that of their sovereigns. The late Tsar's son-in-law and daughter, the Duke and Duchess of Edinburgh, left London at once on receiving the news they had dreaded and expected for so long. They arrived at St Petersburg three days later, and immediately sent a wire home to the Prince and Princess of Wales, assuring them that the new Tsar and Tsarina, 'Sasha' and 'Minnie', would appreciate their presence. Lord Dufferin, English ambassador at St Petersburg, agreed that their attendance would be desirable. Queen Victoria gave her consent reluctantly, warning Dufferin that if anything happened to them she would hold him responsible. From Berlin Emperor William sent his son Crown Prince Frederick William, despite receiving anonymous letters warning him that his life would be in danger if he went. The Tsar and Tsarina were at the Winter Palace, while their guests stayed at Anichkov Palace in conditions of claustrophobia almost beyond endurance. Count Loris-Melikov assured them that they would come to no harm as long as they did not go outside in the Tsar's company. Even so the Prince of Wales was dismayed by the narrow snow-covered garden at the Winter Palace, the only area in which it was considered safe for the Tsar to exercise, and said the area would be unworthy of a London slum.

The body of the deceased lay in a mortuary chapel in the Winter Palace, without any crown on his head or decorations on his breast, contrary to the normal funeral ritual of the Tsars. He had left orders that he wanted no emblems to follow him into the tomb. On the day before the body was taken from the Palace to the Cathedral of the Fortress, Pobedonostsev took the service for the last intercessions. After everyone else had retired, he saw the widowed Princess Catherine enter from the next room, and though her sister was supporting her, she evidently struggled to remain upright and retain her composure. She fell on her knees beside the coffin, pulled the veil aside, and covered the brow and face with long kisses before tottering out. Much as he had resented her, for once he admitted to nothing but sympathy for her plight. That evening she returned, carrying her long hair which she had just cut off, and placed it in her dead husband's hand as a gesture of farewell.

Once a day the Tsar was allowed to leave the Palace and attend a service held beside his father's coffin in the fortress church of St Peter and St Paul. In accordance with Russian custom the dead man's face had to be left exposed to be kissed by all his relatives, an unpleasant ordeal as his features had been damaged by the bomb and decay set in some days before the funeral took place on 15/27 March. To his sons it must have been ironic to see him laid to rest beside their wronged mother whom he had long ceased to love.

Before leaving St Petersburg the Prince of Wales invested his brother-in-law with the Order of the Garter on behalf of Queen Victoria. The ceremony, held at the Anichkov Palace, unintentionally brought a moment of light relief into the lives of those who sorely needed it. As the British heir walked into the Throne Room, leading the procession of five members of his staff carrying the insignia on narrow velvet cushions, as custom demanded, a very loud feminine voice called out in English that they looked exactly like a row of wet-nurses carrying babies. The Princess of Wales and the Tsarina glanced at each other and helplessly collapsed with laughter.

Some sections of Russian opinion fervently believed that revenge for the assassination was not the answer. Much as he abhorred the violent death of his late sovereign Count Leo Tolstoy, the author and philosopher, still begged the new Tsar to spare those responsible. In a long letter he argued that decisive methods of extermination had failed to quell terrorism, as had 'liberal indulgence' – namely partial freedom and steps towards a constitution – and that Christian forgiveness was the answer:

> If you do not pardon, but execute the criminals, you will have uprooted three or four out of hundreds; but evil breeds evil, and

> in place of those three or four, thirty or forty will grow up, and you will have let slip for ever the moment which is worth a whole age – the moment when you might have fulfilled the will of God, but did not do so – and you will pass for ever from the parting of the ways where you could have chosen good instead of evil, and you will sink for ever into that service of evil, called the Interest of the State. . . . One word of forgiveness and Christian love, spoken and carried out from the height of the throne, and the path of Christian rule which is before you, waiting to be trod, can destroy the evil which is corroding Russia. As wax before the fire, all Revolutionary struggles will melt away before the man-Tsar who fulfils the law of Christ.[1]

He persuaded Grand Duke Serge to place it on his desk, and the Tsar read it but contemptuously threw it aside. At the same time the executive committee of the People's Will believed mistakenly that they had brought autocracy to its knees. Their new ruler, they imagined, would surely listen to advice in order to avoid the same fate. In a lengthy open letter they warned him that there were only two possible alternatives – 'either the inevitable revolution, which cannot be obviated by capital punishments; or voluntary compliance with the will of the people on the part of the Government'. They demanded 'a general amnesty of all previous political offenders, for they were no criminals, but mere executors of a hard civic duty'; and 'the convocation of representatives of all the Russian people for a revision and reform of the private laws of the State, according to the will of the nation'. These would be 'the only means of restoring Russia to the paths of peaceful progress', and their party would never be guilty of any act of violence against the measures of a government created by such a parliament. It ended with the words 'Your Majesty has to decide. You have two ways before you; it is for you to choose which you will take.'[2]

Neither appeal had any effect. His Imperial Majesty Alexander III, Tsar of all the Russias, had decided already. Ever since the explosion in the Winter Palace, he had lived in even more dread than his father, and was determined to purge the empire of terrorism. His reign had barely begun before barriers were hurriedly erected at potentially vulnerable sites. Guards were moved regularly around the Winter and Anichkov Palaces, and riflemen were posted at the entrances of government buildings, with armed and mounted patrols in the streets, as the police were ordered to leave no stone unturned in rounding up suspects. The family observed security as strictly as possible, the new Tsar and Tsarina barely stepping outdoors at first. Pobedonostsev personally told the Tsar to lock all doors leading to his bedroom and to lock himself in before retiring to bed. All their children were under round-the-clock surveillance. From Berlin, Chancellor Bismarck ordered the German ambassador in St Petersburg to telegraph him twice a day. If he received no telegram, he would have to assume that the telegraph had been destroyed in the ensuing state of anarchy.

Such a move was symptomatic of total panic, and as the period of calm and lack of revolutionary outrage lengthened into weeks and months, the guards and sentries grew bored with waiting for something to happen. Loris-Melikov refused to share the mood of alarm. Though he had failed to keep his late master safe, he was still sure that the few revolutionaries still at large could be rounded up by ordinary police methods. If the granting of reforms was delayed, he feared, then the vast majority of responsible educated Russians who sympathized with the revolutionaries would be drawn towards them. Some officials believed that the assassination had completely discredited him and that he would soon be dismissed, but Tsar Alexander III was reluctant to take any precipitate decision on the matter. Maybe it was out of reluctance to do anything with haste which could be construed as a public demonstration of rebuttal of his father's policies, or maybe a temporary lack of confidence in his own judgment.

The courts were ordered to bring the assassins to justice as soon as possible. Grinevitsky was dead but Perovskaya was still at large, and with four of her colleagues she was arrested a week later. All five were condemned to death: Zelyabov, who had been in custody when the Tsar was assassinated but still boasted of being the *eminence grise* behind the operation; Kibalchich, the chemist who had made the grenades; Rysakov, who had been the last to volunteer; and Michelovitch, who had attended early meetings at which it had been discussed. Jessica Hellman, who had lent her flat to the conspirators, was spared as she was pregnant, and sentenced to penal servitude.

The others were hanged on 3/15 April in what would be the last public executions ever held at St Petersburg, seated in chairs on large tumbrils, with their backs to the horses. Each bore a large placard bearing the word '*Tsaryubeeyetz*' ('Regicide'). They were followed by two brass bands, playing loudly enough to prevent the condemned persons from addressing the half-approving, half-indignant crowds. The music had been selected with little thought; one band regaled the gathering with *Fatiniza*, and whenever the musicians paused for breath the other band took over with *Kaiser Alexander*, a similarly jaunty lively march. 'The hideous incongruity between the tune and the occasion made one positively shudder,'[3] wrote the diplomat Lord Frederick Hamilton.

Tension subsided in St Petersburg after the executions, but the mood throughout rural Russia was sombre. Sensational versions of what had happened passed from village to village. Some peasants believed that the landed nobility had killed the Tsar Liberator because of his kindness to the peasantry, and they attacked local landlords, seeking revenge. Others imagined, or were told, that the new Tsar intended to make his coronation the occasion for an announcement of plans to distribute the aristocracy's lands, and peasants became impatient at having to wait.

The Tsar was not slow to set his own seal on the direction of Russian affairs during his reign. Autocracy, he firmly believed, was divinely ordained, and nationalism, based on the fact that 'real Russians' were Russian Orthodox by birth and monarchist by conviction, was an essential policy of government.

His first appointment was to make General Nicholas Baranov prefect of St Petersburg with responsibility for the maintenance of law and order. Having been dismissed from the navy by Grand Duke Constantine for fraudulently claiming victory over a Turkish battleship in the war, Baranov's reputation was not spotless. Yet it did not prevent him from joining the army with the full approval of the then Tsarevich, who disliked his uncle Constantine. He had been a firm ally of the Tsarevich and Pobedonostsev, who saw him as one of the 'true Russians' needed to replace liberals in responsible positions. Now he saturated St Petersburg with emergency vigilance, surrounding the city with Cossack patrols to search and intercept everybody who entered or left.

To protect the Tsar and run all revolutionaries to ground he established a committee of volunteers, the committee of public safety, nicknamed by some the Baranov Parliament, *baran* being the Russian for sheep. Its members watched carefully the Tsar's movements, all activities involving members of the imperial family, guarded railway stations and palaces, and reported anything they thought was suspicious. The prefect enlisted an army of volunteers by requiring cab drivers to report all the addresses to which they took their fares, that landlords should divulge the actions of their tenants, and that servants should inform against their masters and fellow-servants. It was heightened by regular announcements from the prefect's office that a plot against the Tsar or state had just been discovered. In the end he overreached himself; patrols interfered with the supply of food and goods so much that they had to be withdrawn, and much of the informants' information was obviously irrelevant, while not everyone took the task seriously in cooperating with informing against everybody else.

Barely had Alexander II taken his last breath before Loris-Melikov asked his successor if he would confirm his father's instructions in publishing the manifesto which would have prepared the Russian people for the long-awaited tentative step which would lead them closer towards representative government. Still numbed by shock, Tsar Alexander III answered that Loris-Melikov was to make no changes to what his father had ordered; 'this shall be his bequest to his people'. He would always respect his father's wishes, and the manifesto should be published the next day. Privately he had had his doubts about Loris-Melikov and his policies, fearing that the constitution to which Tsar Alexander II had been about to append his signature would be dangerous for Russia, yet unsure of himself, he intended to behave with caution and set a new date to consider the matter fully.

That night Pobedonostsev argued that he should wait and countermand publication. A secret meeting by the absolutist clique was determined to suspend the execution of the document as a prelude to its destruction. Tsarevich Alexander had been involved in its approval, but now he seemed – or was being persuaded – to have second thoughts. Grand Duke Constantine, Milyutin, and Alexander Abaza, appointed minister of finance by Loris-Melikov, spoke in its favour; but several more conservative-minded officials were convinced that it should not be allowed to go any further. They advised that the calling of a national congress would be premature, and the matter should be adjourned indefinitely. According to eye-witnesses, by the end of the sitting the Tsar appeared to be 'seized with a sort of faintness'. Never the quickest of thinkers and not versed in the skills of argument or discussion, he was content to let his more articulate and quick-witted ministers and servants convey their opinions, especially where they coincided with his.

Meanwhile he secretly authorized Pobedonstsev to draft a new manifesto expressing firm commitment to autocracy, due to be published at the end of April. It affirmed his promise to respect the will of God that he should govern 'with faith in the power and truth of autocracy', and never to sanction any limitations on his autocratic powers. Pobedonstsev, a bitter enemy of Loris-Melikov, attacked him in a letter to the Tsar, denouncing him as a man who was 'not a Russian patriot', and probably playing a double game. The new constitution, he said, was 'a new, supreme talking-shop on a foreign model', where 'corrupt speeches will be given'. It was filed away bearing a note in the Tsar's handwriting, 'Thank God, this criminal and precipitous step towards a constitution was not taken'.

Loris-Melikov was furious, declaring that the Tsar had 'torn up his own signature!' Bitterly he told Yyacheslav Plehve, the director of the state police department, that as a result of rejecting the constitution the Tsar would be killed, 'and you and I will be hanged on a gallows'.[4] He resigned and left Russia, settling in Nice, to be replaced as minister of the interior by Pobedonostsev's nominee, Count Nicholas Ignatev. There was a virtual sweep of liberal ministers in favour of conservatives. Grand Duke Constantine, whose bitter enemies at court had long resented his reforming zeal as well as his impatient manner, was rumoured throughout the courts of Europe to be implicated in his brother's murder. Such a slander was rightly regarded as nonsense by those who had any personal knowledge of Constantine whatsoever, but in the fraught family atmosphere which pervaded personal relationships during that unhappy year, rumour fed on rumour and his foes had their revenge at last. Thoroughly out of sympathy with his nephew, he had had enough. If hostile forces really wanted to drive him out of public life, he no longer had the will to fight. Resigning all his government posts, he took his mistress and their children off to Paris. He was succeeded as imperial head of the navy by the Tsar's brother Alexis, and as chairman of the state council by his own brother Michael.

In the estimation of Charles Lowe the Tsar's stubborn refusal, or rather his readiness to allow the reactionary counsels of Pobedonostsev and his cronies to overrule him, to honour the quasi-parliamentary intentions which his father had been ready to bequeath Russia, was 'the great mistake of his reign'.[5] Had he not kept his people muzzled but given them some opportunity to express their grievances, their hopes and their aspirations, his reign and thirteen years of reaction might not have been such a dark era for Russia. Nonetheless it was understandable that he looked askance at the fate of his liberal father and felt obliged, not least for his own safety, to follow a diametrically different path.

With her husband's death Princess Yourievsky had lost nearly everything. Her children were her only comfort, and she clung to them as much as they depended on her. They had been left a substantial income in their father's will, and he had made his heir responsible for them as well as their mother. He had reportedly left his eldest son and heir a letter with his will, committing his wife and children to his care, as 'your friendly feelings towards them have always heartened me, and I believe that you will not forsake them and will be their protector when I am gone',[6] though doubts have been cast on the document's authenticity.

Tsar Alexander II had left instructions that she and the children could retain their apartments in the Winter Palace, and much as he might have disapproved of the liaison, her stepson was neither vindictive nor dishonourable. Not only did he put no pressure on her to move, but he also allowed her the use of another dwelling in St Petersburg, *Le Petit Palais Rose*, named after the pink marbled front. She moved there soon after her husband's funeral, taking all the furniture, books and decorations she wanted from his private apartments. With them came his bloodstained uniform, a cross, various icons, his wedding ring and reading glasses, a deathbed portrait which showed all his injuries, and a torn stump of his finger which she had preserved in glass and kept under his bed. These keepsakes remained in her possession for the rest of her life.

She turned one of her rooms into a replica of the study where he had died.

If the attitude of her stepsons (of whom the eldest was not only two years older than her but now her sovereign) and their wives during the previous reign had made it clear that once her husband was dead she could expect no special favours, to their credit they showed her no malice. They were undoubtedly moved by pity, for their loss was hers as well. Maybe they saw her to some extent as a victim of their father's baser desires.

In her memoirs her younger daughter Princess Catherine recalled a game in which she, her brother and sister, were thrown around playfully in a huge net by her eldest half-brother. She could remember fondly the enjoyment and shrieks of childish laughter that always went with it, 'and the amusement of the Emperor, who seemed a playful and kind Goliath amongst all the romping children'.[7] Though such a touching picture may sound like an attempt to look back on infancy through rose-coloured spectacles, there is no reason to doubt her.

All the same, the widow was perpetually haunted by what she had lost. Russia could never be the same for her without her husband, and the increasingly repressive political atmosphere saddened her. Moreover not everybody was anxious to extend the same courtesy to her as his family, and at a railway station zealous functionaries refused to let her use the 'Tsar's Room', a waiting room for administrators and government officials.

Determined to put the past behind them, she and her children set out for France in the spring of 1882, accompanied by her companion and sister-in-law Barbara Shebeko, a household of around twenty people – nurses, governesses and tutors, cooks, maids, footmen, a doctor – and a military escort for security. At the German frontier they changed trains, and after arriving in Paris stayed briefly in an hotel, then in a house in Switzerland, before returning to the French capital where they installed themselves in a house at Avenue Kléber, with a country house at Boulevard des Sablons in the suburb of Neuilly-sur-Seine. In a home which was at last her own, the Princess created a shrine to her late husband. Soon her sister joined her, and as she had been handsomely provided for, her less wealthy brothers regularly came to visit, finding her a useful source of funds. In time several Romanov in-laws came to call as well. That Grand Duke and Duchess Vladimir and Grand Duke Alexis should have been among the first was not surprising, as they were regular visitors to Paris, but that the Duchess of Edinburgh soon followed suggests that she was indeed regarded as one of the family.

While her children often had cause to rue their anomalous position in the world, they must have been thankful for their escape to a more classless society. They settled in Nice in 1888 where the Princess bought a three-storey marble villa, naming it Villa Georges, and furnishing it with treasured reminders of her husband. She brought her children up with the full knowledge that their father had been Tsar of All the Russias, and her bearing was that of an Empress, which she would have been but for fate.

Tsar Alexander III was aged thirty-six at the time of his accession. Six foot three inches tall, broad-shouldered, and extremely strong, he could tear a pack of cards in half with his bare hands. Ungainly in movement with thinning hair and a beard, he had the appearance of a Russian peasant, a look he accentuated by dressing in the baggy trousers and shirt of a *moujik*. He invariably spoke with the voice of a sergeant-major, and issued his orders in a manner that discouraged argument if not discussion as well. When angry he could be terrifying, and his language was often blunt if not crude. As a family man his young nephews and nieces saw a different person altogether, finding him full of fun, always ready to join in their games. Outside the domestic circle he gave an air of sullen taciturnity, reinforced by a distrustful look, confounded with a scowl, blunt replies and brusque movements in order to finish any uncongenial conversation as soon as possible.

All the same his ministers soon learned to like and respect him. Once they were chosen and had proved they could be trusted, he would stand by them and their policies in the face of all opposition. A forbidding exterior concealed a spirit which could be perfectly approachable. When belatedly sending him congratulations on his birthday one year, men of a particular regiment assured His Majesty that they were drinking his health for the fifth day in succession. 'Time to stop!' he replied good-humouredly.

'A confirmed believer in the policies dictated by healthy national egotism, a thorough disciplinarian and a thinker of pronounced scepticism, he brought to the throne a complete freedom from all illusions,' wrote his cousin (and later son-in-law) Grand Duke Alexander. 'He had watched the passing show of the imperial court sufficiently long to acquire contempt for his father's collaborators, while his knowledge of the rulers of contemporary Europe gave birth to his well-motivated distrust of their intentions.'[8] The contempt and distrust were there, though some of his contemporaries might not have recognized 'a thinker of profound scepticism' in their sovereign. He knew his limitations, and while he might have looked or sounded like an autocrat, particularly when in a bad temper, he was prepared to leave the thinking, policy and administration of Russia to ministers whom he knew were better equipped for the task.

Taking threats on his life much more seriously than his father, he accepted a bodyguard without question. When warned that it was impossible to make the Winter Palace secure, after his father's funeral he needed no persuasion to move to the safer, less pretentious Gatchina, about thirty miles from St Petersburg, much as he might grumble about having to 'retreat' after he had faced Turkish guns in wartime.

Although on first sight it seemed almost as grand inside as the Winter Palace, its six hundred rooms were moderately sized and furnished more simply for greater comfort. It stood in the more rural setting of a large park which stretched from forests and thickly wooded mountains to the seashore. Gardens were laid out in the English fashion, with trim walks and neat flower beds, fragments of classical stonework, and the Tsarina's favourite roses, while well-stocked orchards and vineyards were to be found further afield. The Tsar had always enjoyed it during childhood, and during his reign he was never happier anywhere else in Russia. Part of the great Romanov art collections were kept there, but his children were quite unconcerned and thought nothing of playing hide-and-seek in the Chinese Gallery, crouching behind vases twice their size. Fortunately none of these irreplaceable treasures were ever damaged in the process. Except on formal occasions when meals were served in the banqueting hall, the family dined in a large bathroom on the ground floor. But even here security was so strict that nobody in residence, whatever their station or rank, was allowed to lock their doors at any hour of the day or night. The French chef responsible for food was under constant supervision, and sentries guarding the walls of the park were changed every hour so that vigilance could be maintained.

To uphold this increased level of security, including curbs on the Jews and restrictions on the press, called for additional corps of gendarmes; a new division of the department of police, the *Okhrannoe Otdelenie* ('Security Division'), known as the *Okhrana*. Its members were basically undercover agents employed to keep political suspects under close observation by any means possible.

Always a man of simple ways, the Tsar did not change the routine which he had always followed. On rising early each day he washed in cold water, took a stroll in the park, made himself coffee in a glass percolator and sat down to a humble breakfast of boiled eggs and rye bread and butter, sometimes joined by the Tsarina, then went to his desk to begin his day's work. Although there were plenty of servants to wait on him, ready at the touch of bells in his study, he preferred not to disturb them. A session of 'manual labour', such as felling trees and sawing them into planks and planing them to prepare them for the cabinet-maker, or shovelling snow, set him up for the more important if less congenial tasks of paperwork. To these he devoted himself conscientiously, reading and signing large piles of laws and reports, invariably making notes in the margin, his favourite criticisms of particular individuals, 'What a beast he is!', or of various groups of people, 'They are a set of hogs'. Bad news, such as accounts of fire, famine, or failure of crops, was described as 'discouraging'.

Much of the work could have been done just as well by junior officials. One of the roles of His Imperial Majesty was in effect that of a rubber stamp, or chief clerk to the empire. Ministers of the previous two Tsars had sought their permission to submit only matters of major importance, only to be told firmly that it was not for them to decide what was important and what was not. When Loris-Melikov suggested to Alexander III that his council of ministers could relieve him of certain burdens such as approving the appointment of provincial midwives or signing requests for leave from imperial pages, he received the same answer. Even an ever-swelling bureaucracy and subsequent overwork was apparently no excuse for breaking with time-honoured tradition;

what his father and grandfather had done in the normal course of their duties, he would do as well.

Lunch was served at 1 p.m., consisting of three courses including soup. This was followed by another walk in the park, often accompanied by one or more of the family and an adjutant. Next he read or glanced through the newspapers, and listened to a reading of the summary of the previous day's news, consisting of extracts from the Russian and foreign papers selected by officials and copied out in calligraphic script. Although interested in foreign and home news, quite remarkably for one who so treasured family life and abhorred smart society, he also liked hearing gossip and scandal from the fashionable society world of the capital. Next he gave audiences to ministers whose reports were due on that day, discussed matters laid before him, and read over more edicts drawn up for his signature, signing them or putting them aside for further consideration. Four-course dinner was at 8 p.m. *en famille*, then he took tea in the Tsarina's private apartments before retiring to bed.

Once installed in government, Ignatev's immediate priority was the eradication of *kramóla*, which in his eyes meant not merely terrorism but any threat to the social and political order. Within a year most of the known terrorists were under arrest or had fled. Putting an end to seditious activities was easier said than done, and Ignatev spent several months working closely with Baranov on legislation to deal with the problem. Also involved was Phehve, who had been one of Loris-Melikov's protégés but now saw his future lay in joining Ignatev's crusade against liberalism. The result, published in August 1881, was known officially as the Statute Concerning Measures for the Protection of State Security and Social Order, or more generally as the Law on Exceptional Measures. It provided for directives under the local authorities and the minister of the interior, to whom they were responsible, for suspension of legal regulations and administrative practices in any period for any area where there might, according to the central authorities, be need for protection against terrorism, outbreaks of peasant unrest, strikes or student demonstrations. It amounted to the exercising of martial law, with officials in such areas granted exceptional powers to enforce 'protection', even to prohibiting meetings of any kind, even in private homes; search and arrest on their own authority; suspending the operation of schools; closing business establishments; and imposing limited sentences without trial. An inter-ministerial committee, acting on the recommendation of police authorities, might sentence persons considered to be political criminals to terms of exile of up to five years, without trial if necessary.

The attack on *kramóla* was additionally reinforced by the re-introduction of stringent controls on the press. An inter-ministerial commission was empowered to suspend or close down any offending publications, while after three warnings Ignatev himself could subject any title to censorship in the two capitals of St Petersburg and Moscow, where Tsar Alexander II had removed such a repressive measure.

The Tsar's education had been undertaken by Pobedonostsev; known behind his back as the 'Black Tsar', he was one of the most reactionary men in Russia, and his pupil had inherited his prejudices. The Tsar was not uncritical of him, and remarked once that 'one could freeze to death just listening to him all the time'. Pobedonostsev was largely responsible for the savage persecution of Russian Jews, placing them high on his list of subversive elements alongside the Poles. Anti-semitism in Russia was nothing new; in the reign of Catherine the Great they had been confined to land on the western and southern borders of the empire. Alexander II had eased their plight, allowing them to settle anywhere they wished. Now Ignatev encouraged them to emigrate, announcing that the western frontier was 'open' to them. He justified his action in the name of the Tsar by issuing a circular to the local governors pointing out that within the last twenty years Jews had been monopolizing trade and commerce, and had by lease and purchase gradually acquired a considerable portion of the land in which they did not so much aim at increasing the productive power of the country, more at exploiting its Slavonic inhabitants, especially the poorer classes. This, he explained, had been responsible for the recent riots; 'while repressing these acts of violence, the Government at the same time recognized the need of equally rigorous measures for remedying the abnormal relations existing between the Jews and the native population, and for protecting the people from that injurious activity of the Jews which, according to local reports, was the real cause of the agitation'.[9]

Other Russians hated the Jews, denouncing them all as shopkeepers and moneylenders. While racialism and anti-semitism had always been close to violence, under the reign of Tsar Alexander III and the rule of Ignatev and Pobedonostsev, brutality against them became respectable. Anti-Jewish agitation was eagerly endorsed by some of the revolutionaries who despised their financial acumen, and argued that in killing them the masses had embarked on a course of action that could only end in the violent death of all oppressors throughout the borders of Russia. For his part, Ignatev maintained that an international Jewish conspiracy had been fomented by other Powers during the Russo–Turkish war, as proved by Russia's humiliation at the Berlin Congress by that most powerful Jew of all, the late British prime minister, Benjamin Disraeli. Further evidence of Jewish perfidy could be seen in the hand they had had in Polish subversion, and a Polish–Yiddish association that had been responsible for difficulties in the St Petersburg stock exchange. More brutally, Pobedonostsev proclaimed that one-third must die, one-third emigrate, and one-third be converted or assimilate.

Much was made of the fact that Jessica Hellman was Jewish, and that not only the Tsar but also most of his subjects believed that Jews had attempted to frighten the autocracy into conceding political rights and representative institutions which they could exploit to their own advantage, and were heavily implicated in the conspiracies which had claimed the life of his father. Within six weeks of his accession the Jewish quarter of Elizabethgrad was sacked and burned, and a reign of terror against them was unleashed; thousands of homes were destroyed, and many more Russian Jews were reduced to poverty. Fires and looting occurred at Kiev, and 2,000 Jews had the roofs burned over their heads. The Tsar was persuaded unremittingly by his advisers that Jews were 'social parasites, demoralising every community into which they penetrated – a species of human vermin whom every Government should seek to extirpate for the general good',[10] and international Jewry was attempting to end the monarchical system. According to Ignatev Jews exploited peasants, fomented sedition against the government, and hated the Christian world; it was therefore the government's responsibility to protect Christians from them. By the May Laws of 1882, no Jew could hold any administrative post, become a lawyer, or own land; Jewish schools were to be closed; books could not be printed in Hebrew; no Jew could marry a Christian unless he gave up his religion; no Jew had the right of appeal against any court sentence; they were not permitted to engage in business on Sundays or Christian holidays; and only a small proportion of them could attend universities. Within six months of this legislation, an estimated 225,000 destitute Jewish families left Russia for Eastern Europe, much to the Tsar's satisfaction.

While admitting privately that their lot was a hard one, he was convinced that their plight was 'preordained by the Gospels', and that they deserved punishment as they had crucified Christ. Personal prejudices inculcated in him by Pobedonostsev from adolescence had been reinforced by calumnies circulated about the Jews in connection with fraud on a massive scale in the commissariat department during the Russo–Turkish war by men responsible for appropriating money that should have gone to supply soldiers with adequate clothing and food. Had the Tsar spoken out against such persecution, it is questionable as to what effect his words would have had, so ingrained was the feeling among his subjects. When rioters were asked the reason for their behaviour, they retorted that 'our little father, the Tsar' wished it. Throughout Europe these attacks were the subject of hostile criticism, particularly in England. The Russian press shrugged off such attacks from 'self-conceited, hypocritical, and ignorant islanders', and *Novoe Vreyma* retorted that England had much to answer for outside Europe, accusing her of poisoning the Chinese with opium and 'under pretext of abolishing the slave trade, is now exterminating in most wholesale fashion the numerous races of Africa – the concern of a people who do those things is certainly astonishing'.[11]

The main voice of dissent came from Michael Reutern, once Tsar Alexander II's minister of finance and now chairman of the committee of ministers. He argued forcefully that it was necessary to protect everyone from any kind of illegal encroachment; if the Jews were hounded today, next it would be the peasants, who were 'morally the same' except that they belonged to the Orthodox Christian faith, and then the turn of the merchants and landlords. They could all expect 'the most terrible kind of socialism' in the near future. A commission was set up under the equally enlightened

Count Pahlen to examine the status and position of Jews in Russia, and to make recommendations for revision of laws regulating their position in society. At length it concluded that Russian Jews had to be treated as Russians and not foreigners, and advised that the existing repressive and discriminatory laws should be replaced in an orderly fashion by a gradual process of total emancipation. By then, however, the official anti-semitic attitude was so deeply rooted that it would have taken more than the word of a committee chairman to initiate a change in policy. Many Jews had taken the path of least resistance and emigrated, mostly to western Europe or North America, carrying with them a deeply engrained hatred of tsardom which would fall on fertile ground and convert other nations to their cause. Those who had stayed, generally the more intellectual, began to study Marxism and anarchism, forming as they did so an ever-growing disaffected community within the empire which would take only a few years to erupt. The Jewish Social Democratic Party, a direct result of the persecution of the 1880s, would play a major role in encouraging strikes and demonstrations against Russian autocracy, not to mention revolutionary education of the people, during the last years of Romanov rule.

Not all of Ignatev's schemes were directed towards repression. One enlightened idea was the establishment of a *zemsky sobor*, or consultative assembly elected by the peasants, landed nobles and merchants. Rather idealistically he imagined that it would provide a forum for the Tsar and his subjects to meet; delegates would share their hopes and sorrows with him, believing that his 'divinely guided conscience' would lead him to do whatever was best for them. This institution, he decided, should be inaugurated on a suitable occasion, such as the Tsar's coronation, to take place in May 1883. By opening a *zemsky sobor* at the same time, in the Moscow Kremlin, Ignatev hoped he would prove willing to show himself a true father of his people, give the lie to fears that he was a reactionary seeking to turn back the clock, and bring forth a groundswell of loyalty which would make his reign a golden one.

Knowing that Pobedonstsev would be certain to oppose it, Ignatev enlisted the support of Count Ilarion Vorontsov-Dashkov, minister of the court, whose children used to play with those of the Tsar. The Count proved agreeable, but Pobedonostsev's influence was too strong; to permit such a body, he stormed, would mean revolution, the ruin of government, and therefore of Russia. The Tsar abruptly dismissed the suggestion and relieved Ignatev of his post, replacing him with Dmitri Tolstoy.

Nevertheless, there were signs of modest reform, especially in the first years of the reign. Nicholas Bunge, who was minister of finance for five years, worked towards the general improvement of every level of society. For the peasants, reduction of their redemption payments, schemes to increase the availability of land to them, establishment of a national bank to provide means for them to purchase the land, and initial measures for unburdening them of the poll tax; for the financially pressed landlords, a banking system was established to provide government loans; and for industrial workers, inspection systems to ensure adequate safety and better working conditions in factories were introduced.

At the same time the Tsar appointed a committee to serve with Michael Kakhanov, a prominent member of the state council, to work on suggestions for the improvement of local government, using data assembled through Loris-Melikov's investigations. Its final report, in 1885, included recommendations which should have been considered for reform. Unfortunately such initiatives were engulfed in the subsequent mood of reaction. Thanks to the combined influence of Pobedonostsev, Tolstoy and Katkov, distrust and fear dominated the government from 1886 onwards.

By the time of his coronation in May 1883, the Tsar had evidently gained in confidence. Count Vorontsov-Dashkov was in charge of ceremonial for the occasion, and the religious services, public displays, crowning at the Kremlin, and programme of entertainments, all went smoothly. At Khodynka Field, the military training area just outside the city, thousands of his peasant subjects gathered to pay him homage and receive the traditional gifts of sweets, *kolbasa* ('salami'), drink, and souvenirs decorated with an image of the Romanov double-headed eagle. Never again throughout his reign would the Tsar be so close to his people.

From the end of April there was an influx into Moscow of many thousands of visitors from the provinces, as well as representatives of the various royal and imperial families and governments of Europe. Prominent among the guests were the Tsar's brother-in-law the Duke of Edinburgh, the Duke of Aosta, the Prince of Montenegro, and a cousin who would shortly incur his greatest displeasure, another Alexander, Prince of Bulgaria. On 12/24 May the official state entry to Moscow took place, with a procession of Russian Grand Dukes and foreign princes escorting the Tsar to the Kremlin. He rode by himself in front, a squadron of horse guards forming the vanguard, announcing his approach to the troops and to the civilian population lining the streets of their march. A long file of golden carriages followed their cavalcade, the first one containing the Tsarina, her elder daughter, eight-year-old Xenia, and Queen Olga of the Hellenes, the others being reserved for the Russian Grand Duchesses, princesses of royal blood and elder ladies-in-waiting.

A *Te Deum* at the Cathedral of the Archangels, and various entertainments in honour of the imperial family and their guests took place over the next couple of days, prior to the coronation itself on 15/29 May. The resigned expression on the Tsar's face betrayed his true feelings at the pomp and ceremony of the occasion, while the Tsarina, 'covered with crown jewels and looking like some Oriental deity', was in her element with a radiant smile for everyone. Everard Primrose, a member of the British diplomatic service and brother of the future prime minister Lord Rosebery, was overwhelmed by the contrast between Russian pageantry and his own experiences at home, where his own monarch was generally seen in 'a somewhat unattractive bonnet'. 'For the first time one realises the picture of toy books and playing cards and saw Royalty crowned, robed, sceptred and orbed.'[12]

Although security was as tight as ever, the authorities were pleasantly surprised at the lack of nihilist activity or efforts. In fact they had decided that any attempt against the Tsar during his coronation would do their cause more harm than good.

A customary coronation manifesto was issued, providing for the remission of taxes, fines and punishments. Criminals condemned without deprivation of civil rights had one-third of their sentences remitted, while exiles to Siberia for life had their sentences commuted to twenty years' penal servitude, at the discretion of the governor of the province concerned. Yet those who had hoped for a new distribution of land among the peasantry were to be disappointed. At a Moscow banquet for the elders of the rural communes, the Tsar told them to pay no heed to 'absurd rumours' about the subject; 'all property – yours as well as other people's – must be inviolable'.[13] Primrose expressed the general disappointment; the *ukase* was 'an empty document giving back to people some old debt which could never have been collected and promising nothing'.[14]

8

'*The* very bad state *of Society*'

The reign of Tsar Alexander III saw a deepening mood of Russification. In Finland and the Baltic States people were deprived of their hard-won autonomy; censorship was introduced, and the Russian language was made compulsory in all schools. Even German families settled in Russia since the days of Peter the Great were subject to restrictions. A *ukase* aimed at German manufacturers and merchants who had built up large businesses prohibited them from inheriting or acquiring property, and many had to close down their factories and leave. New military uniforms were designed with Russian boots and black lambskin *shapka* replacing all Prussian details or 'foreign frippery'. Speaking German was forbidden at court, and every man with a German name who could be replaced by one with a Russian name was dismissed from government service. When the German chief astronomer of the Russian empire died, the Tsar demanded that his successor should be a Russian and have a genuine Russian name. As the only scientifically qualified astronomer was a Herr Kleber, the post was conferred on an ignorant Russian general.

Despite his mother's Hessian blood, the Tsar regarded himself as Russian to the core. He always chose Russian food to be served at his table, to be included on all menus for the imperial household, and he encouraged others to eat it as much as possible. He enjoyed homegrown wines, particularly those from the Crimean imperial vineyards, and gave orders that at court and in the officers' mess of the guards regiments, no foreign wines should be served except when honouring foreign diplomats or rulers.

When affairs of state required his presence at St Petersburg during the summer months he lived at the more humble Anichkov Palace, using the Winter Palace only for official functions, and even then with reluctance, wandering awkwardly through the huge supper-rooms, or playing bridge in an ante-room. When the winter season finished they returned to Gatchina until summer. The imperial summer residence was Peterhof, though they also visited Krasnoe Selo, site of the guards' summer exercises and the great gathering of St Petersburg society, and the coast of Finland, staying on board the yacht *Polar Star*. The Tsarina had long had a particular affection for the grand duchy of Finland, and regretted the official Russian policy which sought to curtail Finnish autonomy. Although her husband – always more the autocrat in theory than practice – considered himself obliged to respect official Russian policy, he sought to moderate any moves against Finland in deference to her feelings. Early in autumn they attended army manoeuvres, usually in one of the south-western provinces. After that they would entertain a few specially invited guests in a lodge at the imperial hunting preserves of Spala or Skierniewice, before returning to Gatchina for the last weeks of the year, with the occasional trip south to Livadia. Everything was carefully planned, with each journey decided only after consultation with the police and troops who guarded them at every step.

Responsibility for the Tsar's security lay with the palace commandant, who held the rank of general and discharged his duties through three carefully selected military units and a special detail of police. Of the military units, the one designated as the personal escort guarded the grounds of the palaces he occupied and provided a detachment of Cossacks to accompany him on his travels; a joint battalion of guards looked after palace security, indoors and outdoors, and a railroad battalion checked and guarded all his travel routes. Two identical imperial trains were used on every journey, and nobody except the guards knew which one carried the Tsar, his family and entourage. Additional security was provided by the palace police, a group of plain-clothes agents with close ties to the *Okhrana*, who kept under surveillance all persons in areas adjacent to the palaces, and checked on all who came to the court on business, the personnel of the ministry of the court, and all the palace guards.

While the Tsarina loved the social life at court, she generally had to bow to the wishes of a husband who hated court functions and festivities. Frugal to the point of miserliness, the Tsar cut down severely on official entertaining. Economies in food and wine were made, and the expenses of his establishments were pared to the bone. Soap and candles must not be thrown away until fully used, table linen was not to be changed daily, and lights should not be left burning in empty rooms. He insisted that his trousers and other clothes should be repaired as much as possible and not thrown away until completely threadbare, and wore cheap shoes and boots until they were on the point of disintegration. The Tsarina had to inspect him before he showed himself on official occasions or received important audiences, and sometimes she had to send him back for his valet to re-dress him if his tunic was shabby or trousers stained at the knees, or if he was wearing the wrong orders or decorations, as the valet was far too terrified to say so himself.

His favourite food was cabbage and gruel, and while magnanimous enough to admit that his guests would prefer something a little more exciting, they still complained in private that the food at the Tsar's table was poor and frequently inedible, if not sometimes a hazard to health as well.

The children shared in this spartan upbringing. They slept on camp beds with a rough woollen blanket, a single hard pillow and a very thin mattress. A modest carpet covered the floor of their nursery, with no armchairs or sofas, only straight-backed wooden chairs, cane seats, ordinary tables and whatnots for books and toys. The only decoration was in the 'icon' corner with a picture of the Madonna and Child, surrounded by pearls and other gems. A cold bath was taken every morning, regardless of the weather. Their food was plain, with porridge for breakfast, and for tea bread and butter with jam and English biscuits, cake being served only on special occasions. In accordance with family tradition, English nurses were engaged for the children.

At meals the Tsar and Tsarina were always served first, followed by guests, then the children, the youngest being served last. It was considered bad form to hurry or finish the food on their plates, and there was barely time for one or two bites before the servants collected them again. As their nurses strictly forbade eating between meals, they were often hungry. Once the Tsarevich took a golden cross given to him at baptism, filled with beeswax, said to have a tiny sliver of wood from the True Cross embedded in the wax. He ate it and confessed to a feeling of shame, but even so he said it had tasted 'immorally good'.

In many ways far less tolerant and more strict than his father, Tsar Alexander III had his endearing side. Unlike his predecessors he was scrupulously faithful to his wife. What had started out as a political marriage of necessity had blossomed into a genuine love-match. While the Tsarina lacked the beauty of her elder sister Alexandra, Princess of Wales, she had the more forceful personality. The huge husband and his petite wife appeared superficially to have very little in common, but as their children readily admitted, they complemented each other well and their marriage could not have been happier.

Only rarely did they argue in front of others. The Tsarina had always adored horses, whereas her husband never trusted them. Although he rode well, he had been afraid of them ever since an unpleasant childhood experience on a bad-tempered mount. One day at Gatchina she brought her small pony chaise to the entrance to collect him for a drive. As he stepped in, a little nervously, the animals reared back and he leapt out at once. She promptly told him to get back in but he snapped, 'If you want to kill yourself you can do it alone'.[1] The ponies must have been grateful for his decision, for with his massive weight a couple of carthorses would have been more in order.

As a father the Tsar was devoted to his children. When *The Times* foreign correspondent (and subsequently his biographer) Charles Lowe was sent to Moscow in 1883 to cover the coronation, he was personally shown round Anichkov Palace by the Tsar, who, whatever his failings as an autocrat and his lack of fitness for the burdens of office, was a devoted husband and father. (In time, similar praise and criticism could be levelled at the son and successor who in other ways resembled him but little.) The simplicity of their surroundings impressed Lowe, especially the schoolroom with its severity and simplicity, the walls hung with maps, and pasted over with pictures of battles from the Russo–Turkish war from contemporary papers, particularly the *Illustrated London News*. Even when the Tsar returned home late, he never retired to bed without visiting the cots of his smallest children, kissing them as they lay sleeping, and making the sign of the cross over them. In boyhood he had collected miniature glass and china animals, which he kept carefully in a locked drawer in his desk. He always enjoyed showing them to his children, as well as his lovingly preserved album of pen and ink sketches of Mopsopolis, of which he and his late elder brother Nicholas had once been so proud.

The Tsar was particularly fond of his two youngest children, Michael and Olga. If they played pranks on the grown-ups or indulged in mischievous escapades like climbing on the palace roofs to see the moonlight better, he would always roar with laughter when he was told while their mother not only insisted on punishment, but could not even smile at their high-spirited misbehaviour. The only one of their children to whose antics she would turn an indulgent blind eye was George, the born practical joker, who could even get away with putting his foot out to trip up valets carrying heavily laden tea trays. In George's case perhaps she had a premonition that he would not live long.

A rural man at heart, the Tsar's greatest pleasures were simple tasks like mending fences, cooking over an open fire, and cutting firewood. He enjoyed taking Michael and Olga on exciting walks in the countryside, showing them how to light fires, cut down dead trees, roast apples and damp down the fire afterwards, and finding their way home in the dark by the light of a lantern.

Etiquette, as well as security, forbade any member of the imperial family from entering shops, and retailers had to send their goods to the palace on approval. The children were given simple toys, books, gardening tools and similar practical items for Christmas. They had no pocket money, and all their presents were paid for out of the privy purse. Hand-made gifts, such as Olga's cross-stitched red and white slippers for her father, were encouraged more than luxury goods. When Xenia was thirteen she saw a filigree scent bottle studded with sapphires, on approval from Cartier. She begged the ladies-in-waiting to let her give it to her mother for Christmas, a gift which prompted the Tsarina to insist soon afterwards that in future the girls could admire any jewellery brought to the palace – but no more.

At Gatchina the Tsar preferred his favourite old sofas, shabby and well-worn though they might be, to new expensive ones. If members of the household pointed out that an item of furniture needed recovering or repair, he would agree that it was rather worn, but as it had lasted for so many years, it would surely make do a little longer.

His sole extravagance were regular purchases for his family of splendidly jewelled Easter eggs from the St Petersburg workshops of Carl Fabergé, a Russian jeweller of French descent. The Tsarina, who had been brought up in the comparatively humble Danish royal household, did not share his mania for economy. She spent lavishly on clothes, prepared to put up with her husband's scolding her for extravagance, and enjoyed inviting large numbers of guests to functions.

She was always impatient to leave Gatchina after Christmas and return to the lively society of St Petersburg, while her husband used every excuse he could to delay their departure. At palace balls she thoroughly enjoyed herself, the centre of attention in her fine clothes, while he stood to one side or wandered through the rooms impatiently, the look on his face making it clear that he could not wait for proceedings to finish. When he thought the ball had gone on quite long enough, he would go up to the orchestra and start curtly ordering each musician out one by one. As all of them were too frightened to stop playing until he had spoken to them individually they carried on in some trepidation, until each had put down his instrument and left until only a solitary drummer was still present. If guests continued to dance the Tsar would turn the lights off as well, until the Tsarina could ignore the hint no longer and announce to her guests with a gracious smile that it looked as if His Majesty wanted them all to go home.

His favourite form of entertainment was a humble 'beer evening'. As a boy he had been invited to join the palace orchestra, trying his hand with any instrument of his choice, and he chose the trombone. This, and later the cornet as well, remained his sole concession to artistic refinement, and as an adult he would invite fellow musicians to bring their instruments for an informal busking session. They were instructed to wear casual clothes and would drink beer from half-gallon tankards. As Tsar and self-appointed bandleader, his instrument drowned out the others and could be heard throughout the palace, though it is doubtful whether any of the other musicians, or family members within earshot, dared to complain. As a contemporary journalist, the pseudonymous 'Mr E.B. Lanin' wrote tactfully, 'music has a soothing effect upon him . . . but he displays a particular fondness for loud music'.[2]

The Tsar's patronage of Tchaikovsky's music had continued throughout the years. Soon after his accession the composer, as ever in dire financial straits, petitioned him for a loan of 3,000 roubles to be paid gradually from royalties of his works. The Tsar traditionally dispensed such financial assistance at his discretion, and though Tchaikovsky was aware how much he admired his music, he was delighted to be sent the money as a gift from His Majesty in recognition of his work as an official court composer. Embarrassed and deeply moved by such generosity, Tchaikovsky was pleased to produce a coronation march and cantata two years later, expressing himself 'both flattered and pleased to participate in these solemnities . . . I feel much sympathy and love for the sovereign, especially as I know from good sources that he likes my music'.[3] He was notified that he would receive 1,500 roubles for the commission, but his delight turned to disappointment when he was presented with a diamond ring to this value instead of cash, and he lost no time in pawning, redeeming and selling it. Nevertheless, he remained devoted to his imperial patron. In 1884 the Tsar requested a special command performance of *Eugene Onegin* at court as it was his favourite opera, and Tchaikovsky was asked to come to Gatchina to be presented to the Tsar and Tsarina, and for the Cross of St Vladimir to be conferred on him. Deeply moved, he wrote afterwards, 'I think it is only necessary to look once into the Emperor's eyes, in order to remain for ever his most loyal adherent, for it is difficult to express in words all the charm and sympathy of his manner'.[4] The production of the opera later that year at St Petersburg was a great success, marred only slightly by the Tsar's absence. At the last moment he had been persuaded by the police to stay away for fear of a terrorist attack. Four years later he was granted a lifetime annual pension of 3,000 roubles, and wrote to a friend that 'one cannot help being infinitely grateful to a Tsar who attaches significance not only to military and bureaucratic but also to artistic activities'.[5] When the composer died in October 1893, the Tsar readily agreed to bear the costs of the funeral himself and asked the directorate of the imperial theatre to organize the ceremony. Among the floral tributes was a wreath of white roses sent specially by the Tsar.

Like so many of their contemporaries, the Tsar and Tsarina were devoted to the operas of Gilbert and Sullivan. A command performance of *The Mikado* in January 1889 held them and the Tsarevich spellbound; 'we had a lot of fun and laughed a great deal'.[6]

The Tsar dutifully read newspapers and historical journals, but for relaxation he restricted himself to Russian, French and English novels. His favourite authors were Tolstoy ('little though he relishes him as a preacher'), Pierre Loti and Robert Louis Stevenson.

He guarded his autocratic prerogatives jealously, acting the part of a true chief executive. In practice he dispensed with his council of ministers, in which he saw the makings of a cabinet, preferring to deal directly with individual ministers instead. He admired strength in his ministers, but none of them, not even Pobedonostsev, were permitted to dominate him or exceed their stipulated authority. Years later Grand Duchess Olga revealed that Pobedonostsev's influence was generally exaggerated, and that while the Tsar listened to him more attentively than his other ministers, he usually arrived at his decisions independently of the advice of others. Nevertheless the procurator of the holy synod had been such a dominant influence on the thinking of his sovereign that it was unlikely any decisions made by the latter would have brought him into disagreement with his mentor. Rather than preside over the state council, or committee of ministers, he thus ran Russia through private audiences with his ministers and so acquired a rather one-sided view of problems. In his isolation he met far fewer people than his father had done. Even among his close relatives it had to be accepted, partly for reasons of strict security and partly as he loved his privacy, that there could not be unscheduled visits or casual discussions with him. With strict press censorship, he knew Russia purely through what his compliant officials chose to tell him, and was completely in his bureaucracy's hands. He lived in a vicious circle from which there was no exit, putting his trust in his ministers, strictly watched that each one kept to his own business, and did not allow intervention in their neighbours' hands. This, said Kireev, ensured that each minister was completely outside monarchical control.[7]

Count Dmitri Tolstoy was responsible for much of the reactionary tone that coloured later years of the reign. He obstructed the Kakhanov Committee's proposals for reforming local government, and persuaded the Tsar that reform had already made local governing bodies so independent of central authority that they were endangering the basis of Russian autocracy. In 1885 he dissolved the committee, disregarding most of its recommendations, and making readjustments where he felt they were needed. During the next four years until his death Tolstoy worked out proposals for virtually destroying the effectiveness of the *zemstva* and municipal councils as bodies of self-government. They were made subject to strict controls by governors, direct interference from the minister of the interior, and an increase in the proportionate representation of the nobility in their membership. Municipal councils were further reduced in power by the tightening of bureaucratic authority over them and making them less representative, this being done through restricting the urban electorate through increased property qualifications.

Nonetheless the police powers and emergency regulations introduced shortly after Tsar Alexander III's accession and never repealed were interpreted with some flexibility. During his reign about four thousand persons were detained or questioned regarding political offences and less than fifty were executed – all for murder or attempted assassination. The right to travel beyond Russian frontiers was respected, as were property rights, including those of expatriate revolutionaries.

Additional measures put paid to hopes for amelioration of conditions among the peasants. The most far-reaching rescinded many of their self-governing privileges accorded to the village commune in 1861, and restored much administrative and judicial power in the countryside to the nobles. Moreover they reaped no advantages from the abolition of the poll tax, as they had to reimburse the treasury for revenue lost by means of increased tax on matches, spirits and tobacco, while some, the former state peasants, had to make additional allotment payments.

Under Ivan Delyanov, minister of education, reforms were aimed at curbing the spirit of 1866–80 among the youthful intelligentsia. A new university charter revoked their autonomy, making them responsible to the ministry of education; university students were denied the right to act collectively or assemble in groups of more than five; and opportunities for higher education for women, already limited, were further restricted. The ministry of education advised that children of coachmen, servants, laundresses and small shopkeepers should be discouraged from attending secondary schools, and tuition fees were raised as a disincentive.

While the Tsar disapproved of much of the splendour associated with the court and the activities of high society, he felt himself powerless to make far-reaching changes. One measure he did take however was to make substantial reductions in his civil list. The subsequent curtailment of titles and incomes did not find favour with the rest of the family. When Tsar Paul had decreed that the title of Grand Duke or Grand Duchess and a suitable allowance might be conferred on children, grandchildren, great-grandchildren and great-great-grandchildren of Tsars, the family had been much smaller. By the 1880s it was growing so fast that Tsar Alexander III felt obliged to restrict those entitled to the privilege. In 1886 he issued a family statute proclaiming that in future only children and grandchildren of a sovereign would be styled thus. All others would be princes and princesses and their allowances reduced accordingly. His uncle Grand Duke Constantine reacted with fury, seeing it as a measure aimed at his grandchildren, as his daughter-in-law Alexandra, wife of his son Constantine, was expecting her first child. Although the Tsar refused to let his formidable uncle's arguments deflect him from his purpose, he avoided summoning a family meeting about the measure as he knew it would end in confrontation.

Unimpressed with the economies practised at court, the Tsar's brothers and St Petersburg society chose to lead the life they preferred. Grand Dukes Vladimir and Alexis enjoyed wine, women and song. In Paris they spent so freely that coaches advertised sightseeing trips round nightclubs, known as *la tournée des grands ducs*. Vladimir's visits to Paris, according to Grand Duke Alexander, 'meant a red-letter day for the chefs and maîtres-d'hôtel of the Ville Lumière, for after making a terrific row about the "inadequacy" of the menu he would invariably finish the evening by putting a lavish tip in every hand capable of being stretched out'.[8] The clever, artistic Grand Duke and Duchess Vladimir were regarded as the leaders of society. Their balls all but eclipsed the splendour of those held at the Winter Palace, and they regarded the Tsar's establishment at Gatchina as no better than a provincial manor. Unlike the Tsar and Tsarina they did not exclude divorced persons from their functions, and although gambling was frowned on in certain quarters, it was positively encouraged at the Vladimir Palace where they had their own roulette wheel.

While strait-laced where marital fidelity was concerned, the Tsar had little choice but to tolerate their wayward behaviour. Vladimir was appointed president of the academy of fine arts, commander of the imperial guard, and chief of the St Petersburg military district, although he tended to resent the interference of military duties with his pursuit of the arts; he painted well, was an enthusiastic patron of the ballet, and collected ancient icons. He treated the younger Grand Dukes with contempt, and they maintained that none of them could engage him in conversation unless prepared to discuss the fine arts, or the superiority of French cooking. There was little love lost between the Tsar and Vladimir, and they had almost nothing in common apart from their Anglophobia. The Tsar called Queen Victoria 'a pampered, sentimental, selfish old woman',[9] while Vladimir felt that their sister had always been treated most unfairly in Britain. From boyhood the thick-set, broad-shouldered yet spry Vladimir had always had the more forceful personality, and was slightly envious that his bovine, slow-witted elder brother should be heir to the throne once their eldest brother had prematurely died, but as a bachelor he was prepared to accept what divine providence had ordained. After his marriage, his sharp-witted German wife drove an ever-widening wedge between them.

That the sisters-in-law cordially disliked each other made the gap even wider. The Danish-born Tsarina was regarded as a *parvenu* by the younger but aggressively self-assertive Princess from Mecklenburg. Yet she was tactful enough never to say a single unkind word about the Vladimirs. While Tsar Alexander II reigned, a façade of family unity was preserved and rivalries simmered below the surface, but with his assassination matters changed. While he had lain dying from his wounds in the Winter Palace, as the stunned former Tsarevich could do little more than look on in horror, Vladimir had virtually taken control. Though he soon recovered his poise he always remained slightly in awe of his clever, more decisive brother and sister-in-law. It was less easy to extract loyalty and obedience from a brother two years his junior than from a son. The Grand Dukes were forbidden to walk into the Tsar's study without an appointment, but alone among his brothers Vladimir declined to respect this rule. He thus sometimes managed to get his own way with the Tsar, who found it difficult to argue, particularly if caught off his guard, but was often left fuming at his brother's lack of respect.

Vladimir did have one rather back-handed scheme for helping his brother. He organized a 'holy band' to defend the Tsar's life, and over two hundred members of the St Petersburg yacht club (a party loving crowd who would probably have been hard-pressed to recognize a yacht) volunteered to help, as well as younger men of the nobility and the imperial guard. As the secret police could not defend their sovereign, this 'secret league' would undertake the task for them. If it was organized with the best of intentions, which in view of Vladimir's attitude is open to doubt, it soon descended into farce, and was disbanded on the Tsar's orders.

Vladimir was not well liked in St Petersburg. Though he had his friends, few people were indifferent to him. His coarseness and drunkenness made him enemies, as did his pro-German wife. Wisely they spent more time in Paris, where they were popular and where there was less opportunity for friction between them and the Tsar and Tsarina. Though Grand Duke and Duchess Vladimir were always glad to remove themselves to Paris, on at least one occasion the Tsar had to urge them on their way. The Grand Duchess had taken it on herself to act as an unofficial political intermediary between Russia and Germany, carrying on lengthy correspondence with Princess Bismarck in Berlin, describing everything at the court of St Petersburg with a considerably jaundiced pen. One day she was careless enough to leave a characteristically vitriolic letter on her writing table, and one of her husband's aides-de-camp, Count Paul Shuvalov, showed it to the Tsar, feeling that his duty to his sovereign was greater than that to his master's fickle wife. A furious Tsar sent for his brother, told him that his wife would have to give up these political initiatives, and it would be politic for both of them to go abroad for a while. The Grand Duchess never spoke to Shuvalov again.

Another scandal incurred the wrath of the Tsar even more. Grand Duke and Duchess Vladimir and their friends often visited the opera in St Petersburg and afterwards had supper at Cubat, a fashionable restaurant noted for its excellent cuisine. One evening while they were there the Grand Duchess heard voices among which she recognized that of the French actor Lucien Guitry, who was appearing in French plays in St Petersburg at the time. She summoned a waiter, who confirmed that Monsieur Guitry was present, and she asked that he should be presented to her. He was entertaining a lively group of Bohemian friends including his lover Mademoiselle Angèle, and she insisted that his party should join hers. When Guitry, fearing all too accurately that their standards of behaviour might not be compatible with imperial decorum, protested gently that this was impossible, she brushed his objections aside. The enlarged party became more riotous until a rather drunken Vladimir seized Mademoiselle Angèle and kissed her. In his anger Guitry, encouraged by the Grand Duchess, reciprocated by putting his arm around her and kissing her in turn. This was too much for the Grand Duke, who took the actor by the throat and threatened to kill him. Within moments the restaurant resembled a scene from a wild west saloon bar, with other patrons either departing for safety or eagerly joining in. Unable to restore order, the management sent for General Presser, the prefect of St Petersburg.

All was duly reported to the Tsar. Nobody had ever seen him in such a rage before, and even the Tsarina did not dare to speak to him for three days. Once he had calmed down he ordered that Guitry should be sent out of Russia by the next train, and Grand Duke and Duchess Vladimir should follow likewise. If they did not depart as soon as possible, they would be sent somewhere less accommodating than France. When they were forgiven and later allowed to return, it seemed that they had learnt their lesson at last.

There was no such rivalry between the Tsar and their other brothers. After the enforced retirement of Grand Duke Constantine Nicolaievich from naval affairs and public life in 1882, Grand Duke Alexis was created a rear admiral, and six years later made grand admiral of the Russian navy. Tsar Alexander III had been impressed with the necessity for modernizing his navy so that ships could engage enemy vessels on the high seas, and shortly after appointing his brother to the post the annual allocation for Russian naval expenditure was doubled, and a new shipbuilding programme was approved.

Whatever enthusiasm Grand Duke Alexis may have had for his naval responsibilities was not matched by any sustained desire for hard work. It was fortunate for the men under his command that he had two experienced admirals, Ivan Shestakov and Nicholas Chikhachev, to assist him. Too fond of good living and the enemy of anything which smacked of naval reform, it was said not unfairly that he preferred to conduct his naval manoeuvres at Monte Carlo or Paris than on board ship. Weekly conferences with the admirals were conducted in a convivial atmosphere round the dinner table in his palace. A few glasses of Napoleon brandy put them in a receptive frame of mind for his oft-repeated, never varying account of the wreck of the frigate *Alexander Nevsky* off the Danish coast at Skagen many years before. The lengthy narrative would always end (for the more sober, not a moment too soon) when he brought his ample fist crashing down on the table, exclaiming with a thunderous voice: 'And only then, my friends, did the bloody captain recognize the silhouette of the rocks of Skagen!'[10]

Nevertheless he was prepared to try and help the less fortunate members of his family. In 1893 his nephew George, son of Princess Yourievsky, presented himself without any preliminary examination, and was allowed to join the navy. Some people found him charming and amusing, but he had always been outrageously spoilt by his mother, and the despair of his tutor. One of his fellow midshipmen thought he was not only large and extremely fat, but also talked through his nose and spoke appalling Russian. Fortunately for everyone else concerned, the experiment was rapidly seen to be a failure. George resented naval discipline, borrowed money from the other officers with reckless abandon matched only by a lack of consideration as to how to pay it back, and seemed to 'spend' much of it by throwing gold coins at the girls during carnival season. He failed his examinations, and the naval authorities were given confidential instructions 'to examine him until he passes'. George then decided to take unofficial leave of absence, and it was evident that nothing could be done with him. Alexis wrote to his mother that her son was lazy, untidy, refused to accept advice from his superiors, and was the laughing stock of his peers. He was dismissed and transferred to the hussars guards regiment with the lowest possible rank, where he fared little better.

According to Grand Duke Alexander, Alexis was 'a man of the

world to his fingertips, a Beau Brummell and a bon vivant hopelessly spoiled by women, particularly those of Washington DC'.[11] Officially he remained a lifelong bachelor, his marriage with Alexandra Zhukovsky having never been openly acknowledged, but he was not starved of female company. He nursed an anything but secret passion for a distant relative by marriage, Zinaida Beauharnais, wife of the Duke of Leuchtenberg, a grandson of Tsar Nicholas I. According to the inveterate court gossip Princess Catherine Radziwill, writing under the pseudonym of Count Paul Vassili, Zinaida was not only beautiful and much admired, but extremely ambitious, 'devoid of prejudices and scruples, and possessed of an almost royal indifference to the tittle-tattle of gossip-mongers', and 'a being of intoxicates'.

At first Alexis regularly invited himself to stay with Zinaida, and before long he regarded himself as having almost equal conjugal rights with the Duke in what amounted to a *ménage à trois*. All three travelled round Europe together and were often seen in each other's company. The Duke evidently accepted the situation, although how willingly must be a matter for conjecture. The story goes that one night he returned very late from his club, found his wife's room locked, and proceeded to knock on the door loudly, insisting that she let him in. Almost at once the ample figure of Grand Duke Alexis appeared. Even when in his better moods, His Imperial Highness was not a man to be trifled with. Once roused, he was invincible. He kicked the Duke downstairs, bellowing that he could spend the rest of the night on his sofa for all they cared. Still simmering from his injured pride if not his bruises, later that day the Duke went and complained bitterly to the Tsar. Though the latter was not inclined to thank his younger brother for besmirching the family name, he told the Duke coldly that if he was incapable of managing his wife himself he could hardly expect others to help him. Crestfallen, the Duke returned home and thereafter slept in his study.

The two youngest Grand Dukes were prepared to choose their own wives, rather than help themselves to somebody else's. The tall slim Serge was a shy young man whose initially reserved temperament eventually hardened into haughtiness. The kindly German Crown Princess was readier than most to make allowances for the chilly exterior, writing to Queen Victoria

(15 December 1883); 'there is something quiet and gentle, in fact rather melancholy about him, and his appearance and manners have something high bred and *distingué* which one misses in some of his brothers'.[12] In March 1884 Princess Elizabeth ('Ella') of Hesse, who had just become engaged to him, wrote to the Queen, her grandmother: 'I am so glad you will see Serge when you come next month & *hope* he will make a favourable impression on you, all who know him like him & say he has such a true and noble character.'[13]

As she knew, the Queen had had deep misgivings about the family. Her profound distrust of the Romanovs and their country was not easily appeased. The good impression made by the visit of Tsar Alexander II had been rapidly swept away by the ensuing war, the persecution of the Jews that had outraged opinion in Britain, and also an incident in which British India had been threatened by the sudden arrival of a Russian diplomatic mission in Afghanistan when a new Amir, exiled in Russia for several years, had entered the country shortly after an unsuccessful British invasion and seized power.

Memories of the tragic fate of another Hessian Princess who had married into the family and been profoundly unhappy, Tsar Alexander II's ill-starred wife, came back to haunt her. Only six months earlier she had warned Ella's elder sister Victoria about 'the *very bad state* of Society & its *total want of principle*, from the *Grand Dukes downwards* . . . Serge & Paul are exceptions but I hear the former is not improved of late'.[14] Yet it was to no avail. While Ella had no great enthusiasm for Russia in general, the more she saw of Serge the more she felt they had in common as personalities – religious, serious-minded, cultured – and she was determined not to be pressurized into marrying any other equally eligible prince her grandmother had in mind for her. By October 1883 she had made her mind up, and early the following year they were formally betrothed.

Serge had the Romanov eye for fine jewellery, and on their engagement he presented her with a cases of splendid rubies, emeralds and diamonds. He insisted that she should try them all on, and helped to decorate her with them till she could hardly stand underneath the weight, while he admired the result. With laughter she recalled that she looked like a Christmas tree, and that they spent a long time removing them afterwards, 'as we couldn't find the clasps'.

He and Elizabeth were married in St Petersburg at the Winter Palace on 3/15 June 1884, and spent their honeymoon at Ilinskoie, an estate about an hour's drive from Moscow, inherited by Serge from his mother. It had no palace, but instead it was dominated by a wooden, two-storey house, its back windows overlooking the banks of the Moskva. Beyond a small, well-timbered park lay the village at the edge of a large wood. The Duches of Edinburgh visited them in July, and wrote to Queen Victoria to assure her how happy they were. Paul, who was also there at the time, was 'very discrete and never in the way; his great pleasure is riding about the country for hours'; while Ella 'enjoys being here, it is such a nice healthy life for her and she can do exactly as she likes and need not tire herself in any way'.[15]

They led a simple unpretentious life exploring the river and woods, hunting for mushrooms and wild berries. Elizabeth would bring a sketch book with her and a box of watercolours, painting while Serge read aloud to her and she copied wild flowers or trees. Then they drove on towards a remote wood to dine under the spreading branches of an old oak, Elizabeth cooking on a portable stove.

Stepping out into the village brought them face to face with the harsh realities of life, far removed from the gilded splendour of court. Serge had always been prepared to accept the status quo; the life of the peasant was indeed hard, but drink was his ruin, and if he was to close the *Kabaks*, there would be mutiny. Nevertheless there was always room for basic welfare improvements. When Ella discovered to her amazement that no midwife was in the neighbourhood, with a subsequent high mortality rate among newborn infants – something which everybody took for granted – and told him, he said nothing at first, but within weeks a trained midwife was installed in the village.

As the most Anglophile couple in the family, it was inevitable that Serge and Elizabeth should be chosen by Tsar Alexander III to represent him at Queen Victoria's golden jubilee celebrations in London in June 1887. Serge was among those members of the family (grandsons-in-law) to be honoured with official decorations bestowed by the Queen, in this case the Grand Cross of the Bath. The jubilee was not an occasion of unalloyed happiness, for though the Grand

Duchess was glad to see her favourite sister Victoria again, she sensed that her grandmother might disapprove of her 'Russification'. Perhaps there were further reasons for discomfort; as some time after their return to Russia, she wrote to the Queen that 'all I can repeat is that I am perfectly happy',[16] suggesting that already she found it necessary to deny that her marriage was in trouble. Most of the family strongly resented Serge's attitude to his wife in public and his habit of addressing her in front of others as 'my child'. Within a few months of their wedding it was rumoured around Europe that he had forbidden her to read Tolstoy's *Anna Karenina*, a novel portraying the empty marriage of a beautiful woman to a condescending pompous husband, on the grounds that both characters were uncannily like themselves, and that she was seeking a divorce.

Though he was often ill at ease in public, Serge did not lack a sense of humour in private. Ella had not been in Russia for long when she and her husband visited a certain monastery for the first time together. Standing in front were several beggars, one of whom, a woman, threw herself at Ella's feet and clung to her knee as hard as she could. A frightened Ella screamed as she swung her parasol around, eventually throwing it away. Serge and the attendants were so helpless with laughter that for a time they could not come to her assistance.

Serge and Paul, the two youngest brothers, had always been close. Paul, a particularly sensitive young man, was tall and thin with wide shoulders, a small head, small feet for his height, delicate hands, and a charming manner. He had been shattered after the death of their adored mother when told about their father's liaison with Catherine Dolgorouky, although Serge had tried to shield him from the truth as long as possible. Their father's assassination shortly afterwards also haunted him, and he clung to Serge for protection in the first few years of their brother's reign. When Serge went to England shortly before marrying Ella to be vetted by Queen Victoria, Paul came too.

Ella, Serge and Paul shared the same household for some time. Serge and Paul enjoyed reading aloud in the evenings, and acted together in productions at the Hermitage Theatre. An Italian actor watching them commented that it was a great loss to the stage. Paul also enjoyed dancing, and gossips at St Petersburg noticed how frequently he danced with his sister-in-law. The rumours of this unusual living arrangement were disregarded by the persons involved. They had nothing to hide, although in the early days of her marriage Ella had a reputation for being something of a flirt, loving beautiful clothes, dancing until dawn, and talking to the guards who served under her husband, single and married. Never showing any jealousy, Serge often helped her to fill out her dance card, and sometimes suggested with which officers she should dance. Once, noticing how much time she spent talking to their wives, he asked her why afterwards, saying with a smile that she could hardly dance with the officers' wives. Only when Ella's passion for dancing with Paul threatened to start a scandal did he intervene. Her hated sister-in-law, the sharp-tongued Grand Duchess Vladimir, commented on this, suggesting that Paul was trying to steal his brother's wife. The rumour reached Serge, who trusted them implicitly but felt morally obliged to warn them against appearing too friendly.

Although Grand Duke and Duchess Vladimir had initially objected to the marriage of Serge and the too-English Ella, they soon accepted her as a sister-in-law. Sometimes they would stay together and act comic plays or take part in charades.

In the autumn of 1887 they visited Turkey together, and Paul went to Greece afterwards on medical advice. In 1888 the Tsar asked them to go to Jerusalem and attend the consecration of a Russian memorial church on the Mount of Olives, dedicated to their mother. Although Ella still retained her Lutheran faith, she was pleased to have the chance of making a pilgrimage to the Holy Land. (Not until 1891 did she enter the Russian Orthodox Church, and even then it was rumoured that her husband had coerced her into taking the step.) Taking part in the consecration ceremony and visiting the Church of the Nativity of Bethlehem had a profound effect on Ella, and marked the beginning of her turning to religion as a solace. Perhaps it made her ponder on the problems of a childless marriage to a man whose faults she had not fully realized until they were married, whom she respected but did not really love; perhaps it was from this time that she became convinced of her ultimate vocation.

After leaving the Holy Land they went to Athens, where King George and Queen Olga were celebrating their silver wedding. Paul proposed to their daughter Alexandra; she accepted him, and they were married at St Petersburg on 5/17 June 1889. Among the guests who came to witness their wedding at the Chapel of the Winter Palace were the King and Queen, with their sons acting as the bride's groomsmen. Alexandra was her parents' favourite child, and it was with sadness that they saw her go to the altar. They were not to know that her married happiness would be cruelly brief.

The Tsarevich, Grand Duke Alexander.

Princess Marie of Hesse and the Rhine, at the time of her betrothal to the Tsarevich, whose framed portrait can be seen to her left. By kind permission of the Trustees of the Broadlands Archives.

The Tsarevich, Grand Duke Nicholas, and Princess Dagmar of Denmark, at the time of their betrothal.

The Tsarevich, Grand Duke Alexander, in early adult life.

The wedding of Grand Duke Alexander, Tsarevich of Russia, and Princess Dagmar of Denmark, in the Winter Palace, St Petersburg, 28 October/9 November 1866. By kind permission of Theo Aronson Collection.

Grand Duchess Marie Feodorovna, shortly after her marriage. By kind permission of Theo Aronson Collection.

Princess Catherine Dolgorouky, *c.* 1866.

Tsar Alexander II and his family at the Winter Palace, *c.* 1870. Seated, left to right: the Tsar; Grand Duchess Marie Feodorovna with Grand Duke Nicholas on her knee; Empress Marie. Standing, left to right: Grand Duke Paul; Grand Duke Serge; Grand Duchess Marie; Grand Duke Alexis; the Tsarevich, Grand Duke Alexander; Grand Duke Vladimir.

Tsar Alexander II and his daughter Grand Duchess Marie, at about the time of the latter's betrothal.

'The New (North) Star'. From a cartoon by Sir John Tenniel celebrating the state visit of Tsar Alexander II to England, *Punch*, 16 May 1874.

PUNCH, OR THE LONDON CHARIVARI.—MAY 16, 1874.

THE NEW (NORTH) "STAR."

FREEDOM AND LOVE, GO FORTH TO MEET
THE CZAR ON WELCOME'S WINGS;
YOURS ARE THE SMILES THE GUEST TO GREET
WHO SUCH CREDENTIALS BRINGS.

IN THIS HAND, HIS AND OUR LOVED CHILD,
WHOM TO OUR PRINCE HE GAVE;
IN THAT, THE COLLAR THAT HE FILED
FROM THE NECK OF THE SLAVE.

Empress Marie and her grandson Prince Alfred of Edinburgh, 1875.

Tsar Alexander III. By kind permission of Theo Aronson Collection.

Empress Marie. By kind permission of Theo Aronson Collection.

Three souvenirs – an antimacassar, a pottery mug and platter – issued to commemorate the coronation of Tsar Alexander III, 1883. By kind permission of the Commemorative Collectors' Society.

Grand Duke Vladimir.

Grand Duchess Vladimir.

Grand Duke Alexis.

Grand Duke Serge.

Grand Duke Paul.

Princess Olga Yourievsky; Prince George; Princess Catherine, c. 1892.

Grand Duke Paul, Queen Olga of the Hellenes and Princess Alexandra.

Grand Duchess Serge (second from right) with her sisters Irene, later Princess Henry of Prussia; Victoria, Princess Louis of Battenberg and Alix, later Tsarina, 1885.

Family group at Livadia, Denmark, summer 1893. Standing, left to right: Nicholas, George, Olga, Xenia. Seated, left to right: Empress Marie, Michael (at front), Tsar Alexander III.

Grand Duke Paul with Olga, Countess Hohenfelsen and their daughter Irina, 1914.

The Russian imperial family, c. 1914. Seated, left to right: Grand Duchess Olga; Tsar Nicholas II; Grand Duchess Anastasia; the Tsarevich, Grand Duke Alexis; Grand Duchess Tatiana. Standing: Grand Duchess Marie; Empress Alexandra.

Grand Duke Michael, who was nominated by his brother Tsar Nicholas II to succeed him but declined to accept the crown.

Grand Duchess Serge, 1917, the last known photograph before she was killed at Alapaevsk the following summer.

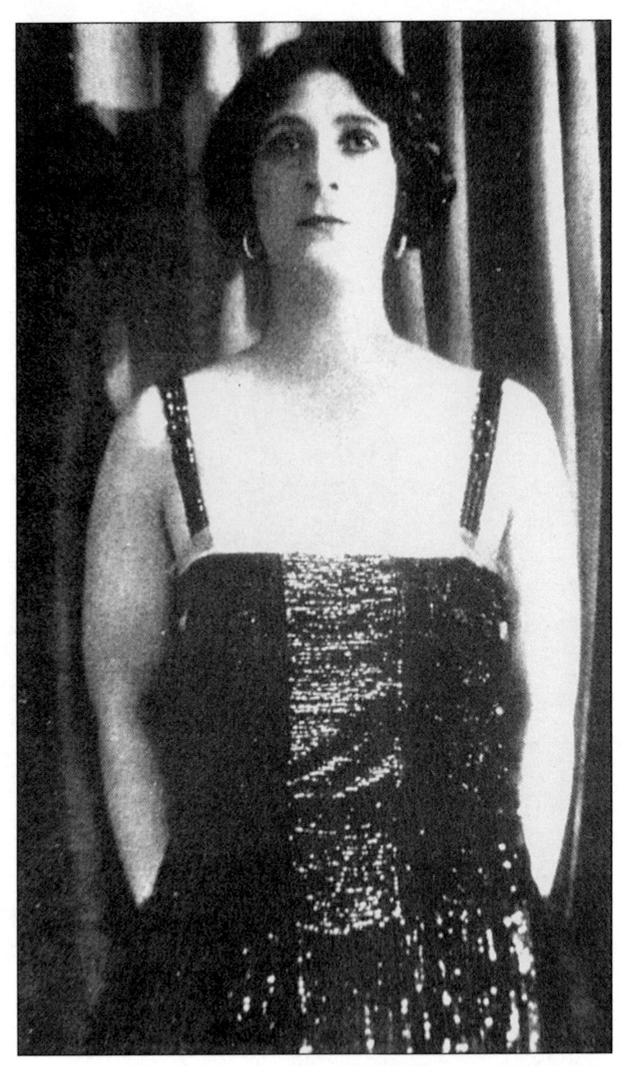

Princess Catherine Yourievsky, c. 1920, from a photograph used for publicity material during her career as a professional concert performer.

9

'Morally high and sensible'

Well aware that the least lapse in vigilance could cost him his life as it had that of his father, the Tsar found it difficult to relax properly in Russia. Activities in the country with his children helped him to unwind more than anything. Yet only on foreign trips could he really feel at ease. Away from home, he was prepared to put up with the grandeur appropriate to his station as he, his wife, family and suite set sail each summer aboard the royal yacht for family reunions at Fredensborg or Bernstorff hosted by his parents-in-law, King Christian IX and Queen Louise of Denmark. No expense was spared for once, with over a hundred servants accompanying them, and twenty railway trucks taking their luggage from Peterhof to St Petersburg and from there by barges to Kronstadt. Even some of the pets came too, although the Tsar and Tsarina drew the line at bringing Olga's pet hare and wolf cub. All the same, a cow was taken on board as the Tsarina considered fresh milk essential during the three day voyage, and the yacht was said to resemble Noah's Ark. The family gatherings included relatives from England, Greece, Germany and the other Scandinavian countries. As there were so many guests the children usually slept on camp beds (part of the luggage) in huts in the park.

Political discussion was strictly forbidden on these holidays. The Fredensborg reunions, Olga recalled many years later, were 'a wedding market' if anything, but Bismarck's grumblings about a 'whispering gallery' were mere paranoia. In Denmark, the family experienced much greater freedom. No members of the *Okhrana* were there to prevent the younger Grand Dukes and Duchesses from driving into Copenhagen to wander about the streets or go into shops and buy things over the counter, like any ordinary citizen. It was more than fun, they thought; it was an education. Such behaviour at home in Russia was out of the question without stringent security. Well might Tsar Alexander III of Russia declare from the depths of his soul that he wished he was King of Denmark instead.

Indeed, none of the visitors seemed to relish being in Denmark more. The Tsar seemed ten years younger as he led his children into muddy ponds to look for tadpoles, or into orchards to steal King Christian's apples, or turned a hose on the pompous unpopular King Oscar II of Sweden. He joined in all their games and made them late for meals, and their hosts never minded. If His Imperial Majesty was responsible, it was impossible for anybody to complain. Once the children solemnly handed him a document informing him that he was 'too corpulent to take part in the excursions and activities' of their cycling club, but they would make him Honorary President. He took the joke in good part, pretending to treat this promotion in all seriousness and gravely reading the letter regarding his presidency out loud to the other adults. 'I always felt that the boy had never really died in the man,'[1] Grand Duchess Olga said of her father; while after meeting him in Denmark in September 1883 Gladstone 'was much pleased to observe that [the Tsar] appeared to be entirely released from the immediate pressure of his anxieties supposed to weigh much upon his mind'.[2] When these all too brief reunions came to an end for another year, he would say to the Prince and Princess of Wales with a sigh that they were returning to their happy English home, and he to his Russian prison. On one occasion he and his wife broke down and howled like children, the Princess wrote, describing her sister 'standing on the top of the steps in utter despair, her eyes streaming over with tears, and trying to hold me as long as she could. Poor Sacha too felt the parting very much and cried dreadfully.'[3]

At home the Tsar's simple blunt personality did not impress the more sophisticated or cosmopolitan members of Russian society. Some, however, could readily appreciate his positive qualities. General Alexander Mosolov had nothing but respect for his personality, 'Poorly gifted but morally high and sensible'. However the foreign minister Count Vladimir Lambsdorff found the Tsar and his family strangely commonplace and ill-bred, lacking intellectual interests and refinement, too fond of ordinary anecdotes and banter rather than stimulating discussion. Others who dined with them found him and his brothers lively enough but lacking depth, more than making up for it with crudeness and vulgarity. When the Tsar's aunt, Queen Olga of Württemberg, visited Russia in 1891 she was horrified by the change at court since the time of her father, Tsar Nicholas I, and her brother, Tsar Alexander II. In those days, she remarked to Lambsdorff with asperity, there were always several guests who could talk about serious or political matters. Now her ill-mannered nephew and his children found throwing pellets of bread across the table at each other the height of amusement.

Even his own children sometimes found their father's leisure activities verged on the distasteful. The Tsar loved a regular game of cards with his suite, who in the excitement of winning or losing, 'uninhibited by the Sovereign's presence, allowed themselves impermissible pranks and expressions'. Just to see and hear them put the reserved Tsarevich off cards for life, while the Tsarina regarded this pastime of her husband's as merely something to be tolerated. 'Papa plays cards with the gentlemen,' she wrote to the Tsarevich in June 1887 on a cruise on the imperial yacht, 'and they are a great nuisance with their noise and conversation.'[4]

In Russia security was kept tight, but terrorism was never entirely extinguished. The police were ever diligent in rounding up suspects in their hundreds, with regular mass trials, and the hounding of subversive organizations out of existence where traced, but terrorist incidents still occurred. In 1882 General Strelnikov, public prosecutor of Kiev, was assassinated while sitting on the boulevard in Odessa. A few weeks later a mine was discovered in the Kremlin where preparations were under way for the Tsar's coronation. At Easter the head of the Moscow police received a basketful of artificial eggs, several containing dynamite. Though the coronation went off without incident, at the end of the year General Sudeiken, chief of the St Petersburg police, was found battered to death in his flat.

The Tsar generally slept with a pistol under his pillow. After retiring to his study for a rest one afternoon, the Tsarina was horrified to hear a shot coming from the room. Opening the door in panic, fearing the worst, she saw an aide-de-camp at the Tsar's feet, a bullet through his head, while the dazed Tsar sat on his sofa with the smoking revolver in his hand. An investigation concluded that the man had come into his study with some papers, and saw the Tsar dozing with a constricted look on his face. Trying to loosen his collar, the Tsar awoke to find fingers round his throat – and drew the worst possible conclusion. The young aide came from one of the most loyal aristocratic families in Russia, and there was no evidence to connect him with the nihilists. It appeared to be simply a tragic accident symptomatic of the nervous tension which was never far from the surface.

Various stories, which may or may not have been true, were told of terrorist infiltration into the household. One concerned a family photograph album which the Tsar was turning over one afternoon, and he suddenly came face to face with a signed picture of one of the nihilists executed for his part in the murder of Tsar Alexander II. All the servants, it was said, were thoroughly questioned, but how the picture came to be there remained a mystery. Another was of an immaculately painted Easter egg that the Tsar picked up at Livadia. He opened it to reveal a small silver dagger, two death's heads carved in ivory, and a piece of paper bearing the words, 'Christ is risen – We shall also rise again'.

As the killings decreased, public opinion breathed a sigh of relief at feeling that terrorism was on the decline. Then in the spring of 1887 a student, Alexander Ulyanov, was arrested with a bomb concealed inside his medical encyclopaedia. His sister Anne, who had been visiting him when the police arrived at his rooms, was also arrested. It had been his mission to assassinate the Tsar. At his trial he did not beg for mercy and refused all chances to escape abroad, declaring that he wanted to die for his country, and he was executed on 8/20 May. His younger brother Vladimir, whom the world would know some thirty years hence as Lenin, never forgot his example.

The most serious threat to the Tsar's life came on 17/29 October 1888 when the imperial train was derailed near Borki en route from the Caucasus. Two engines were pulling twelve coaches when there was a violent lurch, the sound of splintering glass, the creak of breaking wood, and a thunderous noise as carriages fell down the embankment. At the time the Tsar and Tsarina were lunching with their children in the dining car. The roof caved in, the carriage fell onto its side and the floor buckled. The Tsar's strength was put to the test as he freed himself from the debris which threatened to crush him, and held up the roof of the coach according to one account, or landed on his feet and caught the falling roof on his shoulders according to another, so that his wife, children, nannies and other servants could crawl to safety. Soldiers came running up to him where he was groaning under the strain, and seized pieces of wood to shore up the structure so he could struggle in on hands and knees, looking for everyone in a daze. Six-year-old Olga, who had been thrown clear of the wreckage, terrified but otherwise unhurt, screaming, 'Now they'll come and murder us all!' A soldier handed her to his father as he wandered towards the wreckage, looking for his wife.

Once she was assured that her husband and children were safe, the Tsarina looked after as many of the wounded as she could, making bandages out of her underwear. Bruised all over with cuts on her arms and legs from splintered glass, she insisted that nothing was the matter with her. A relief train arrived later, but although she and her husband were tired and in shock, they would not board it until all the wounded were settled in and the fatalities, properly covered, were taken on board. Twenty-one people were killed, and between two and three hundred were injured, some crippled for life. Officials maintained that the accident had been caused by an old engine which had gone off the rails, pulling the carriages after it, or a combination of rotten railway sleepers and overladen carriages. An enquiry failed to locate the cause. Nevertheless, it was believed that the route had been bombed and the Tsar was disturbed by these sensational and possibly unfounded reports. In official nineteenth-century Russia, it was easy to suppress the truth.

Even at such a grim moment the Tsar could permit himself one little joke about the ongoing rivalry between him and his brother. His three sons had been with him aboard the train, and had they been killed, the reign of His Majesty Tsar Vladimir would have begun that day. As Tsar Alexander climbed from the wreckage he remarked wryly, 'Imagine Vladimir's disappointment when he hears that we all escaped alive'.[5]

Vladimir and his wife were in their beloved Paris at the time. They were evidently undisturbed, and did not hasten back to Russia. As the Tsar and his family were safe there would have been no purpose in them altering their plans, beyond a fraternal mission to express their joy at the sparing of their lives, but the

Tsar was indignant that he should show his lack of feelings in such a way.

Though the Tsar and Tsarina might make light of their narrow escape, they were never quite the same afterwards. Both suffered from delayed shock, and the images of death and destruction took their toll of the Tsarina, who suffered from nervous prostration for some time. As for the Tsar, his strength was not quite as superhuman as had been supposed. Aged forty-three at the time, he gradually became more sedentary and easily tired. A medical examination might have revealed the physical damage, particularly to his kidneys, which became all too evident within five years and brought about his early death a year later.

Whereas his father had been drawn into the Russo–Turkish war with grave reluctance, Tsar Alexander III had supported the call to arms as a wholehearted Panslavist. Although the experience had made him anxious to avoid war as far as possible, his sympathies had not changed with time, and he was still indignant at Russia's failure to dominate the Balkans and seize control of the Straits, thus obtaining access to the Mediterranean. Bulgaria had been split in two by the Congress of Berlin, one part ruled by his cousin Prince Alexander. The Tsar wanted to reunite Bulgaria and place it under Russian control, and establish subservient governments in Serbia and Greece.

Aware that the imperial coffers were in no state to finance another campaign, the Tsar and Giers, his foreign minister, waged what amounted to virtual 'cold war'. Russian revolutionaries, ruthlessly hunted at home, were encouraged abroad to stir up disaffection in the Balkans. Matters came to a head in Bulgaria, which Russia had a vested interest in maintaining as a weak undeveloped neighbour. In the words of Pastor Koch, the new state was to be isolated 'and content itself with the crumbs of culture that fell from Holy Moscow's meagre furnished table'.[6] Prince Alexander, intelligent enough to see through his cousin's motives, refused to act as a Russian puppet. In 1886 Bulgarian nationalists and Prince Alexander brought about the unification of Bulgarian territory by the annexation of Turkish controlled Eastern Roumelia. From Russia's point of view Bulgar initiative was going too far. Russian agents whipped up a mutiny in the Bulgarian army, with the aid of certain Bulgarian officers kidnapped the Prince at gunpoint and forced him to sign a deed of abdication. He was taken as a prisoner to Russia, but after protests from other European powers, he was allowed to go to Austria. His morale broken, he refused all demands to return to Bulgaria, but joined the Austrian army and took the name of Count Hartenau. In fact the Tsar's plan had misfired because the new regime, under Prince Ferdinand and his patriotic chief minister Stamboulov, proved equally resistant to Russian pressure, and he had no alternative but to withdraw all Russian army officers from the principality.

When ministers at Vienna objected to what it called Russia's 'continuous interference in the zone of influence of the Dual Monarchy', the Austrian ambassador in St Petersburg tried to warn Tsar Alexander III of the possible consequences. At a state dinner he began discussing the Balkan question, advising him that Austria might be forced to mobilize two or three army corps. The Tsar picked up a silver fork, twisted it into a knot and threw it at the Ambassador, saying that he would do exactly the same to the army corps.

To his government, the Tsar would proclaim that they had two allies in the world, their army and their navy. 'Everybody else will turn on us on a second's notice.'[7]

In order to bring Russia from international isolation brought about by the Russo–Turkish war, the Tsar put his personal dislike of the Habsburgs to one side and consented to renewal of the *Dreikaiserbund*, the Three Emperors' League, between Austria, Germany and Russia. The terms of the alliance, agreed in 1881 and kept secret for almost three years, assured him that Russia would not be without allies in case of conflict with another power.

Although the Romanovs had had little affection for the Habsburgs, better relations were restored by a meeting between Tsar Alexander III and Emperor Francis Joseph of Austria in August 1885 at the town of Kremsier in Moravia, a meeting arranged by Bismarck, now chancellor and minister-president of the German Empire, to try and strengthen the *Dreikaiserbund*. Kremsier had been chosen as the meeting place rather than Vienna, as it would be easier to guard the Tsar there. He had brought his own guards along, making the task of the Austrian police difficult, as to them every Russian looked like a nihilist. A company from the Burgtheater had been brought to Kremsier to perform in the garden theatre. The Tsar enjoyed the performance so much, not least that of Katherine Schratt (whom he had seen act in St Petersburg), and who was about to become the Emperor's mistress, that he suggested that the ladies who had provided them with such a delightful evening's entertainment should be invited to take supper with them. In the rigid etiquette of the Habsburg court such an idea was well nigh unthinkable, but as the Tsar was his guest of honour, the horrified Emperor and his court officials could hardly refuse.

For the Tsar and Bismarck, both of whom were rather drunk, it was a thoroughly convivial evening and in no time they were exchanging bawdy stories amid much laughter. The fastidious Emperor, a light drinker himself, was thoroughly embarrassed, particularly in the presence of the Empress Elizabeth, the Tsarina and the ladies of the Burgtheater. On the other hand the Empress found that what had promised to be just another stuffy state reception was proving to be more fun than she had anticipated. She could barely contain her amusement when the Tsar drunkenly paid Madame Schratt undue attention. Next morning Emperor Francis Joseph was further irritated when informed by his chief of police that a Russian aide-de-camp had called on Madame Schratt's quarters with a bouquet of a hundred roses and an emerald brooch from the Tsar. Much to the Empress's amusement, the Emperor complained that the Tsar's behaviour had been 'quite unpardonable'.

Though there was no love lost between Tsar Alexander III and Queen Victoria, he knew better than to let petty animosities stand in the way of better Anglo–Russian relations. Although the Prince of Wales had been moved to fury against his wife's brother-in-law, Tsar Alexander III, by the advance of his troops in Central Asia and his treatment of Alexander, Prince of Bulgaria, he too was persuaded that cultivation of Russian friendship could only be to British advantage, especially as Bismarck's Germany could no longer be trusted.

In September 1887 the Tsar and the Prince of Wales were among the party at Fredensborg, the last place for anything approaching political dissension or debate. It was not so much the congenial and relaxed family atmosphere of Denmark which united them, more their mutual distrust of Prince William of Prussia. The German

Emperor William I, aged ninety, was evidently in declining health; his son and heir, Crown Prince Frederick William, was gravely ill with suspected cancer, as yet a furtively whispered diagnosis which was to be realized all too soon, and from Gatchina and Sandringham, as well as their respective capitals, the premature accession of Prince William to the imperial throne of Germany was not a prospect to contemplate with equanimity. William had already made himself look foolish by endeavouring to blacken his uncle Bertie's character verbally to the Tsar by thinking he was pandering to traditional Romanov hostility towards England, ill thought out conversations the validity of which the Prince of Wales had no difficulty in dispelling. In Berlin Prince William heard of this meeting with alarm. When the Tsar returned to Russia through Germany, the Prince decided to pay him an unannounced visit and boarded his train at Wittenberg before daybreak. Summoned at an unearthly hour to ask if he would receive His Imperial Highness the Prince William, the furious Tsar retorted that he was too sleepy.

In the winter of 1887 Lord and Lady Randolph Churchill visited the Tsar and Tsarina at Gatchina, and Lord Randolph was particularly impressed with his host's 'conviction of sincerity and earnestness'. The conversation, he reported, 'began in French, which was a great disappointment to me, for he can speak English perfectly; and sometimes he talked rather low and in his beard, so that I, who do not hear very well, missed some of his remarks'. He advised the Tsar not to take any notice of the English national press, since 'no public man in England ever cared a rap for anything they said'. The Tsar assured him that if England desired peace and friendship with Russia, she must not involve herself in the Black Sea or the Dardanelles. They would never permit any other power than the Turks or themselves to hold the Dardanelles, 'and if the Turks ultimately go out, it is by Russians that they will be succeeded'.[8]

The Tsar always held the Prince of Wales in warm regard. From St Petersburg Lord Randolph wrote to the Prince that the Tsar had asked much about English men, matters and politics, and would much have liked to visit England to see the Prince. On the subject of Afghanistan and the south-east of Europe, he thought the Tsar 'seemed most pacifically inclined', a view confirmed by what he had heard elsewhere; above all, 'there can be no doubt in my mind as to his extreme desire for friendly relations with England; and

H.M. told me moreover that there was a strong party in Russia who desired firm friendship with England'.[9] Tsar Alexander III was three years younger than the Prince of Wales, and must have looked forward to the day when they would meet as fellow sovereigns. Harmony between the British lion and the Russian bear would surely follow the accession of King Edward VII.

In 1887 Bismarck persuaded the Tsar to sign a Reinsurance Treaty with Germany, in effect a renewal of the Three Emperors' League, by which both empires pledged neutrality if the other went to war. He was keen to continue friendship with the Hohenzollerns by which his father had set such store, and his aversion to German ways at the court of St Petersburg did not extend to willingness of the loss of Germany as a friendly power. Nobody could have foreseen that this accord between both imperial nations had only three years left to run. He had always had the utmost respect for Emperor William I, who died in March 1888, and was ready to deal with his successor, Frederick III, but the latter was plainly dying when he ascended the throne, to be succeeded three months later by his unpredictable son as Emperor William II. The self-proclaimed 'All-Highest', personified all that the Tsarina had bitterly hated in Germany and associated with the robbery of her father's kingdom. Compounded with this was her personal dislike, and that of her sister the Princess of Wales, for the young Emperor who behaved so callously towards his dying father and now his widowed mother, the Empress Frederick.

The Tsar had nothing but contempt for this upstart of an Emperor, whom he called 'an exhibitionist and a nuisance',[10] and once told him to his face not to act like a whirling dervish. William had gone to St Petersburg in July 1888, barely a month after his father's death, to make his first 'duty call'. The reception went satisfactorily enough, with magnificent hospitality from the Russian court, although the Tsar's attitude towards the younger man was evidently reserved. There was a world of difference between them. Alexander might have been an Emperor, but he cared nothing for empty theatricality, for pomp and circumstance, for glamour (or sheer tedium, as he would have seen it) of fine uniforms and changing them two or three times a day. William's martial showiness and obsession with pageantry provided his subjects with a monarch and war leader who looked the part, but such ways were utterly incomprehensible to his host.

In October 1889 the Tsar returned the visit and went to Berlin. Surprise was expressed that he had waited so long, particularly as he did not travel from Russia, but on his way back from Denmark, as if it was an afterthought. As Emperor Francis Joseph of Austria and King Humbert of Italy had been visited by Emperor William afterwards, and returned the compliment promptly, the Tsar's reception was cool, made more so by his preference for lodging at the Russian Embassy in Berlin instead of at the Schloss as His Majesty's personal guest. Observers thought the meeting of both sovereigns artificial and constrained, with the Tsar barely bothering to conceal his boredom. At the grand state banquet in the White Salon of the Schloss there was a marked lack of conversation between them, and while the German Emperor's speech was effusive in the extreme, the Tsar's brief reply was confined to perfunctory thanks for his hospitality, with no comments of a political nature.

In a report which combined paranoia with extraordinary naïvety, Emperor William wrote to Emperor Francis Joseph in October 1889 that the Tsar 'has also been told personally many lies about me personally [sic], to make him as suspicious as possible, but all that was got rid of with a magician's wand. He was cheerful, satisfied, felt at home, and at breakfast with the Alexander Regiment was so lively that he gave a German toast and drank with almost all his lieutenants. . . . He started his homeward journey in the best of spirits and invited me to his grand manoeuvres at Krasnoye Selo next year, a result that came as quite a surprise to the Chancellor, but a very pleasant one . . .'[11]

Journalists and political commentators in both respective capitals were less easily deceived, and after the visit the German press could not but admit that nothing had changed in the political relations of their countries, while in St Petersburg it was felt that the day had passed for ever 'when we permitted Denmark, the guardian of the Baltic, to be dismembered, and the European equilibrium to be disturbed by the defeat of France and Austria, receiving in return for our generosity nothing but a platonic right to keep a few ironclads in the Black Sea'.[12] Bismarck resigned in 1890, the year the treaty expired, and Emperor William declined to renew it on the grounds that his foreign office claimed it was incompatible with the spirit of Germany's obligations to Austria.

Traditionally France and Russia had never been friends. An alliance between Alexander I and Napoleon Bonaparte had been shortlived, and their enmity was underlined by an Anglo–French alliance at the time of the Crimean war. During the 1860s both lands had remained far apart politically, and Russia's close relationship with Prussia was seen as one factor in Germany's victorious conduct of the Franco–Prussian war. In 1889 Tsar Alexander III had ruefully remarked that Russia had 'only one true and sincere friend', namely Nicholas, sovereign Prince of Montenegro – hardly a prestigious European monarchical ally. France, whose reputation as the centre of revolution, regicide and republicanism instantly handicapped her *vis-à-vis* the matter of alliances with fellow monarchical powers, was a pariah. Nevertheless, she was a solvent one, and had impressed her neighbours with her economic recovery since the defeat of 1871. In addition she was an excellent source of armaments and financial loans, and a counterweight to Germany under the brash young Emperor.

When the Russian government, suspicious of ostentatious demonstrations of Austro–German friendship, failed to raise a loan in Berlin and appealed to Paris, the response was unequivocal. A proposal was accepted in St Petersburg for joint consultation in case of a war crisis, and at length the Tsar came to see France in a different light, resulting in the signing of a Russo–French military treaty. In 1891 the Tsar welcomed a unit of the French navy at Kronstadt, having approved arrangements for national banners flying side by side and a band playing *La Marseillaise*, the revolutionary hymn previously forbidden in Russia. Secret negotiations led to a military convention and the ratification of a treaty early in 1894 aimed against the Triple Alliance powers of Germany, Austria-Hungary and Italy.

In August 1890 Emperor William had paid a second visit to Russia, where he was met at Reval by Grand Duke Vladimir and conducted to Narva to witness a display of sham-fighting, including a cavalry charge which he was invited to lead. The visit was returned in June 1892 when the Tsar dropped anchor at Kiel on his way from Copenhagen, where he had been attending celebrations for the golden wedding of King Christian IX and Queen Louise. That the German Emperor had to make a day's journey to receive the Tsar at Kiel instead of remaining in Berlin was considered by some of his subjects to be a strangely humble gesture. They drew comparisons between Mahomed and the mountain, arguing that His Imperial Majesty William II was the mountain, and ought not to move in order to meet the convenience and caprice of the Russian Mahomed. Despite an enthusiastic banquet at the Kiel Schloss, at which the Tsar was made an Admiral of the German Fleet, as he steamed out into the Baltic back to Russia on the *Pole Star* with memories of fireworks from German warships, nobody had any doubt that nothing had been done to bring the empires closer together. If Emperor William was trying to play him off against France, it did not succeed.

Shielded by intensive security and rarely meeting anybody not of his own choosing – and certainly none of his subjects – the Tsar was assured of considerable privacy. Though he sometimes called his existence in Russia 'imprisonment', by and large such a way of life suited him, for a while. But by 1889 he and Grand Duke Vladimir both bewailed their isolation; he had become disillusioned with oppressive security and privacy, necessary as they were. When the latter complained of this state of affairs to Alexander Polovtsov, a member of the state council, he was told that 'both the Emperor and you live in conditions which make it very difficult if not impossible to know people. . . . You live your lives under lock and key, see people at official receptions and speak to two or three whom fate or intrigue have brought close to you and who find in you a means to the attainment of their goals.' To the Tsar, he pointed out that the throne had once been surrounded by a hereditary aristocracy, whose members could tell the monarch the truth, if not in the course of official service, then in everyday social intercourse and during entertainments. 'Now the aristocracy has been destroyed and high society itself scarcely exists any more. The Emperor is only accessible to servile bureaucrats who see in him a means to the achievement of their own egotistical goals.'[13]

Count Vladimir Lambsdorff from the foreign ministry also appreciated the adverse effects that isolation was having on his sovereign. He seemed to be developing a dangerous sense of his own infallibility, and was 'more and more becoming the autocrat'. His 'drunkenness with power' was due to the absence in his entourage of men with enough courage and independence to tell him the truth.[14]

The Tsar never trusted Grand Duke Vladimir and was ill at ease with his German influence and his ever-partisan German wife. Serge was the brother he liked and trusted most, in spite of the latter's dubious private life and a series of scandals involving him, Prince Vladimir Meshchersky and others.

Since 1872 Meshchersky, a long-standing friend of the Tsar, had published *The Citizen*, a reactionary government subsidized journal, and was regarded as a leading pillar of the Russian autocracy. He was also a notorious homosexual. In July 1887 he had become infatuated with a young bugler in the imperial guards battalion and recommended him to the Tsar, asking him to enlist the youth in the court music choir. The Tsar accordingly asked Count Feodor Keller, the battalion commander, to transfer the bugler to the court ministry. Knowing exactly why, Keller not only neglected to effect the transfer but also caught Meshchersky and the bugler red-handed at a quiet rendezvous, and placed the matter before the public prosecutor. The latter quailed at initiating proceedings without permission from the minister of justice, who feared imperial wrath and forbade it. Meshchersky complained to the Tsar about the high-handed action of Keller, who was discharged, but he had various influential connections in St Petersburg society, and his punishment caused an uproar. Pobedonostsev was appointed to investigate the matter and Keller was reinstated, while Meshchersky was cold-shouldered by almost everyone. He laid low for a while and eventually won back the Tsar's support so well that two years later the ministers could comment on the close resemblance between Meshchersky's editorials in *The Citizen* and the Tsar's official speeches.

Although it may not have been evident at the time of his betrothal and marriage, by now Grand Duke Serge's homosexuality was no secret either. He had established an exclusive male club in St Petersburg whose members were young men from the imperial guards and the aristocracy. The Tsar turned a blind eye to their activities until a series of scandals involving the guards, actors from the Alexandrinsky Theatre, Serge (and perhaps other members of the imperial family, who were more successful at hushing up their proclivities) and Meshchersky persuaded him to take action. Twenty officers from the guards were dismissed from their posts without trial, while Serge was removed from St Petersburg and appointed governor-general of Moscow in 1891. Until then, wags said, Moscow had stood on seven hills, but now she must stand on one hillock. The Russian for hillock was *bugor*, similar to the French *bougre* and the English *bugger*.[15]

In the light of recent unrest in the city, both brothers believed in strong government and ruthless suppression of dissent to crush what appeared a hotbed of radicalism. Such responsibility brought out the worst in Serge, who became increasingly earnest, efficient to a fault, and prepared to regard the exercise of ruthless autocracy as a necessary evil. His stern rule was popular with the clergy, nobility and merchants, but it made him few friends elsewhere. During the Passover in 1892 he ordered that the city's 20,000 Jews should be expelled. They were allowed a few months to settle their affairs and for traders to sell their businesses, usually for a fraction of their real value. Whether he shared the prevailing anti-Semitism or not is open to question, but he felt morally obliged to carry out his brother's policy in the interests of loyalty. It was said that some of the richer Jews bribed him in order to stay, and that young Jewish girls were exempted from expulsion if they registered themselves as prostitutes. Students and professors at Moscow University were made subject to new restrictions, and many were driven straight into the arms of the revolutionaries.

Keeping his own counsel more and more, Serge ceased to discuss such matters with Ella. Though she kept her feelings to herself, she must have been shocked by his increasingly illiberal ways if not his personal life, though as her brother Ernest was also reputed to have a markedly unfortunate interest in young servant boys, this aspect of her husband's personality may have been easier to tolerate. Nonetheless, any hopes she may have had as a young bride of influencing or reforming his character, let alone having children, were surely fading. While she never complained, she too became more reserved in her manner.

Serge has come down through history with a reputation far worse than any of his brothers. Yet for all his faults, he was probably the most hard-working and arguably the most capable of the sons of Tsar Alexander II. However, his reserved manner and the coldness in his grey-green eyes did nothing for his popularity with others. A similar criticism was levelled against his brother-in-law Alfred. Though prone to colour her descriptions of people with a certain amount of imagination, his niece Princess Marie of Edinburgh conveyed in her memoirs something of the enigmatic personality of the Romanov uncle whom they found the most frightening and their 'chosen favourite' at the same time;

> his lips were thin and closed in a firm line that was almost cruel. . . . As abrupt of movement as he was short of speech, he had a particular way of holding his hands in front of him, the fingers of one hand clasping the wrist of the other, making a chain bracelet he wore continually jingle against his cuff. His eyes were steely grey and his pupils could narrow like those of a cat, till they became mere pin-points, and then there was something almost menacing about him. But oh, how handsome he was, so inconceivably upright, with such a magnificent figure, though no doubt there was in his face something of the fanatic that he was at heart.[16]

Proud and reserved, devoid of self-advertisement, Serge could be charming, but had a hasty temper as well as a tendency to withdraw into himself behind a stern and inflexible front. He liked tidiness, order and discipline, and expected to be obeyed as a matter of course. Cultured in the Western sense, he was a great reader and a passionate lover of music, and ever since visiting Italy as a young man had loved Italian art. The contrast with his wife was acute; gossips at court were disconcerted by the difference between him and the Grand Duchess who loved court balls, dancing, seemed so beautiful, and in the early years of her marriage a cheerful figure, her face often lit up by laughter. His grave manner made him seem much older than her, though only seven years separated them. Were they really happy? Was there a streak of cruelty and meanness in the Grand Duke? That she was known to have grown up much under the influence of Queen Victoria, and was regarded as more English than German, did not bode well for her popularity in Russia.

Yet because she gave no other grounds for criticism, it was easier for gossips to attack him than her. No story, it seemed, was too bad to tell about him. He had raped his wife and thereafter they never shared a bed, thereby accounting for their lack of children; he was not only homosexual, but a sadist and paedophile as well, if not more. A theory was widely held that he had been so traumatized by the effect of losing his parents that he was unable to consummate his marriage. His greatest defender was his brother-in-law Ernest, Grand Duke of Hesse (whose rumoured homosexual tendencies contributed to the breakdown of his first marriage, though his second was happy enough), whose defence however has counted for less than a whispering campaign of inveterate enemies among the family which constantly blackened him.

The German Emperor William II had always been especially fond of his cousin Ella and had once nursed hopes of marrying her himself; he was bitterly jealous that Serge should have succeeded where he failed. While ready to speak well of the Tsar and Grand Dukes Vladimir and Alexis in a report from St Petersburg in May 1884 to his grandfather, Emperor William I, the then Prince William had no kind words for Serge, whom he said had 'latterly occupied a specially isolated position in the family . . . is always monosyllabic, always shows a discontented countenance, and is the only one who in my case has never passed beyond the most frigid politeness'.[17] Serge's engagement to Ella had been announced earlier in the year, and this was written three weeks before their wedding.*

That the strait-laced family man Tsar Alexander III would have appointed him governor of Moscow, and that his equally moral son Nicholas II would later allow him to become guardian of his niece and nephew if he had been guilty of all the vices ascribed to him, speaks for itself. Yet as far as his posthumous reputation goes, this seems to have counted for less than the verdict of Grand Duke Alexander, who could not find a single redeeming feature in his character, calling him obstinate, arrogant, disagreeable and 'a complete ignoramus in administrative affairs'.[19]

His other arch-critic in Russia was his sister-in-law Grand Duchess Vladimir, who resented his friendship with Tsar Alexander III, his English sympathies, and later his encouragement of the

* Grand Duke Serge's feelings for the Emperor were mutual. Soon after Queen Victoria's death in 1901 he told his wife, 'Thank heaven your Uncle Bertie is King of England. Willie will never dare plunge into anything – he is mortally afraid of his uncle.'[18]

match between Princess Alix of Hesse, whom she and her husband detested. The beautiful and universally loved Ella was difficult to blacken; Serge was an easier target. Prince William of Prussia was much impressed with Grand Duchess Vladimir who, he told his grandfather, was working 'magnificently for the German cause'. The secret police discovered that she wrote privately to Bismarck, and the furious Tsar ordered her to stop forthwith. Vladimir was outraged at what he regarded as interference, and also as he feared that his wife would be misrepresented as a German agent.

Never ready to blacken others, but equally unlikely to whitewash them either, Prince Nicholas of Greece considered that Serge had 'a rather haughty expression which he cultivated, perhaps purposely, in order to counteract something indefinably effeminate in his general appearance'.[20]

The joint household of Grand Duke and Duchess Serge and Grand Duke and Duchess Paul was happy but cruelly shortlived. The former Princess Alexandra of Greece and Denmark, who had come to Russia as the bride of Grand Duke Paul, had a cheering influence on the brothers, but her lively demeanour was not achieved without effort on her part. Ten years younger than her husband, whose regimental duties took him away a good deal, she found it difficult to adjust to married life. She soon became pregnant, lonely and homesick. Her daughter Marie was born in April 1890 and Serge, who was delighted when asked to be the baby's godfather, carried her to the font. At about the same time Ella entered the Orthodox Church. Her decision to remain a Protestant for the first few years of their marriage had always perturbed Serge, as one of the many things in life they could not share, and he was pleased when she did so – perhaps, partly, as a result of Alexandra's encouragement.

That autumn Paul took his wife back to her homeland for a holiday, which helped to restore her spirits. On their return to Russia he was appointed commander of the imperial horse guards, and such promotion inevitably took him away from home even more. They were given rooms in the Great Palace at Tsarskoe-Selo, but husband and wife only saw each other at weekends. Increased responsibilities meant anxieties for both brothers. Serge took up his appointment as governor-general of Moscow with reluctance, not because he dreaded the task ahead of him so much, more as it meant leaving the brother whom he had always treated more like a son.

Little did they know that Paul would soon need his elder brother's moral support more than ever. Both couples spent what promised to be a happy summer together at Ilinskoie, until Alexandra's second pregnancy gave some cause for concern and ended in tragedy. In her seventh month she went into a convulsive fit. The only medical help available was a village midwife, who delivered her of an undersized and apparently dead son. While Marie's nurse noticed faint signs of life in him, everybody else concentrated on trying to save the mother, but she never regained consciousness and died after six days in a coma.

At the funeral Paul was beside himself with grief. His niece Princess Marie of Edinburgh, who had accompanied her mother to the ceremonies, long recalled his tearful face and and how Serge 'took him in his arms when he made a desperate gesture of protest when at last they laid the coffin lid over the sweet face he had loved'.[21] Even the Tsar, whose bear-like appearance was at odds with an emotional nature, had been devoted to his sister-in-law and was bitterly upset. The Princess's brother, Prince Nicholas of Greece, reported him as 'shaking with sobs, his voice broken with emotion', as he asked, 'Why should this Angel be taken from those who adored her, and we old ones remain?'[22]

Meanwhile the baby son, christened Dmitri on the third anniversary of his parents' engagement, was nursed tenderly to health in Serge's household. Paul was absent much of the time, trying to bury his grief in military work, and Serge and Ella became in effect virtually the parents of Marie and Dmitri, treating them as the children they never had. As they were devoted to children it was a source of eternal sadness to them that they never had any of their own. Marie and Dmitri were left at Ilinskoie for the next few months, and not until Dmitri was considered strong enough to travel did they return to St Petersburg to live with their father in his palace. They occupied a nursery suite on the second floor, looked after by nurses and attendants, entirely isolated from the rest of the palace. The head nurse and her assistant were both English, and until Marie was six years old she heard virtually no words of Russian; the immediate household and all the family spoke English.

Paul came upstairs twice a day to see his children, but never displayed any spontaneous tenderness towards them, embracing them only when he said good morning or good night. Only occasionally did a sense of humour break through the shy reserve. One Easter he slipped a hen's egg under the children's pet hare, persuading them that the hare had laid the egg. Yet it was as if he was unable to come to terms with the living presence of the children who reminded him so poignantly of the beloved wife he had lost.

10

'The preservation of an unbroken peace'

In 1892 Tsar Alexander III appointed Serge Witte his minister of communications, and later his minister of finance. Witte wasted little time in negotiating foreign loans to develop Russia's industrial potential. A start was made on building the Trans-Siberian Railway, and after a severe famine in the winter of 1890–91 which had sent thousands of peasants to the towns and cities seeking work, several factories opened up, with textiles and engineering firms providing large-scale employment in Moscow and St Petersburg. Other European countries provided not only finance but also engineers, managers and technical experts to advise on planning and techniques. Coal output in the Ukraine doubled during the next few years, while oil production in the Caucasus multiplied several times over. It was Witte's conviction that modernization could only be achieved through a form of state capitalism, or through effective use of state power to direct and control the economy, while the Tsar and his other ministers supported his industrial aims not with the intention of creating a new capitalist class in Russia, but in order to improve the military might as well as international standing of the empire.

With an eye on the future, Witte suggested involving the Tsarevich in matters concerning the empire's industrial expansion. Like heirs to the throne before him, the Tsarevich had been appointed a member of the state council and the committee of ministers, as well as to the chairmanship of a special committee on famine relief. Now Witte told the Tsar that he thought the heir to the throne should be made chairman of a committee dealing with the construction of the Trans-Siberian Railway. The Tsar was reluctant, telling the minister that the Tsarevich was still a child with only infantile judgments but Witte persisted, warning his sovereign that if he did not make any effort to initiate his son and heir in affairs of state he would never understand them. He got his way, but the Tsar was proved right. The Tsarevich was appointed chairman, with Nicholas Bunge, a professor of economics, former finance minister, and one time tutor to the Tsarevich vice-chairman. While the heir made a painstaking effort to take an interest in the work of the committee, he would freely admit to the end of his life that he was no businessman and had never understood economics.

Grand Duke Nicholas was a well-meaning kindly youth, but lacking in powers of concentration. A proficient linguist, he spoke English, French and German well, and passages from his diary reveal an uncommon gift for descriptive prose; according to one modern biographer, Eduard Radzinsky, 'he wrote with the power of a Hemingway'. Like her sister Alexandra, Princess of Wales, and George, King of the Hellenes, his possessive mother never recognized that her adult children were not perpetual infants. She raised objections when her elder daughter, Grand Duchess Xenia, wished to marry her cousin Grand Duke Alexander Michaelovich, and forced the youngest daughter, Grand Duchess Olga, into a travesty of a short-lived marriage with her homosexual cousin Prince Peter of Oldenburg. Her sons remained 'darling children' well into maturity, and her over-protective influence was partly responsible for Nicholas's unreadiness for the throne on his accession. Nonetheless Witte, who never liked nor respected the Tsarevich before or after his accession to the throne and compared him unfavourably as a personality with his father, admitted that the quick-minded Nicholas learnt more easily than his father. Even so he was content with the carefree life of a young aristocratic officer with nights on the town, regimental dinners, being carried back to his villa dead drunk by comrades, and above all the pleasures of his mistress Matilda Kchessinska from the Imperial Ballet.

In October 1890 he left Gatchina on a tour which was to include much of Europe, north Africa and the far east, returning through Siberia, accompanied by his cousin, Prince George of Greece and Denmark. Not as naïve as his elders might have supposed, he thought the trip was 'senseless', as with strict security and protocol he was not permitted to travel incognito; 'palaces and generals are the same the world over and that is all I am permitted to see. I could just as well have stayed at home.'[1]

In Japan a policeman, offended by some apparent breach of etiquette, attacked him violently with his sword, and only the prompt intervention of Prince George saved his life. They cut short their trip and he came home to convalesce. Still with his head in bandages, he joined a family visit to Denmark, and then represented his father at the wedding of his cousin George, Duke of York, to Princess Victoria Mary of Teck in London in July 1893. Having none of his father's antipathy to Queen Victoria he enjoyed his stay in London, much amused at being congratulated on having found himself such a splendid bride, for his facial resemblance to his cousin George was remarkable. Even so he cut an uninspiring figure. After a visit to the House of Commons, the Irish Nationalist member T.P. O'Connor wrote that he found it hard to believe that 'this slim, not very tall, and decidedly delicate-looking stripling was the son of the giant who could twist tin plates in the hollow of one of his brawny hands'. The young man 'seemed shy, uncertain, indecisive, looked back as if to get a hint; and altogether went to his place with much awkwardness and shame-facedness. There was something suggestive of the lonely and perilous elevation to which he will so soon attain in this little scene – of all its solitude, desertion, and uncertainty in the midst of the millions of adoring subjects and thousands of servile courtiers.'[2]

On only one matter could the Tsarevich make up his mind. He had sown his wild oats with Madame Kchessinska, and established her in a residence formerly occupied by the mistress of his great-uncle Constantine, next door to the quarters of his uncle Alexis. As he was heir to the throne – though he had no reason to expect this situation to change for another ten or fifteen years – it was imperative that he should think seriously about marriage. Whether he would follow the example of his father, the first Tsar to keep both the peace and the Seventh Commandment, or do his dynastic duty and sustain a mistress as well, was up to him. Yet a suitable wife must be found.

So often hesitant and unassertive, in this case he had virtually decided for himself. As a youth of sixteen he had met Princess

Alix of Hesse, who came to Russia as a girl of twelve in 1884 to attend the wedding of her elder sister Ella and Grand Duke Serge.

It has often been claimed, and just as often disputed, that his parents looked with disfavour on the choice. The Tsar was close to the Hessians; he had been Alix's godfather, he himself was partly Hessian. The Tsarina loathed all things German, ever since Prussia had declared war on her father's kingdom of Denmark in 1864. Bitter rivalry with her husband's sister-in-law Grand Duchess Vladimir had only reinforced her views. However the Hessians, who had fought against Bismarck's Prussia in 1866 and lost, likewise hated the Prussians, and the Tsarina was wise enough not to condemn Hesse at the same time.

All the same, Alix had made a bad impression on Russian society when visiting her elder sister. Pathologically shy, clumsy and ill at ease at the court of St Petersburg, anybody who looked less like a future Empress would be hard to imagine. While the Tsar could not have been deaf to such criticisms when scanning unmarried princesses of Europe for the right daughter-in-law, he could hardly have failed to recall the mutterings of those who had dismissed him as a gauche, clumsy youth and contrasted him painfully with his more accomplished elder brother.

For a while the German Emperor's youngest sister Margaret was thought to be a candidate for Nicholas's hand. Although Prussian, 'Mossy' was never at one with her eldest brother and his deplorable treatment of their widowed mother, the Empress Frederick. While certainly not the personification of ugliness she was sometimes made out to be, she was said to be 'not regularly pretty', and the Tsarevich vowed he would sooner enter a monastery than marry her. It was rumoured that the Tsar looked with disfavour on her as her father had died of cancer of the larynx and he did not want his son to marry a Princess who might be affected by tainted blood; if so, in the light of future events, it was an ironic comment. Likewise Princess Helene, daughter of the Comte de Paris, pretender to the French throne, would be more suitable as long as she agreed to change her religion. Above all, marriage to her would strengthen the Franco–Russian pact, especially in the eyes of French society. Helene saved them the trouble by making it plain that she could never renounce her Roman Catholicism.

Nicholas swore that he would marry Alix or nobody. By Christmas 1890 Queen Victoria had heard that Alix's sister and Romanov brother-in-law were doing their best to assist the matchmaking process; 'Ella & S. [Serge] do *all* they *can* to bring it *about*, encouraging & even urging the Boy to do it!'[3] In January 1892 when the dissipated Prince Albert Victor, Duke of Clarence and heir to the British throne after his father the Prince of Wales, succumbed to influenza, he hoped fervently that he would not have to go to England and represent his father at the funeral as it would be better for him and Alix not to meet. To his relief Grand Duke Alexis was sent to Windsor instead.

In August 1893 the death of the dissolute Ernest, Duke of Saxe-Coburg Gotha, brought his nephew Alfred, Duke of Edinburgh, to the duchy. Her Imperial Highness Marie Alexandrovna of Russia, who had long given her English in-laws the impression that by becoming the wife of a mere Prince and Duke she had married beneath her, could now consider herself advanced in rank. As her sister-in-law the Empress Frederick observed, she 'will love being No. 1, and reigning Duchess'.[4]

Princess Alix, a devout Protestant, seemed unlikely to renounce her faith for the Tsarevich. Yet he would not be dissuaded. A massive gallery of European royalty was to descend on Coburg in April 1894 for her brother Grand Duke Ernest's marriage with Princess Victoria Melita of Edinburgh. Among them were Queen Victoria, the Prince of Wales and his brother the Duke of Connaught, the German Emperor William and the Empress Frederick. The Tsar sent his brothers Vladimir and Paul, while the Tsarevich begged to go, intending to make one last effort to ask for Alix's hand. Once he was there, it seemed that some guests were less preoccupied with the nuptials of the bride and groom (whose marriage was destined to last but seven years) than with speculation as to whether Alix would be betrothed to the heir to the Romanov empire by the time of their departure home.

According to some, her cousin Emperor William saw that a Russo–Hessian (and therefore Russo–German) marriage alliance would go some way towards counter-balancing more politically negative aspects of the Franco–Russian treaty. The Emperor had a friendly talk with his hesitant guest, took him to his room, placed roses in his hand and said, 'Now we will go and ask for Alix'. She was in turmoil, insisting with tears in her eyes that she could not. Two hours of persuasion on his part failed to move her, and the Emperor resolved to sort matters out. He went to see her himself, then drove her to the house where the Tsarevich was staying, pushed them into a room together – and the deed was done.

Others consider that no matter how much pressure there was from relatives, it made less difference than the fact that she was passionately in love with the Tsarevich; that the advice of her sister Ella, who had become a voluntary and passionate convert to the Orthodox religion, helped her over the crisis of conscience; and that with the marriage of her brother 'Ernie', she would have to yield her position as first lady of the duchy to a female cousin whom she cordially disliked. The last reason is open to doubt. Though in years to come Alix would have her differences with the woman who was at present Princess Victoria Melita of Saxe-Coburg Gotha, there is no reason to believe that her warm-hearted description in a letter to Queen Victoria, written in December 1893, of 'my darling Ernie and the sweet little Wife whom he is soon going to fetch' was a hollow one at variance with her true feelings.[5]

Overwhelmed with joy, the Tsarevich wrote to his mother, admitting that his hand trembled so much that it was no easy task, but 'the whole world is changed for me; nature, mankind, everything; and all seemed to be good and lovable and happy'.[6] His parents immediately wrote to him of their delight at the news, mingled with regret that they could not have been with him at such a happy time. The Tsarina told him that they were both 'overcome with joy knowing you to be so happy', while the Tsar assured him of 'the happiness and rejoicing with which everyone greeted the news'; and asked him to thank his dear bride-to-be for consenting to marry him, 'and how I wish her to flourish for the joy, comfort and peace she has given us by deciding to agree to be your wife!'[7]

The joy was not unanimous. Society in St Petersburg still looked coldly on the marriage, taking its cue from the Grand Duke and Duchess Vladimir that the Tsarevich would fall completely under the spell of the British element, particularly his uncle Serge and his betrothed's grandmother Queen Victoria. Though Tsar Alexander III was no admirer of the Queen, maybe he felt that in her mid-seventies she had little time left. He liked and respected the Prince of Wales, who would surely soon succeed her on the English throne, and who would be a far more suitable role model and influence as well as monarchical ally for his son.

There was one other reason for the Tsar's acquiescence in a Romanov–Hesse marriage alliance, one which he hardly dared to speak of as yet. Marriage would stabilize the young man, as well as provide him and the Russian empire with heirs – and the sooner the better. Already he was beginning to fear that his own time on earth was running out. During recent months he had begun to complain of ill-health. He became more sedentary, less interested in going on long walks, chopping wood or hunting, than sitting down to doze in his chair even when family guests were present. Obesity, the long-term effect of injuries and the physical strain of holding up the wrecked train at Borki in 1888, years of living under the threat of assassination and its effect on his nerves, had all aged him prematurely. A year after the Borki incident he suffered from a severe attack of influenza from which he recovered slowly, and after that he was never quite the same again. In August 1893 a massive nosebleed left him weakened, and a ready prey to bronchial trouble throughout the autumn.*

In January 1894 he was weakened further by an even worse attack of influenza. By early March immediate fears for his life had passed, but Count Lambsdorff reported that he appeared thinner, especially in the face; his skin had become flabby and he had aged greatly.

* Prince Alexander of Battenberg, the former Sovereign Prince of Bulgaria, who had retired into private life and adopted the name Count Hartenau, died of peritonitis in November 1893 at the early age of thirty-six. It was noted at the time that all bar one of the sovereigns of Europe, even the German Emperor William II – who had firmly opposed the Prince's intentions of marrying his sister, Princess Victoria of Prussia – sent Countess Hartenau telegrams of condolence on her husband's death, as well as representatives to the funeral. The exception was Tsar Alexander III. How much this omission could be ascribed to the Tsar's ill-health, and how much, as his biographer Charles Lowe asserts, was due to the Tsar's personal campaign of persecution and spite, is debatable.

One spring morning at Gatchina he took his youngest daughter Olga, then aged eleven, for a ramble in the woods. To her alarm she noticed that where he used to outpace her effortlessly with long strides, he now had difficulty keeping up with her. Smiling sadly as he asked her to keep it to herself, he told her that he felt tired and they ought to go home.

By summer he was rapidly losing even more weight and complaining of constant tiredness. When his elder daughter Xenia was married in July 1894 to Grand Duke Alexander Michaelovich, he seemed outwardly well, but only the immediate family knew what an effort he was making to take part in the celebrations. A cruise on the yacht *Tsarevna* that summer failed to set him up. 'I hope it will do a great deal of good to Papa who wanted a rest and a change of air badly,' the Tsarina wrote on board the yacht between Jungfrusund and Korpo to her eldest son, then in England. 'I found him looking very poorly again and so very tired, just the same as when he left Gatchina. At Peterhof all this time he has been suffering from *insomnia*, which was surely caused by overwork and by the fact that he goes to bed much too late; so I do hope that this little cruise will be good for him from every point of view.'[8]

At forty-nine he could have reasonably expected to live for another fifteen or twenty years. The doctors' diagnosis was kidney trouble, resulting partly from internal damage after the Borki train accident, or nephritis, complicated by chronic mental exhaustion. Professor Zacharin of Moscow found signs of nephritis, including a weak pulse, sleeplessness, nausea and enlargement of the left ventricle of the heart. In his official report he noted that his patient's habit of being out in all weathers was a contributory cause, particularly after the damp and cold of the previous summer. The ground floor of the imperial apartments of the Alexandra Palace near Peterhof, and above all his freezing wet bedroom, were much to blame. As the Tsar disliked heat he always sought somewhere cool. By the time the professor saw these rooms and made him change to another on the second floor, he had occupied the damp one for nearly three months, from May to August.

The family's annual summer expedition to Denmark was cancelled, and the doctors recommended a change of air. First he had one final duty to discharge as Tsar – the annual review of his troops at Krasnoe Selo. Watching him in the green tunic of the

Preobrazhensky Guards, mounted on a grey charger, the family saw how pale and tired he was, and sensed instinctively that it was a farewell to his men.

Increasingly anxious, the Tsarevich blamed his father's condition on his driving himself too hard; 'he hardly can sleep for more than a couple of hours in the night, which of course wears him out completely for the rest of the day'. All he could hope for was that the annual summer break would benefit him; 'with the change of place, of air, of life naturally – this bad condition of his shall pass, as it did in winter'.[9]

Exhaustion and physical weakness delayed their departure to his hunting lodge at Bieloviecz, Poland, for a few days. A 30,000-acre forest with no nearby railway station was the least suitable place for somebody in his state of health, but he insisted. At first he joined the others for shooting, but they saw that he had lost all enthusiasm for the sport. He would not even join them in the dining room, having his food brought to the study instead. As his appetite was dwindling fast, he probably disposed of the contents of his dishes secretly rather than force himself to consume them. When the sight and smell of food prepared for the rest of the family made him physically sick he was put on a special diet, but to little effect. Another specialist was summoned from Moscow but gave his patient no confidence, as he wandered around at night complaining he could not sleep because the ticking of the tower clock was too loud.

After a few days the family moved to another Polish hunting lodge, Spala. The Tsar was deteriorating fast, and his legs began to swell. 'To see that great man, always so respected, so dignified and yet so full of fun, tormented morally and physically by his cruel disease, was sad indeed,' wrote Prince Nicholas of Greece. 'It was like seeing a magnificent building crumbling.'[10] At the insistence of Grand Duke Vladimir, he reluctantly permitted the German specialist Dr Ernest Leyden to examine him and consult with his doctors. Leyden diagnosed virulent dropsy, and when pressed by the Tsar to tell him the worst, admitted sadly that there was no hope of a cure.

The Tsar's first reaction was to telegraph his second surviving son George and ask him to come to Spala as soon as possible. George had always been sickly, and since consumption was diagnosed in 1890 when he was aged nineteen, he had lived in a sanatorium in the foothills of the Caucasus. As his father could now face the truth that he was dying, he wanted to see his son for the last time. George looked much the worse of the two, and the family were astonished when the Tsar spent hours watching by his bedside at night. They would have been even more astonished if they had known that George had five years left, while for his father it was a matter of weeks.

The sad news spread to the other royal and imperial families in no time. Queen Olga of Greece offered the Tsar the use of her villa Mon Repos on the isle of Corfu. Dr Leyden agreed that a warm climate might at least make him comfortable, and the family made arrangements to go there, stopping at Livadia on the way. It was the beginning of October, and the sun was still warm. However once they were there he was evidently in no fit state to travel any further. His clothes hung on the once massive frame, his skin was pale and his cheeks were hollow. He could hardly bear to lie in bed, and only felt comfortable when his chair was wheeled to the window so he could look at the view outside. Every movement was an agony, yet he was so suspicious of drugs that he would not let his doctors give him anything to alleviate the pain. When they forbade him to eat ice cream, he waited until he and his daughter Olga were alone one day, then asked her in a whisper to fetch him some and not to let anybody else find out. The nurse caught her, but wisely said that her father had so few pleasures left in life now that a helping of his favourite ice cream could not possibly do him any harm.

By the beginning of October he was sometimes confined to bed all day, and the Tsarevich was starting to read state documents on his behalf. Grand Dukes Serge and Paul arrived at his bedside from Moscow, and assumed many of the duties of dealing with matters needing imperial attention, ignoring their nephew. A couple of days later Alix came, to the Tsar's evident delight. On her arrival he kept her in his room for a long time, talking to her and undoubtedly giving her such paternal encouragement as he could in the task she had ahead of her sooner than she had expected. Otherwise the Tsarevich was the only one to give her more than perfunctory attention. She in turn tried to impress on him that as he was his father's son, it was important that he was told and asked about everything; 'Show your own mind and don't let others forget who you are.' The Duke and Duchess of Saxe-Coburg came too, the

Duchess telling her brother to his face with questionable tact, 'Thank God I've arrived in time to see you once more'.[11]

Unemotional to the last, the Tsar wanted to be spared any deathbed histrionics. To quote Grand Duke Alexander, on 20 October/1 November, 'He died as he had lived, a bitter enemy of resounding phrases, a confirmed hater of melodrama. Just muttered a short prayer and kissed his wife.'[12] Grand Duchess Olga recorded a slightly different picture, with the entire family gathered in the room. Father John of Kronstadt, his confessor, had been there for a couple of hours, and placed his hands on the Tsar's head. As the clock struck three in the afternoon, and the damp mist embraced everything outside, the dying man's head dropped on his wife's breast, and the first prayer for the rest of his soul was read to the grieving, kneeling company.[13]

'The poor Emperor's end came suddenly,' Charlotte Knollys, in the Prince of Wales's suite, wrote to her brother Francis. They had left England as soon as possible but heard of his death when they stopped to dine at Vienna. 'He was sitting in his armchair, fully dressed, holding the Empress's hand and a moment before he had said he felt better, then he gave one sigh, his head fell back against the Empress and then all was over. The Empress remained sitting with her hand still in his till she fainted dead away.'[14]

His eldest son's reaction was heartfelt; 'This was the death of a Saint! God help us in these sad days! Poor dear Mama.'[15]

From the early days of his reign, Tsar Alexander III was condemned for his reversion of the reform programme begun by his father, and thus widening the gap between his regime and contemporary Russian society, thereby contributing to the overthrow of the dynasty within less than twenty-five years. His first biographer Charles Lowe, writing within a year of his death, noted that 'with an intellectual outfit scarcely equal to the task of ruling a hundred of his fellow-men', he had been given the responsibility of ruling a hundred million of them. An honest man determined to govern to the best of his ability, Lowe maintained, 'the worst of him was that he let himself be guided by the counsel of men who, his superiors in mind, were inferior to him in the qualities of the heart'.[16] The greatest mistake of his reign was to withhold the quasi-parliamentary privileges which his father had been ready to grant; 'at first also he was for confirming this bequest, but reactionary counsels gained the upper hand over him, and he refused to grant concessions which might seem to have been wrung from him by the threats of the terrorists'.[17]

This was not how his achievements were seen at the time. By most of his family, and by ministers and officials whom he appointed and with whom he worked most successfully, he was praised for restoring the self-confidence and prestige of government and empire after the crisis of 1878–81, marked by virtual bankruptcy after the Russo–Turkish war and the terrorist campaign culminating in his father's assassination in March 1881. While he had to share some of the credit with others, a firm hand against the revolutionary underground, and tightening of government control over the universities and *zemstvos*, made Russia strong, as did his reduction of expenditure, particularly in the field of defence, and avoidance of confrontation with foreign powers. Although the Russian empire had faced rupture with Great Britain over the question of Afghanistan, while the Tsar had no love for England, he had even less for war. He salvaged state finances and restored international prestige; his last years witnessed unprecedented industrial growth in the empire; he left Russia much more stable and prosperous than it had been at his accession. The courtier General Alexander Kireev commented after his funeral; 'A good, honest heart, a Tsar who loved peace and was a very hard worker; a man who could serve as an example to every one of his subjects both in his private and his public life.'[18]

If his father had been the 'Tsar Liberator', Lowe judged that should Alexander III be known throughout history by any special title at all, it would be not so much the 'Tsar Peacekeeper' as the 'Tsar Persecutor', or even the 'Tsar Prisoner'. 'His was a reign of terror, and terror of the kind that kills. Never at the best endowed with physical courage of the highest kind, his nerves proved quite unequal to the double strain of coping with his secret foes and at the same time of carrying on the colossal business of his one-man rule. He attempted an impossible task, and he broke his back with the effort.'[19]

During his reign Russia had been vigorously criticized in England, and he would have appreciated the irony that in London *The Times* was unstinting in its praise when his death was announced.

> Russia mourns the loss of a ruler who has spared no effort to promote the grandeur and greatness of the country over which he has borne sway, but who has known and acknowledged that for Russia, as for Europe generally, the chief blessing is the preservation of an unbroken peace. To have directed Russian policy in accordance with this conviction, to have had the power of a despot to work his will and to have used it for beneficent ends – these are his enduring titles to the gratitude of Russia and of Europe.[20]

Beyond the frontiers of Russia, the Tsar had indeed helped to maintain peace. Had he been more of a modernizer at heart, or less susceptible to the malign influence of Pobedonostsev, he might have left his son a more secure inheritance. Tsar Nicholas II was ill-equipped by personality to withstand the maelstrom that forces beyond the control of any one man would shortly unleash; but had his father and predecessor allowed a more enlightened political climate at home in keeping with the spirit of the times, the task he faced on his accession might have been a little less daunting.

Part III: Tsar Nicholas II and after, 1849–1959

11

'There was sure to be trouble'

At twenty-six, Grand Duke Nicholas Alexandrovich was Tsar of all the Russias. Rarely had an heir to the throne been so ill-prepared for his inheritance. His sister Grand Duchess Olga recalled later that he kept telling them he did not know what would become of them all, and that he was wholly unfit to reign. Intelligent and courageous he may have been, but he had no knowledge about governmental matters. 'Nicky had been trained as a soldier. He should have been taught statesmanship, and he was not.'[1] While he had had some token experience as chairman of committees, his grounding in the machinery of government had been inadequate, and of Russian foreign policy, such as the recent Franco–Russian alliance, he knew nothing. Tsar Alexander III had been in failing health for some time, and though he and his wife might have been reluctant to admit to the outside world that the end was not far off, that he had done so little to ease the path of his son and heir showed an alarming lack of forethought.

The only person who tried to encourage him in his new position was his betrothed, Princess Alix of Hesse. On her arrival at Livadia she had been astonished to see how everyone ignored him, and felt quite rightly that the blame lay with his parents. The Tsar had been too sick to do anything, but the Tsarina still treated her son like a boy. She issued orders in the name of her dying husband, as it never occurred to her to delegate anything to the son about to succeed him. Alix impressed on her future husband that he must make the doctors come directly to him; 'show your own mind and don't let others forget *who you are*'.[2]

She was not the only one to notice the ascendancy of the Dowager Empress over her son. When the Prince and Princess of Wales, who had set out as soon as they heard of the Tsar's illness, arrived to attend the funeral, the former found the Tsar 'quite touching in his deference and regard for her and hardly likes to assume his new position'.[3]

On reaching St Petersburg the Prince of Wales telegraphed for his son the Duke of York to join them immediately, 'out of respect for poor dear Uncle Sasha's memory'.[4] Though royalty was safer there in 1894 than in 1881, to Grand Duchess Augusta of Mecklenburg-Strelitz it was 'quite enough to have *one* Heir apparent in Russia and that *Two* are too much!'[5] The Duke dutifully came to the obsequies, and at intervals he was treated to sightseeing tours by Grand Duke Vladimir, who perhaps suspected that the young man shared the anti-German prejudices of his mother and aunt. While he and his wife had been uneasy about the increasing anti-German drift during his brother's reign, he may have hoped to moderate a future King of England's views towards the German Reich as well as make him a dependable Russian ally at the same time. In fact Prince George liked his cousin Emperor William, although when he came to succeed his father on the British throne some fifteen years later, relations between Britain, Germany and Russia had advanced beyond the influence of their crowned heads.

For seventeen days the body of Tsar Alexander III lay in an open coffin in the fortress church of St Peter and St Paul, as thousands of his subjects passed through the church day and night to pay their last respects. Each day his family gathered in the church in full uniform for a service during which they were required to walk up to the open coffin and kiss the icon in the dead man's hand. The funeral was held on 7/19 November at a service lasting two and a half hours, when he was laid to rest in the vault where his predecessors were buried.

One week later the Tsar and Princess Alix were married. He had wanted the ceremony to take place as soon as possible, and even hoped to do so two days after his father's death. Alix and the Dowager Tsarina had agreed, but his uncles all opposed the decision, insisting they must wait until they could marry in a semi-public ceremony to attract attention to the new reign in a positive manner, and he gave in. Grand Duke Vladimir tried to go further, 'insisting forcefully, but unsuccessfully' that the bride ought to be driven to her wedding in a golden coach, and that certain pieces of jewellery should be presented to her as she was a future Empress.[6] It was the Dowager Empress's birthday, and court mourning could be suspended for one day. Even so, in the city her husband's subjects spoke sorrowfully of the Tsarina as 'the funeral bride'.

Whereas Alexander III had lost little time in making it clear that he stood firmly against his father's faltering steps towards democratic reform, Nicholas II declared that he would only do what 'dear saintly Papa' would have approved. On receiving a deputation from the Tver *zemstvo* at the Anichkov Palace, which had come to offer congratulations on the imperial marriage, he dismissed 'the senseless dream of participation by *zemstvos* representatives in affairs of internal administration' (he said afterwards that he had meant to say 'unrealizable dream'), and that he resolved to let everybody know that he would 'safeguard the principles of autocracy as firmly and unswervingly as did my late, unforgettable father'.[7] The liberals now knew they could expect nothing from him.

He believed that he had inherited God-given responsibilities that the whole family should respect. Unlike his father, he was not prepared to turn a blind eye to the all too human failings of the Grand Dukes. For other members of the Romanov family to put individual happiness before family loyalty by marrying commoners or divorcees was to invite punishment.

That Tsar Alexander III did not live long enough for Nicholas to gain experience of administration and working with officials was not the latter's only misfortune. That he lacked Alexander III's authoritative manner was an additional handicap, and he felt that he was replacing his father very inadequately. As an adult, at five foot seven he had only just reached his father's shoulders. He knew that he was, and always would be, compared unfavourably with him.

Soon after becoming Tsar he confided in Grand Duke Vladimir, his eldest surviving uncle, how hard it was for him because he had been kept so far from government affairs in the past. Although Vladimir had little affection or respect for his nephew, he did at least tell him comfortingly that he remembered clearly the accessions of the last two Tsars. On each occasion Russia had been in a very difficult and troubled situation, unlike 1894 when she had enjoyed peace for thirteen years. This state of affairs, he assured him, was a legacy of Tsar Alexander III's policy of 'Russia for the Russians'. Changes would be required, but there was no need to hurry; 'One should not give anyone grounds to think that the son condemns the order created by his father or the choice of people whom the latter had summoned to work with him. Initially one should suspend changes and should follow the main line of his father's policy.'[8]

The Tsar's uncles should have been ideally placed to act as his mentors and give him support during the first years of his reign, when he most lacked experience and confidence. Thanks largely to the memoirs of Grand Duke Alexander Michaelovich, a picture has been handed down to posterity of a diminutive, mouse-like Tsar Nicholas, trembling behind his desk while his larger than life uncles banged their fists down in front of him, shouting, cajoling and threatening him in order to get their way. This was undoubtedly colourful exaggeration. At the start of his reign his second cousin Grand Duke Constantine Constantinovich noted in his diary that he was already aware of talk that the Tsar's uncles were trying to influence him, 'but I think these rumours are fuelled by envy and are only empty gossip'.[9]

In the case of Vladimir perhaps it contains an element of truth, for Vladimir had never concealed the fact that he regarded himself just as good if not better than his elder brother, and was sure he would have made a better Tsar. In 1894 he was commander-in-chief of the guards and of the St Petersburg military district. Almost as overpowering in stature as his late sovereign, he had sometimes taken a firm hand in chastisement to the Tsar as a child (there were twenty-one years between them), and he was disinclined to start being deferential now. Likewise there was little rapport between the Tsar and Grand Duke Alexis, general admiral and naval overlord, who with his beard and vast girth looked like a younger, rather more elegantly attired version of Tsar Alexander III. His fondness for wine, women and ships was not matched by dedication to public service.

Serge proved the most sympathetic and reliable confidante. Already closely related by marriage to Alix, the governor-general was now the Tsarina's brother-in-law as well as the Tsar's uncle. He was more than willing to take on the role of adviser and elder brother, but that 'Nicky's' closest ally among the elder generation should have been a man with so many detractors and enemies in public life and few friends was an additional disadvantage. The youngest uncle, Paul, still scarred by the sudden loss of his beloved wife, was not yet temperamentally able to offer a ready shoulder to lean on, although circumstances would drive him into the role some years later – if not too late.

If the Tsar was determined to keep a distance from most of his uncles, he was not inclined to establish a ready rapport with Princess Yourievsky either. When her elder daughter Olga became betrothed to Count George Merenberg, son of Prince Nicholas of Nassau and grandson of Pushkin, and married him on 30 April/12 May 1895, he was asked to act as sponsor. The Dowager Empress made plain her disapproval; 'Mama was in despair at the idea,' he wrote to his brother George, 'so I very politely but firmly declined, and she was deeply offended!'[10]

The Tsar had made an unpromising start with his peoples; with his family he cut an equally pathetic figure. Nicholas and Alexandra Feodorovna, the name she assumed on marriage, were not allowed by the Dowager Empress to set up their own household until they had reigned for three months, and had to share her home, the Anichkov Palace. No rooms were ready at the Winter Palace or Tsarskoe-Selo until well into 1895, as the marriage had been arranged so hurriedly and the court had been so preoccupied with Tsar Alexander III's declining health, yet reluctant to admit that he was dying. In May 1895 they moved into a small palace at Peterhof, then into the Alexander Palace at Tsarskoe-Selo, destined to become their main home. The Tsarina could not avoid the conclusion that her mother-in-law was a selfish woman determined to retain her privileges jealously, with no intention of relinquishing her rights before she had to. Tsar Paul I had promulgated the decree whereby the reigning Empress had to yield precedence to the Dowager, and it had never been repealed. Both Empresses, so different in personality and background, remained on coldly polite terms.

What Alix made up for in seriousness, better education and intelligence, she lacked in social skills, tact, vivacity and health. According to one of her ladies-in-waiting she was a practical Englishwoman on the surface and a mystical Russian underneath. It did not take her long to hear gossip comparing her unfavourably with her mother-in-law. The Dowager Empress was continually reminding her son of what he had to do or whom he had to see. In short, she behaved like the stereotype of a mother-in-law whose child and spouse had to live under her roof at the start of their marriage. Alix was still learning Russian; she spoke French very badly, and felt uncomfortable about using it. Nobody at court spoke German, so derided by the late Tsar, and she was restricted largely to speaking English with the imperial family – and few others, as very few people, especially the servants, could speak in it.

Even the official Orthodox liturgy became a bone of contention. It was customary for the names of the Tsar and Tsarina to be coupled in the liturgy. Marie insisted that her name should immediately follow that of her son. A furious Alexandra referred the matter to the holy synod, to be assured that the reigning Empress should take precedence over the Dowager, but the matter rankled for a long time. Grand Duchess Serge was ready to blame mischievous factions at court when she said, 'I know there are brutes who already turn from Minnie & will do all to spoil the relationship of her with Alix',[11] but it scarcely needed spiteful tongues in high places to spoil the relationship between two stubborn and diametrically different personalities, one married to the Tsar and the other his mother.

Nevertheless Ella spoke more than a grain of truth. She had been close to Grand Duke and Duchess Vladimir for the first five years of her marriage, but her conversion to the Orthodox Church angered Grand Duchess Vladimir, who felt isolated and betrayed by her sister-in-law's action and never forgave her. Always a dominating personality, the latter was a useful person to have as a friend, but the last woman of whom to make an enemy. Having known the Hesse family since she was a child, she had been eager to smooth the path of Alix and help to prepare her for her life as Empress or, as Countess Kleinmichel had put it, approaching her like 'a governess eager to guide all her movements'. She was certainly not averse to the idea of getting her under her own influence, rather than that of the Empress Marie. Torn between two mutually antipathetic sisters-in-law, the shy Alix withdrew even more into herself. In doing so she inadvertently made a lifelong enemy of Grand Duchess Vladimir.

The Dowager Empress found her very unsympathetic and unsmiling. The late Tsar's brothers were equally aware of the bad start she had made, and while Serge and Paul were gentlemen, Grand Duke and Duchess Vladimir and Grand Duke Alexis were not slow to criticize her behind her back for her chilly nature, dull clothes, lack of sense of humour, prudery and poor Russian. They scoffed that the Tsar had no palate at all because he and the Tsarina ate such simple meals except on formal occasions. Although they liked to see national dishes served at their table, like Tsar Alexander III, they were not particular about their food.

Ever the least Anglophile of the brothers, Vladimir held that the British had been 'at the bottom of every trouble in the world', and was aware how much the new Tsarina had been influenced by Queen Victoria, who had always had a special place for her motherless Hessian grandchild. Their palaces at the Quay in St Petersburg and their country place at Ropsha were virtually the centres of Russian society. As they did not see eye to eye with the Dowager Empress, or with Grand Duke and Grand Duchess Serge, for whom their initial dislike had mellowed into little more than tolerance, there was little family unity among the older generation.

At least their mutual dislike of 'the Vladimirs' gave the Empresses something in common. Early in 1895 Grand Duke and Duchess Vladimir disregarded court mourning for the late Tsar, supposed to last for one year, and gave a lavish not to say riotous wedding anniversary party, at which it was said every member of the gipsy orchestra had been thoroughly drunk.

Matters went from bad to worse. The Tsar's coronation, in May 1896, should have been an occasion of celebration, but the ceremony itself was rapidly followed by tragedy. As part of the preparations, Serge had introduced the novelty of electric light to Moscow. The arrival of the imperial party in the city went ahead as planned, the bells of all Moscow's churches pealing out, cannon booming, massed choirs singing 'God save the Tsar', and regimental bands playing stirring marches. The ceremony itself was held in the Cathedral of the Assumption, beginning with a magnificent ritual during which Nicholas received the imperial crown from the hands of Metropolitan Palladius and, in a time-honoured gesture symbolizing autocracy, placed it on his own head. As he mounted the steps to the gates of the high altar to give himself Communion, during the stillness of the ceremony almost everyone heard the jangle as St Andrew's chain fell off his neck on to the floor. To the superstitious it was a bad omen.

Following this was a week of festivities, including receptions, opera, balls and ballet. The conclusion of the popular festival was set for 6/18 May. It was the custom of the Tsar to distribute a handkerchief containing gifts, a piece of bread and a commemorative enamel beaker bearing his and his consort's cypher and the double-headed eagle of the Romanovs, to spectators at Khodynka Field. By sunrise a crowd of nearly half a million had gathered. Shortly before the distribution, due to take place at 10 a.m., it was rumoured that there would not be enough for everybody. The crowd pushed forward, panic-stricken officials began to hand gifts out, those at the edges and behind pressed forward, until the result turned into a disorderly stampede in which many spectators (estimates vary between one and five thousand) were trampled to death.

The immediate impulse of the horrified Tsar and Tsarina was to cancel a ball being given that night by the French Ambassador, the Comte de Montebello. Vladimir, Alexis and Serge persuaded them to continue with the ball as if nothing had happened, as it would not be expedient to offend the French government by cancelling. The public, and many members of the imperial family, were shocked that the Emperor could dance at the French Embassy under such circumstances. Those who looked carefully might have noticed the anguish in the faces of their sovereign and his wife, who had spent the afternoon visiting the wounded in city hospitals, and Alexandra's eyes were red from weeping.

The cause of the tragedy was largely the result of a row over jurisdiction between the ministry of the imperial court, headed by Count Vorontsov-Dashkov, and Serge in his capacity as governor-general of Moscow. After the catastrophe both vied with each other in apportioning blame. General Kireev, no friend of Vorontsov-Dashkov, insisted that the ministry of the court had organized proceedings far less efficiently than Count Adlerberg had in 1883, and they had treated Serge and the Moscow administration tactlessly by pushing them aside and seeking to monopolize arrangements.

On the other hand even the family were divided. Some of the Romanovs, led by Vladimir, and the Tsar's cousin and brother-in-law, Grand Duke Alexander Michaelovich, said Serge was to blame by not bothering to take any precautions to control the crowd. As about thirty people had been crushed to death at the same place in similar though less distressing (and better hushed up) circumstances at the coronation festivities of 1883, they argued, Serge should have known better. Alexander's wife, the Tsar's sister Xenia, found Serge's behaviour 'beneath comment'; he had washed his hands off the whole matter, saying it was nothing to do with him, and that Vorontsov was responsible for everything. He did not even take the trouble to visit the scene of the disaster. When she tried to tell Ella her opinion, the latter replied with astonishing innocence or naïvety, 'Thank God Serge has nothing to do with all this'.[12]

Alexander and his brothers demanded the immediate dismissal of Serge and the cancellation of all remaining coronation festivities. Alexis, whose rivalry with the ever-critical and less experienced Alexander made relations with him and his brothers difficult, angrily told the Tsar that the 'Michailovichi', the sons of Grand Duke Michael, were 'inclined to play to the radical grandstand', openly siding with the revolution and attempting to wrest the governorship of Moscow for one of themselves. The Michailovichi pointedly left the moment the dancing at the ball began, Alexis proclaiming, 'There go the four imperial followers of Robespierre.'[13]

While Grand Duke Constantine Constantinovich readily admitted that Serge was to blame for the lack of foresight, he admitted that he was not personally responsible for the disaster. However he was his own worst enemy and had done himself great harm by not going to the scene of the incident, or at least putting in an appearance at the victims' funeral. On the contrary, that same day he had arranged to have a group photograph taken in his courtyard with the Preobrajensky officers staying in his house. When they heard about the disaster they began to disperse, thinking that this was no time for photography, but Serge had them sent for and the session went ahead.

At length Serge was sufficiently convinced by the weight of opinion to accept responsibility and offered his immediate resignation, but the Tsar refused to accept it. An enquiry was carried out under Count Constantine von der Pahlen, a former minister of justice, who concluded that 'whenever a Grand Duke was given a responsible post there was sure to be trouble'. Pahlen never received a substantial appointment again for such blunt speaking. However, junior officials took most of the blame, especially Colonel Vlasonvsky, chief of the Moscow police, who was dismissed.

Despite Vladimir's initial reaction, he closed ranks with his brothers when they made it clear that if Serge was made a scapegoat for the disaster, they would stand shoulder to shoulder with him and withdraw from court. In retrospect it might have boded better for the reputation of uncle and nephew if Serge had resigned after all. Though he was just as arrogant and convinced of his own superiority as Count Vorontsov-Dashkov, who never offered to resign, in the defence of Grand Duke Serge it should be admitted that he was an extremely conscientious governor-general whose term of office was not the disaster often suggested. Through the years he had worked unceasingly, paying great attention to detail and attending personally to matters which could have been left to subordinates, punishing corruption and fraud. He often went about Moscow incognito to see conditions for himself, distressed by the poverty he saw everywhere and anxious to do what he could to improve general living standards. It was his great misfortune that one lapse in planning and supervision, for which the Count was theoretically no less responsible, should have had such appalling consequences.

Once the Khodynka dead had been buried, a whispering campaign began against Serge and Ella, and the reputed miseries of their home life. The Grand Duchess became increasingly defensive, writing to Queen Victoria to assure her that they were not unhappy. 'The abominable lies,' she said, 'were simply disgusting but one day I trust all the truth will come out and the great thing is to have a clear conscience before God as who can change the unkindness of the world, in this case a set of jealous intriguers . . . people I suppose could not believe that we were harmless and happy so began trying to prove the contrary – really we want nothing . . .'.[14]

Although Serge was often condemned as a complete reactionary during his governorship, his brother-in-law Ernest, Grand Duke of Hesse, told a different story. In politics, he maintained, Serge was considered much too progressive by conservatives because he strove for improvements which were not acceptable to them, and liberals hated him because they thought he would hold their cause back. He thought many of their plans were impractical, or else believed that the time was not ripe for them. His father had been perpetually criticized behind his back for a reforming zeal which, in return, had arguably been a case of 'too much too soon'. Puritan and humourless, at least in public, he thought that drunkenness lay at the root of many of the national troubles and believed that prohibition would go a long way towards eradicating them. Tsar Alexander III would probably never have taken such a fiercely moral view. Hardly abstemious himself where alcohol was concerned, he would not have begrudged the peasant one of his few joys in life, as long as mass drunkenness did not get out of hand.

However, Serge had few other defenders. Prince Felix Youssupov was one of many who greatly admired his wife but disliked him, finding his stare disconcerting. Besides, the Grand Duke was rather a figure of fun, with his corsets and white summer uniform and tunic through which his bones showed all too clearly. As a child Felix found it amusing to touch them, a prank which irritated Serge intensely.

As governor-general of Moscow, Serge was the Tsar's personal representative and viceroy, beyond the jurisdiction of the minister of internal affairs. At the same time he was the Tsar's uncle and brother-in-law, and both were very close. The Tsar regarded him as a useful counterweight to some of his ministers and officials and would always readily take his side. When disturbances broke out in the university the Tsar was grateful for his prompt action and that of the authorities which promptly restored order, while regretting the 'sad phenomenon of students letting themselves be enticed so easily along the wrong path, incited and led astray by a few dozen scoundrels and rascals!'[15]

Vladimir was a less dependable helpmeet and ally. Six months after the coronation, when he had persisted in ignoring his nephew's wishes respecting making guards appointments, the Tsar lost his patience and wrote with a mixture of assertiveness and humility that 'his stupid kindness' was responsible for the matter; 'Only in order not to quarrel and not to disturb family relationships, I have constantly given in . . . a blockhead, without will and without character. Now I do not simply ask, I command you to carry out my *previously expressed will*.'[16]

He got his own way, but any extra respect for him on the part of Vladimir was shortlived. The Grand Duke and Duchess, who had begun to accentuate family divisions in the previous reign, continued to go their own mischievous way in providing a centre for gossip and family scheming. When a fancy dress ball was held at the Marinsky Theatre early in the new year of 1897, the Tsar warned Vladimir firmly that if he and the Empress attended, he forbade guests to enter their box or stay for supper in their room. He was very hurt that this should have happened on a previous occasion without his permission, as 'nothing of the kind ever happened in Papa's day'. It was unfair to try and take advantage of him as he was so young, and his nephew, but he was head of the family and had no right to turn a blind eye to the actions of any member of the family that he felt wrong or inappropriate. More than ever the family needed to remain united and firm, 'and you ought to be the first to help me in this'.[17]

As Empress, Alexandra proved a grave disappointment. To her St Petersburg society was rotten to the core, racked with frivolity and insincerity. Balls at the Winter Palace ceased, and the Tsar and Tsarina retired quietly to Tsarskoe-Selo. Between 1895 and 1901 the Tsarina gave birth to four daughters, Olga, Tatiana, Marie and Anastasia. Her failure to produce an heir troubled her greatly, and his distress was more acute each time.

The Tsarina's troubles made it easier for Vladimir, his wife and their rival court to dominate Russian society with a pre-eminence to which none of his brothers could aspire. As president of the academy of arts he took a special interest in the ballet, and later he befriended the impresario Diaghilev, who had found the management of the Maryinsky theatre too conservative. It was Diaghilev's ambition to form a troupe of artists from the Maryinsky and take them abroad from May to September when the Russian theatre was closed, where he could introduce them to new dances and new music. Vladimir provided Diaghilev with generous financial aid, which made it possible for him to dazzle the capitals of western Europe with his revolutionary blend of music, poetry, painting and dancing.

Meanwhile in Germany, as in England, Grand Duchess Marie Alexandrovna's life had not been happy. Successively Duchess of Edinburgh and Duchess of Saxe-Coburg Gotha, she had chafed at the court of Queen Victoria and was only too happy to base herself at Coburg. Such happiness as she found in her marriage to Alfred was shortlived, and though she presented him with five children (plus one stillborn), by the 1890s they were leading virtually separate lives. A shared love of music had helped to bring them together in the first place, but it was not enough to hold them throughout the passing years. By her early forties she was writing with sadness to a friend of 'young people' staying with her at Ilinskoie, inviting her to take part in a double duet with two pianos in the height of the summer season, 'I who no longer touch the piano'. Alfred had taught himself the violin during boyhood, and for years he took part in orchestras and musical *soirées*, but in later years his musical ear, if not enthusiasm, declined in direct proportion to his increased consumption of alcohol.

Marie had always been homesick for the land of her birth, and only there could she find true contentment. 'Nowhere does one enjoy the summer more than in Russia,' she wrote on a stay at Peterhof to Lady Randolph Churchill (2 August 1886), 'and I must say that it is really heavenly weather when the summer is fine, for we have the very long days and hardly any night.'[18] Eighteen months later, from Malta where they lived officially while the Duke of Edinburgh was commander-in-chief of the Mediterranean squadron, she told the same correspondent, 'My countrymen and women are very lively and demonstrative: they have kind, warm hearts, and are really fond of one. I feel that more and more when I go back to Russia.'[19]

Arguments over their two eldest children drove a wedge further between husband and wife. In 1892 Marie had actively promoted the engagement and marriage of their eldest daughter, another Marie, to the unprepossessing Ferdinand of Roumania, knowing that the Duke was keen to see her betrothed to her cousin and 'beloved chum' George, only surviving son of the Prince of Wales. No daughter of hers would marry an English prince if she could help it. By the time guests gathered to celebrate the couple's silver wedding in January 1899, their only son and heir Alfred was dying. High living as a junior officer and venereal disease had undermined his health, and when he morganatically married an Irish girl his mother insisted that the marriage should be annulled even though she was expecting a child. He shot and wounded himself, and despite the protests of her husband and the doctors, she ordered that he must be sent away for a period of convalescence to Meran in the Tyrol, with only a tutor for company. Aghast at her unfeeling attitude, the doctors warned her that he would die within a week, and they were proved right.

Stricken by remorse, Marie broke down at the funeral at the Friedenstein Church, Gotha. Rarely a demonstrative woman, she sank to her knees as the funeral march began, crossing herself several times and sobbing brokenly as her equally sorrowing daughters strove to comfort her. Afterwards she gave every impression of bearing her erring son's death stoically, but Alfred was heartbroken. His health had already given cause for concern, but knowing he now had nothing to live for, he took to the bottle even more heavily. In the end it was not liver failure but cancer of the larynx which made his last few months on earth sheer agony. By May 1900 he was unable to swallow, and could only be fed by tube. The following month a consultation of specialists at Vienna confirmed that his condition was inoperable, and he returned to Coburg, assured that he had no more than six months to live. The Duchess and their youngest daughter Beatrice returned from a visit to Windsor as guests of Queen Victoria on 17 July. They had seen so little of him during the last few months that they were unaware how ill he was. Thirteen days later he passed away in his sleep.

At length the widower Grand Duke Paul would find consolation, but in the process he succeeded in alienating himself from most of his family. About four years after the death of his wife he began an affair with Olga von Pistolkors, the wife of a captain in his regiment and aide-de-camp to Grand Duke Vladimir. She had three young children, and soon after Paul was moved to a different regimental command to try and avoid scandal, she was expecting a fourth – but the father was not the captain.

In January 1897 a son was born and named Vladimir. The liaison was to make Paul a completely different person; he virtually cut himself off from his family, almost as if he was ashamed of having let them down. To all outward appearances he lost interest in Marie and Dmitri, stopped visiting Ilinskoie, and instead took Olga abroad for holidays. He had left his wife's clothes untouched since her death, but as if determined to sweep the past away and build a new life for himself and the mother of his youngest son, now he sorted them out and gave them away. Come what may, he was determined to marry Olga.

In 1900 he bought a house in Paris from the Youssupovs, and indicated that he was considering remarriage. Although the Tsar had been close to this gentle uncle, he who had found such happiness in his own marriage could not condone the behaviour of a senior family member whose adulterous relationship had apparently broken up another couple's marriage. If Paul did marry, he insisted, he would lose his position, his income, his right to live in Russia, and the guardianship of his children. As Paul's actions had demonstrated, none of this would be much of a sacrifice. For once, Vladimir was unequivocally on the side of the nephew for whom he had previously had little respect. He was furious with Paul for having stolen the wife of his aide-de-camp.

The affair between Paul and Olga was common knowledge throughout St Petersburg. Neither of them had any real enemies and their relationship was accepted without criticism by most, apart from the rest of the imperial family. It might have continued indefinitely, but for an incident which Olga had probably instigated in order to bring matters to a head. At a ball at the Winter Palace she openly wore some diamonds which, it was well known, had been bequeathed to Paul by his mother. They were recognized by the Dowager Tsarina, who was outraged and promptly sought out the Tsarina, asking her to exert her authority to have Madame Pistolkors expelled from the ball. A chamberlain was accordingly given the task of asking her to leave at once. Next day St Petersburg could talk of nothing else, and Captain Pistolkors was faced with the choice of resigning his commission and leaving the army, or divorcing his wife. He chose the latter. Ostracized by society, Olga von Pistolkors fled to Italy.

Guests from throughout the courts of Europe were gathering in St Petersburg for another Russo–Greek wedding in August 1902 – that of Prince Nicholas of Greece and Denmark, one of the late Princess Alexandra's brothers, to Grand Duchess Helen, daughter of Vladimir. Paul could hardly be excluded from the occasion, but it might have been better for all concerned if he had absented himself. King George of the Hellenes, who had been equally distraught at his daughter's sudden death in 1889, was making his first visit to Russia since that tragic occasion. Although he showed his grandchildren Marie and Dmitri every possible kindness, he went out of his way to avoid Paul, who was evidently ill at ease, and preoccupied with other matters. At a family dinner he attempted to argue with Serge, who naturally did not want to let a happy family occasion be soured by one refractory member's personal dilemmas. Declining to discuss the matter, he said with a forced smile as he rose from the table, 'My boy, you are simply in a very bad mood; you ought to take better care of yourself'.[20]

While the bride and groom remained the centre of attention, Paul quietly slipped out of Russia by train, having arranged for a court official to meet him at the station with sufficient funds. He had told his children that he was leaving and they went to wave him off, forlornly convinced that they would never see him again. His destination was Italy, where he was followed once the wedding festivities were over by Serge and Ella who implored him to reconsider his responsibilities in Russia, particularly to his son and daughter. It was to no avail.

Paul married Olga in the Greek church at Leghorn, then wrote to his children explaining what he had just done. In his letter he emphasized how lonely he had been and how great was his love for his second wife; that nothing could ever lessen his affection for his children, and that he hoped they would think of his wife without ill-feeling. His daughter Marie's first reaction was one of shock, feeling that she and her brother meant nothing to him; and how dare this woman take their father from them. When Serge and Ella returned from Italy Serge was filled with anger against Mme Pistolkors, whom he said had divorced an excellent husband to ruin Paul's life and future, and had taken him from his children. Paul had married morganatically, and without the Tsar's permission.

Henceforth he was banished from Russia, deprived of all his rights, and all his official revenues were confiscated. As the Tsar wrote to his mother, he was duty bound to uphold the statutes pertaining to the imperial family which laid down that morganatic marriages were forbidden, and that no match contracted without permission could be considered valid. The matrimonial union between his grandfather and Catherine Dolgorouky had set an unfortunate precedent, but Tsar Alexander II could hardly have withheld permission for his own second wedding. Nevertheless Alexander III had taken an unequivocally firm line in 1891 with his cousin Grand Duke Michael Michaelovich, who contracted a morganatic marriage without permission and was banished to England. His son, who feared the prospect of 'a whole colony of the imperial family' settling in Paris with their 'semi-legal or illegal wives', was not being vindictive; he was doing no more than exercising his rights as head of the family.

The rest of them were equally unforgiving. Vladimir was 'quite undone' by the whole affair, claiming that Paul had given his word, to the Tsar through him, Vladimir, that he would not marry Mme von Pistolkors,[21] an undertaking Paul later denied. 'The most painful thing about it all is the fact that it is adored Papa's own brother who has taken such a step,' the Tsar wrote to his mother; 'is it possible that the lofty example of Papa's life, of his unceasing efforts all through his reign to create order not only in the land, but in the family also, has been of no avail at all?'[22] Trying to find excuses for him, the Dowager Empress wrote that 'One can only be sorry for the poor man, because he seems completely blinded and thinks he has acted honourably by marrying her, and forgets everything else'.[23]

Serge became Marie and Dmitri's legal guardian, thus formalizing a state of affairs which had existed for over a decade. Although he was saddened by his brother's behaviour, Marie felt that he could not conceal the joy he felt at the fact that from then he would be able to keep them entirely to himself. She thought Serge gave an impression of coldness and inflexibility to the outside world, but to her and her brother Dmitri 'he displayed a tenderness almost feminine'. Introspective and diffident by nature, he could be capable of extreme sensitivity; 'those few who knew him well were deeply devoted to him, but even his intimates feared him'. While she was convinced that he loved them deeply, enjoying their company near him and giving them freely of his spare time, she sensed that he was always jealous of them and he would have been 'maddened' to know the full extent of their devotion to their father.[24]

Whether he would really have begrudged them affection for their father is questionable. He had certainly made great self-sacrifices to give them the family life that the brother whom he had always helped so much seemed to have relinquished. But like his wife, he must have felt a sense of anguish at knowing that they were never the children of him and his wife. The Grand Duchess's jealousy was only too evident, Marie noted; during his lifetime, she showed no interest in them or anything that concerned them, and she saw as little of them as she could. 'She appeared to resent our presence in the household, and our uncle's evident affection for us.' Unforgiving, she saw marriage as an insoluble tie, and thought that remarriage, with a former partner living, was violation of the seventh commandment. Though Paul was later pardoned and allowed to return to Russia, there was never any record of Ella having visited Mme von Pistolkors, and in conversation she once remarked coldly that their son Vladimir was not 'of the family'; in other words, he was not a true Romanov.

Selfish as his actions seemed to the rest of his family, Paul had gained a new strength of character. He was no longer protected by his parents or elder brother, even if he risked total estrangement from his favourite brother, children and sovereign. Back in Moscow, as Marie and Dmitri were settling down in the governor-general's palace, Serge told them that their father had another daughter, Irina, born to Olga on 22 November/5 December 1903. Later Marie learned that Paul had desperately wanted to ask her to be her stepsister's godmother, and had consulted Serge, who bluntly refused to entertain the idea. Even where his favourite brother was concerned, there could be no forgiveness. At first mother and children had no legal title or even surname, but in 1904 the Prince Regent of Bavaria created Olga Countess of Hohenfelsen, with the right to pass her title on to her male descendants. She was allowed to see the children by her first marriage on their holidays.

Nevertheless, Marie and Dmitri could not accept that their father had abandoned them. They persisted in seeing him as a wounded hero, mistreated by his family. Serge and Ella found it impossible to forgive him. Marie could not bear to put him out of her mind, and often spoke to her uncle Serge about him. 'He gave me patient but unsympathetic answers, speaking of my father without open criticism, but in a manner half jealous, half condescending, that hurt me deeply.'[25]

A year after Paul's banishment, Marie and Dmitri were told they could see their father again. The meeting would be on neutral territory at Tegernsee, the villa belonging to their aunt

Marie, widowed Duchess of Saxe-Coburg, in Bavaria. Three years after losing the husband whom she had loved but briefly, she had settled into a comfortable existence. Her manner was as brusque and intimidating towards strangers as ever, and her brothers still teased her about 'her grand airs', but she took it in good part. Never afraid to voice her opinions, she still said exactly what she thought as she sat 'installed in a large arm-chair with an interminable piece of knitting in her hands, looking over her big spectacles at the bustling and plotting of the people who moved around her; seeing everything, judging everything with a kind of serene mockery'.[26]

The meeting between Paul and the children whom he had not seen for a year took place initially alone with Marie. He talked much, treating her almost as a confidential equal, but she was struck by his preoccupied manner. With some trepidation she asked after her stepmother by name. Surprised and visibly touched, he embraced her warmly. It created a new bond between them, which all Serge's efforts to separate her in spirit from her father could not destroy. The brothers spoke during this visit, but relations were still strained, and the meeting came to an end when Serge shrugged his shoulders, saying that he considered he himself possessed full rights as guardian of the children that his brother had relinquished, and could exercise them without consulting Paul. The latter knew he was powerless to act or protest.

12

'A terrible war of hatred'

While Tsar Alexander III had kept Russia free from armed conflict, his son was less prudent. Within ten years of the accession of Nicholas II, an ill-fated, ill-advised attempt at expansion into the Far East resulted in total humiliation.

Russia's only Pacific port, Vladivostok, was ice-bound for three months each year. In 1895 Japan occupied several Chinese territories coveted by Russia, including the highly prized warm-water Port Arthur. When Russia declared that this constituted a threat to peace in the Far East Japan, keen to negotiate rather than fight, relinquished her claim to Port Arthur, and three years later Russia extracted a lease of ninety-nine years from China. During the Boxer rebellion of 1900 the Tsar's forces occupied Manchuria against the advice of Witte and other far-sighted ministers who foresaw tension with Japan. One bone of contention remained, namely Korea, which Japan saw as an essential bulwark for her security. Largely through the weasel words of Emperor William II, who told his own ministers in Berlin that Germany had a vested interest in seeing Russia's attention distracted by problems in the East rather than possible expansion in the Balkans where she would clash with Germany's time-honoured ally, Austria-Hungary, Nicholas II allowed himself to be attracted by wresting Korea from the 'yellow peril'. A band of Russian adventurers, led by a retired cavalry officer, Bezobrazov, planned to establish a private company there, move Russian soldiers disguised as workmen into the peninsula, and take control of the area by stealth. Less naïve than Russia supposed, the Japanese government asked to resolve the matter amicably, and sent their emissaries to St Petersburg. When ministers refused to receive them, and when the ambassador was likewise denied an audience, they withdrew in disgust. The Tsar rashly financed Bezobrazov's venture, and appointed the bellicose Admiral Eugene Alexiev to a new post, Viceroy of the Far East.

Had the Russian navy enjoyed stronger leadership it might have fulfilled Alexiev's boast that they would give the Japanese a thrashing they would never forget. However under Grand Duke Alexis this was not the case; still very much the *bon vivant*, preferring to conduct his nautical manoeuvres at Monte Carlo or Paris than aboard a Russian ship, his knowledge of naval affairs still rooted firmly in the days of sail, boring the assembled company at naval meetings with interminable stories about his sailing days on board the *Svetlana*, he was not the right choice to be given responsibility for naval operations. Plans to send auxiliary naval assistance, if needed, to strengthen the squadron based at Port Arthur were forestalled by a Japanese attack early in 1904, and war was declared. After initial patriotic fervour, public support in Russia soon evaporated. Though the Russian army was much larger than the Japanese, it was hampered by inadequate railways and poor leadership. With the third largest navy in the world, after England and France, they hoped for maritime superiority, but a succession of catastrophic defeats at sea and the strategic position of Japanese mines soon put paid to that. The war was a disaster for Russia, and Alexis's only solution to restore the empire's naval strength in the theatre of war was to send out a number of reconditioned ships from the Baltic fleet as a second Pacific Squadron, to replace the first squadron which met overwhelming defeat.

Affairs at home likewise went from bad to worse. In July 1904 Vyacheslav Plehve, minister of internal affairs, was assassinated, and succeeded by Prince Peter Svyatopolk-Mirsky, governor-general of Lithuania. The Dowager Tsarina had distrusted Plehve and feared his policy would lead to revolution. A confirmed liberal, Svyatopolk-Mirsky spoke freely of a new era of trust and reconciliation between government and society. In December 1904 he delivered a ten-point programme of reforms, including a promise of civil rights, and a proposal that elected representatives of society should participate in discussing legislation and central government policy. Serge warned his nephew that this proposal was a long step towards a constitution. The Tsarina believed that he was doing great harm, and he and the Tsar soon realized that they could not work in harmony.

One happy event *en famille* had marked the summer. On 30 July/12 August, after four daughters, the Tsarina gave birth to the long-awaited heir. However, the Russians had waited so long for their Tsar to have a son, and so many times they had been disappointed, that now it had come to pass the reaction was largely one of indifference throughout the embattled empire. Had it happened at a time of peace, or in the wake of victory, enthusiasm would surely have been greater. The child was christened Alexis at a grand ceremony attended by all the family, except for Grand Duke Paul. All too soon their happiness turned to horror; within a few months it was discovered that he had inherited the scourge of haemophilia, the bleeding disease. It was another sorrow to add to his mother's catalogue of woes; with ill-health and constant worry over her son, she cut herself off more and more from everyday life.

There was little joy in the household of Grand Duke and Duchess Serge either. The gap between him and his niece Marie and nephew Dmitri widened, particularly when he appointed an aged priest to give them religious instruction and they found him so intolerable that they complained first to Serge, who reproached them roundly for their lack of respect, then to their father. What Paul said when writing to Serge can only be guessed, but Serge called Marie into his study and scolded her for going behind his back. While she appreciated that he had their best interests at heart, his preoccupation with the smallest details of their education and upbringing were not calculated to appeal to them; 'he was a man limited in his affections and extremely jealous'.[1] He could never forget that, for all his faults, they still loved their absent father.

Serge's responsibility for two refractory adolescents was dwarfed by another worry; war had multiplied the anxiety and strain on him as governor-general of Moscow. When victories over Japan that Russia had taken for granted failed to materialize, and discontent and demonstrations multiplied, so did the pressure on Serge to maintain order. Had he been the fierce authoritarian reactionary of popular legend, he might have been more ruthless – and more successful. When Marie told one of his friends that she thought the crowds who were demonstrating used their patriotic emotions only as an excuse for brawling and that she thought the authorities were wrong not to intervene, the friend reported her opinions to her uncle and he admonished her, saying that the voice of the people was the voice of

God, and in her mistrust of the crowd's temper she was guilty of lack of respect for traditions.

Yet as unrest escalated, Serge's attitude began to harden. After a time he realized that only the utmost severity could put an end to revolutionary ferment. He had strongly disapproved of Syvatopolk-Mirsky's policy, and of the Tsar's partisanship of what he felt to be ill-considered reforms for which Russia was not yet ready. Feeling that he had failed to curb unrest in the city, thoroughly disillusioned with the whole situation, and deciding it was the right time to retire into private life, he resigned his post as governor-general of Moscow, though he retained command of the city's military forces.

In January 1905 a strike broke out in engineering works at St Petersburg and rapidly spread to other factories. Father Gapon, leader of a labour union authorized by the police, led a peaceful demonstration of workers to the Winter Palace, where he was to present a petition to the Tsar. The paper called for a constituent assembly, an eight hour day, freedom of speech and religion, and an amnesty for political prisoners. The Tsar was informed of the petition the night before, but did not travel to the Winter Palace to receive it. Maintenance of order was left to the St Petersburg police, who called in the army. As the crowd moved towards the Palace, carrying icons and religious banners, troops opened fire, and over two thousand were killed or wounded.

For this disaster, thereafter known as 'Bloody Sunday', the Tsar apportioned blame between Father Gapon, the 'socialist priest', who had made good his escape, staying in hiding for a few days and then fleeing the country, for misleading the people; and between Syvatopolk-Mirsky, who had created a climate favourable to such dangerous licence. The latter's resignation was demanded, and he was replaced by Alexander Bulygin, who had proved his capability while working as an assistant to Serge in Moscow.

Ministers recommended that the good name of government should be restored after this fiasco by a dramatic act of benevolence. After being convinced that there was no alternative, the Tsar consented with reluctance to the establishment of an elective consultative assembly, or *Duma*, and he would grant to his people the right of petition.

After his resignation Serge, Ella and the children moved out of the governor's house to the Neskuchnoie Palace, but he continued to go to the new governor's house each afternoon to set his affairs in order and clear out his private possessions. Otherwise he and Ella rarely ventured outside, and at home they only received their closest friends. He realized that he was a marked man, 'trying to avoid a death that was already inescapable, already creeping up on him'.[2]

One evening both of them and the children attended a war benefit concert at the Moscow Opera House. A terrorist organization who knew his route had planned to assassinate him, but when one of them saw the children in the carriage he thought better of it and decided not to wave the handkerchief which he had agreed to use as a signal to one of his comrades ready to throw the bomb. To execute a thoroughly detested Grand Duke was their aim; but to kill his wife and two innocent children in cold blood would surely send a wave of revulsion throughout the empire and set back their cause by years.

Serge had appointed his nephew Count Alexis Belevsky-Zhukovsky his aide-de-camp. The Count had married Marie, Princess Troubetskoy, and they had two young children. Their son was a godson of Serge, and Ella was godmother to their daughter. On 3/16 February Serge begged the Countess to persuade her husband not to come on duty in attendance on him the following day as he himself had received threatening letters. Though he did not fear for his own safety, he felt it was unfair to take the Count with him as he had a young family.

The Grand Ducal premonitions were all too correct. Next day, as he set out past the Kremlin, an explosion shook the Palace and rattled the windows. He had often forbidden his wife to go driving with him, as he feared that it was 1881 all over again and he had had a foreboding that he would meet a similar fate to that of his father.

Instinctively Ella knew what had happened. She hurried out in the cold to the scene where a crowd had gathered amid the smell of gunpowder and a cloud of smoke. Men were holding the assassin, Ivan Kalyaev, who had hung around for several days with a bomb in his pocket, waiting until the Grand Duke was driving without his wife. She saw fragments of wood and wheels, mangled and twisted horses, and the coachman lying mortally injured on the ground, while soldiers were using their cloaks to try and cover the fragments of mangled flesh. Grief-stricken, she went later to visit the coachman in hospital. When he asked for news of the Grand Duke, she assured him bravely that he had sent her to him, and he died of his injuries a few hours later. She begged the Tsar to spare Kalyaev, and when he refused her request she decided to see him herself in prison. Telling him that he must have suffered much to take the decision to perform such a deed, he retorted that 'a terrible war of hatred' was being fought against the people. Citing the events of Bloody Sunday, he told her that 'you' (inferring the imperial family) had declared war on the people, and he was merely taking up the challenge. As for the Grand Duke, he had 'assumed a specific political role'.[3] She declined to enter into political discussion with him, merely saying that the Grand Duke forgave him and that she would pray for him. Before getting up to leave she begged him to accept an icon in memory of her. Three months later he was put on trial, condemned to death and hanged.

Serge had been the Tsar's favourite uncle, the only one he could trust and readily consulted, and his assassination was a devastating personal blow. Because of the threat to the family, he had to accept even stricter personal protection, and remained at Tsarskoe-Selo under heavy guard, avoiding public appearances, even in St Petersburg.

In Paris Grand Duke Paul was bitterly shaken by the news. That his favourite brother should have met a violent death while they were still estranged was a sorrow he carried with him to the grave. He was granted permission to come home for the funeral held six days later, but his meetings with Ella and the children were awkward for all of them. Though she had admitted to them soon after her husband's murder that she had suffered inwardly because of the affection which her husband had always shown them, and resolved to make amends, she could neither forgive her brother-in-law nor forget the past.

Most of the family were advised to absent themselves from the funeral for fear of inviting further catastrophe. The Tsar, his wife and mother all longed to pay their last respects, but the authorities warned that it was not safe for them to leave Tsarskoe-Selo. All the Grand Dukes were informed by letter that they were not merely forbidden to go to Moscow, but also barred from attending requiem services at either the Kazan or Isaac Cathedral. When Alexis expressed his determination to go at all costs, the Tsar asked Paul to dissuade him. As Alexis was almost old enough to be the Tsar's father he quailed at the thought of forbidding him directly, but insisted he had 'irrefutable proof' that Alexis was being hunted like a wild beast.[4] Vladimir was likewise prohibited from appearing in public for weeks afterwards, if his presence was advertised in advance. Paul was the only surviving brother permitted to go. The Tsar presumably relented, partly on the grounds that both had been particularly close in happier days, but more importantly perhaps as Paul, having lived in Paris recently and not incurred the wrath of the terrorists, was the least likely target for an assassination attempt.

Among those who braved the threat were Grand Duke Constantine, a cousin of Serge; Ella's eldest sister Victoria, Princess Louis of Battenberg; his sister Marie, Dowager Duchess of Saxe-Coburg, and her youngest daughter Beatrice. The Dowager Duchess was evidently growing hardened to what had become an occupational hazard for her family. In May 1906, fifteen months later, she was among guests at the wedding of King Alfonso XIII and Princess Ena of Battenberg in Madrid. A bomb thrown at the wedding procession after the marriage ceremony narrowly missed its royal targets but killed some twenty soldiers and bystanders and wounded over sixty more. *'Je suis tellement accoutumée à ces choses'* ('I am so used to these things'), she shrugged.

Also present were the Grand Duke and Duchess of Hesse. Ernest had married for the second time only that week, his bride being Princess Eleonore of Solms-Hohensolms-Lich. Their honeymoon in Germany had been rudely interrupted by news of Serge's violent death, and Eleonore refused to leave Ernest. After attending the funeral they continued their honeymoon at Tsarskoe-Selo.*

* Grand Duke Serge was buried in a vault in the crypt of the Chudov monastery at the Kremlin, and a memorial cross was erected on the spot where he was killed. It is said that after the downfall of the Romanovs Lenin assisted personally in destroying the cross, and the monastery was demolished in 1928. In 1990 building workers in the Kremlin discovered the blocked up entrance to the burial vault. The coffin was examined and found to contain the Grand Duke's remains, covered with the military greatcoat of the Kiev regiment, decorations, and an icon. He had left written instructions that he was to be buried in the Preobrajensky uniform, but as his body was so badly disfigured this proved impossible. In 1995 the coffin was officially exhumed, and after a service in the Kremlin Cathedral of the Archangel, it was removed for reburial in a vault of the Novospassky monastery.

After the funeral Paul asked permission to spend more time with his children, but Ella would not listen. She saw the continued guardianship of them as a sacred duty bequeathed to her by her late husband and officially sanctioned by the Tsar. Unwilling to accept that they were growing up, she held steadfast to his principle that they must remain as innocent little children while in her care. She never discussed any family or political subject with them, or advised them of any changes. They nearly always heard news first from their household; when she decided to tell them these things herself and found out that they already knew, she was displeased. Paul was allowed to return to Russia at intervals with his wife, but permission for them to live there was still withheld. Still numb with shock at the fate of his favourite brother, he did not feel inclined to press his case for the time being, and went back to Paris gloomily resigned to the situation.

After Serge's assassination the Tsar was increasingly isolated. Three of his uncles were left, but he had never enjoyed a close relationship with them. Family rivalry and recent events had created a gulf between him, Vladimir and Paul. That only left Alexis, whose self-esteem and reputation as admiral were shortly to be shattered by the navy's crushing defeat at the Battle of Tsushima in the summer of 1905. He was wrongly blamed by press and public alike for these naval disasters, and though he was not responsible for the decision to send the Baltic fleet to avenge earlier Russian losses, he had no choice but to offer his resignation. Grand Duke Alexander's cynical verdict on the Romanov whose life 'was a case of fast women and slow ships'[5] was less than fair, but for him there could be no way back into public life.

Though he had become virtually a family outcast, Paul was much happier in Paris than he could ever have been at home in Russia. According to Grand Duke Alexander, who had always found him the most pleasant of the Grand Dukes despite his tendency to mount the high horse, 'he benefited considerably by his forced exile through meeting people of intelligence and importance. It changed his character, bringing out human traits formerly hidden under a mask of nonsensical haughtiness.'[6] In France he and Olga led a relatively simple life, and their house at Boulogne-sur-Seine became a magnet for writers, artists and holidaying Russians. Sometimes it seemed like an outpost of the

Russian Embassy. The names of Grand Duke Paul and Countess Hohenfelsen headed the guest list at many social functions, evenings at the opera and ballet, and services at the Russian church. He became acquainted with a wider range of people and ideas than he would ever have met in Russia, built up an impressive collection of antiques and works of art, and extended his house to accommodate them all.

Nevertheless he was still bitter at being treated as an outcast by his own family in Russia. When he planned a visit to Russia in the spring of 1905, a few weeks after Serge's funeral, the Tsar sent word through a telegram to Alexis that he was permitted to return – alone. Paul wrote angrily to his nephew, pointing out that apart from the pain of being separated from his wife, it put him in an extremely embarrassing situation with regard to the embassy in Paris, as he had informed the staff there that he and his wife would be travelling together. Nobody but her children would see her, and she particularly wanted to come at this time as her son was about to be promoted and she had been so looking forward to congratulating him on that special day. He begged the Tsar not to deny him this request, but the Tsar stood firm. Paul therefore made the journey to Tsarskoe-Selo on his own, was noticeably short-tempered with everybody, and according to Grand Duchess Xenia, was 'cold and unaffectionate with the children, and they are visibly shy of him!'[7]

As for Vladimir, he still regarded himself as the father of the rival Tsar-in-waiting. He would never wear the imperial crown himself, but one of his sons might. His eldest son Cyril had served with the Russian navy as first officer on board the flagship *Petropavlovsk*, and had been fortunate to escape with his life when the vessel was blown up by a Japanese mine at Port Arthur in April 1904, one of only eighty to be saved out of over seven hundred on board. Badly burnt, suffering from shell shock and major damage to the muscles of his back, he was in no fit state for further service. Vladimir and Marie were at the head of those who received him on his return to St Petersburg as a war hero, Vladimir 'terribly distressed,' constantly repeating that it was a miracle to see him still alive, and Marie was in tears. An even worse defeat occurred in May 1905 at Tsushima, when the Japanese navy took less than an hour to destroy eight Russian battleships, seven out of twelve cruisers and six out of nine destroyers. The Russian fleet had been almost annihilated, and when the scale of the disaster became known, a council of war was held at Tsarskoe-Selo.

While the Tsar was reluctant to agree with his government and chief officials that a cessation of hostilities was the only obvious answer, Vladimir, it was reported by Sir Charles Hardinge, British ambassador at St Petersburg, 'with his characteristic frankness of speech is stated to have said in the presence of the Emperor that the war was now so hopeless that the best course to pursue would be to send a blank paper with His Majesty's signature at its foot to Tôkiô and to ask the Japanese to fill in their conditions of peace'.[8] More than his nephew, he could appreciate the hopeless state of affairs; but in speaking out, his motives could have been misinterpreted as an effort to put himself at the head of any peace party which might form, in case the Tsar should be overthrown. The Grand Duke was outvoted by the military and naval representatives, reluctant to face reality, but others knew better. Count Paul Benckendorff, grand marshal of the court, felt that after defeat at the hands of the Japanese, Russia had become 'at best a second-rank power for two generations', and might even be destroyed by the conflict. There was no alternative to peace. Witte, who had attempted to dissuade his sovereign and country from provoking Japan in the first place, took his place at the negotiating table, and a treaty was signed at Portsmouth, New Hampshire, in September. Thus ended Russia's efforts at expansion in the Far East.

On 17/30 October 1905 Tsar Nicholas II signed an imperial manifesto which promised freedom of conscience, speech, assembly and association, and granted an elected parliament, the *Duma*. Even so, the Tsar remained the most powerful constitutional monarch in the world; and the delineation of power was so ambiguous that in 1906 the *Almanach de Gotha* referred to Russia as a constitutional monarchy ruled by an autocrat.

Among the elder generation, nobody was more angry than Vladimir. While he had welcomed the cessation of Russo–Japanese hostilities, he was infuriated by the creation of a *Duma* ('a congress of chatterers'), seeing it as craven defeat and concession to the masses. There was another reason for his fury; the treatment meted out to his eldest son. Cyril, who was lucky to be alive, had fallen in love with his cousin Victoria Melita, the divorced former Grand Duchess of Hesse. That he wanted to marry a divorcée was bad enough; but that she should be the ex-wife of the Tsarina's brother, and have been at the centre of a family case which had caused so much grief to the family, made matters worse. Well aware of his cousin's intentions, the Tsar had warned Cyril bluntly that if he persisted in this *mésalliance* he would be deprived of the revenues from his appanages and dismissed from the armed services. Cyril was offended at being informed through a third party, the court minister Baron Fredericks, but would not be dissuaded. The marriage took place at a private ceremony at Amorbach on 25 September/8 October 1905 and they both came back defiantly to Russia, whereupon the Tsar ordered them to leave the country.

Until 1904 the heir to the throne was the Tsar's only surviving brother Michael, who was still a bachelor and two years later contracted an unapproved marriage with Natalie Wulfert, a twice-married daughter of a Moscow solicitor, who had become his mistress while still married to her second husband. The Tsar denied them permission to marry, and a secret wedding ceremony was conducted by a Serbian priest in Vienna. They were officially forbidden to return to Russia until the outbreak of the First World War in 1914, when the Grand Duke's wife was granted the title of Countess Brassova, but neither the Tsar, the Tsarina or Dowager Empress Marie ever received her. The next heirs were the sons of Grand Duke and Grand Duchess Vladimir, but tension between Nicholas and family and the Vladimirs was never far below the surface, especially because of Marie's dislike of Alexandra, and an unseemly row over the banishment of Cyril and his wife.

In the spring of 1907 Grand Duchess Marie, seventeen years old, was betrothed to Prince William of Sweden, a matter in which she had no choice. He was invited to Russia to visit her, and even when she went down with a fever Ella told her that she could not keep the Prince waiting for a decision any longer. He must be given an answer one way or another. Realizing she was cornered, she assented on condition that she would not be married before she was eighteen. When she asked if her father had agreed and what did he say, Ella told her that she had the consent and approval of the Tsar, and as her father was abroad 'you shall write to him yourself very soon'. The letter was dictated by Ella, and as Marie had expected, he was quite upset. To him, the haste with which his daughter's future had been planned was incomprehensible; she was too young to marry or to have developed sufficient independence of judgement. Moreover, he deeply resented the fact that all arrangements had been made without his having been consulted or even notified.

Paul was bitterly angry with his sister-in-law and his nephew. At first he said he would not attend either the engagement ceremony or the wedding of his daughter, because of the hostile attitude shown to him and his wife; 'after five years of exemplary family life I have the right to expect a different attitude towards us both.' He could not participate in the wedding celebrations of even his beloved daughter without his wife, as he did not make the break and sacrifice everything he had to let her 'be humiliated and insulted without reason'. If she was to be forbidden from coming to Russia because of her divorce, then the recent marriage of Grand Duke Nicholas Nicholaievich, the Tsar's uncle, to a divorced woman, to which the Tsar had given his permission and blessing, had surely broken all the rules. Moreover, he could not attend Marie's wedding 'as long as this shameful wardship is in force'. As the children were wards, their father had been given no chance to meet the prince and pronounce himself for or against the wedding, or to voice his opinion that she was too young to be given away in marriage. The wardship had decided so many questions without reference to him that the children had been distanced from him to the utmost possible degree, all 'because of the severe attitude you and Alix have towards me'.[9] His position deserved nothing but sympathy, although Grand Duchess Xenia condemned his behaviour as 'incredible heartlessness', declaring that he had 'spoilt everything' for his daughter. On reflection the Tsar had to admit that there was no justification for maintaining the exclusion on Paul's wife, and in the autumn he sent word through Alexis that they could return to Russia to visit.

In 1907 Paul and Countess Hohenfelsen returned to Russia so the latter could be with her eldest daughter by her first marriage, who was expecting a child. The Tsar could not withhold permission, but Ella did not want him to return, or more specifically did not wish for Marie and Dmitri to meet him again.

Nevertheless she could hardly prevent them, but she did her best to give their reunion a coldly formal atmosphere. Despite Paul's best efforts to be welcoming, it was an uncomfortable occasion. They had another meeting at St Petersburg, but she was present there as well. Paul saw the futility of it all, and did not press for a third. Marie was comforted by seeing that he was evidently happy and at peace, but otherwise she felt that one advantage of her impending marriage would be that in future nothing could prevent her from seeing her father whenever she wanted.

When Paul came to Tsarskoe-Selo for his daughter's marriage the following spring, his suspicions were soon confirmed. It was evident that Ella had 'too easily disposed' of her; he held her responsible and told her so. Her lack of commonsense and normal feelings, her detachment and lack of interest in family matters exasperated him, and he found her so distant and so different from her old self as to be incomprehensible. Marie saw her father in Paris shortly after her wedding, and met her half-brother and half-sisters for the first time. His house at Boulogne was comfortable, peaceful and simple, and his lack of regrets for the forbidding palace that he had left at St Petersburg, his happiness in his second marriage, were obvious.

Within three months Paul lost his two surviving elder brothers. On 1/14 November 1908 Alexis contracted pneumonia and died after a week's illness at the age of fifty-eight. He had relinquished his naval posts after the Russo–Japanese war and retired for good to his true spiritual home, Paris. At his house in Avenue Gabriel he kept open door for writers, painters, actors and especially actresses. Like Vladimir he had always been less interested in the armed services than in art and fashion, and he had long since been recognized as a connoisseur of the social, artistic and literary life of the capital. His massive frame was a familiar sight at restaurants and theatres, particularly on first nights. It was appropriate that his last public appearance, a week before his death, should have been at the dress rehearsal of a new play at the Vaudeville.

Though to some he was little more than a byword for good living, he was remembered with affection by the rest of his family who had always appreciated his generosity and goodness of heart. At the coronation of Tsar Nicholas II he had walked beside the Dowager empress, the sister-in-law who needed a supportive arm to lean on. five years later, when she lost her second George to tuberculosis, he had accompanied her on that desolate journey to the Caucasus to bring his body home for burial. 'My favourite uncle is dead, a noble, honourable, courageous soul!' the Tsar wrote in his diary. 'May the Kingdom of Heaven be his!'[10] On his death President Fallières, who had regularly invited him to take part in state shooting parties, sent his condolences to Grand Duke Paul. Yet as a Grand Duke of Russia, albeit one who had done little to advance the reputation of his family there, Alexis was destined to rest in peace in his homeland, and his body was returned to St Petersburg for burial.*

The funeral of Alexis took place at the Fortress of St Peter and St Paul eight days after his death, at a ceremony attended by the Tsarina and her mother-in-law, and what was the Tsar's first public appearance for some years. Also present was Cyril, who had been permitted by the Tsar as a gesture of reconciliation to return briefly from Paris to Russia for the last rites for his uncle.

Three months later Vladimir followed Alexis to the grave. Alone among the brothers he lived to celebrate his sixtieth birthday, but his last years were dogged by ill-health, and sadness at the belief that he had been responsible for ordering forces to fire on the demonstrators on 'Bloody Sunday'. On 4/17 February 1909 he suffered a major cerebral haemorrhage and within minutes he had passed away. Ever loyal to his memory a Colonel Beresford, former military attaché at St Petersburg, found it necessary to declare in the press that the Grand Duke was on sick leave from his duty as commander-in-chief of the city troops in January 1905, and therefore did not give orders for the troops to be called out, an accusation made against him which he had always felt keenly.[11]

With these two deaths in the elder generation, Tsar Nicholas II felt more secure as head of the family. Alexis had long been little more than a figure of fun, particularly after his move to Paris, but he had always been in awe of the sharp-tongued Vladimir, even though he had mellowed a little in his last years. A full pardon for his cousin Cyril not only allowed him and his wife Victoria Melita

* No mention was made in his obituary in *The Times*, 16 November 1908, of his putative wife (who had died in 1899) or son, Count Alexis Belevsky-Zhukovsky, former equerry to his uncle Serge, was appointed an equerry at the imperial court in 1913, and executed by the Bolsheviks at Tiflis, Georgia, in 1932.

back for the funeral of his father, but also let them make their home in Russia. To the widowed Grand Duchess Vladimir he gave the appointment of head of a dragoon regiment of the imperial guard. At her request he appointed her President of the Imperial Academy of Arts, the position held by her husband. These were kindly gestures to the widow for whom he felt much sympathy, but whom he and his wife could not but regard as something of a rival. During the previous year the Grand Duchess who had defiantly adhered to her Protestant faith for thirty-four years of marriage to a Grand Duke of Russia had converted to the Orthodox Church. Knowing that only the sickly Tsarevich stood between the imperial throne and her eldest son Cyril, she was determined to ease his path to succession in any way she could.

Nevertheless, it seemed to be a time for family reconciliations. In 1912 Princess Yourievsky returned to Russia to visit her husband's grave. The official attitude towards her had mellowed at last. Tsar Nicholas welcomed her, and her existence was reported in the press for the first time. She had still maintained a palace in Russia, and the Tsar's youngest sister Olga used to visit her. 'Whenever I called on her I felt I was stepping into a page of history. She lived entirely in the past. Time stopped for her on the day my grandfather was assassinated. She always talked about him. She kept all his uniforms and clothes, even his dressing-gown, in glass cases in her private chapel.'[12]

Of Princess Yourievsky's three children who had survived to maturity, George had married Countess Alexandra Zarnekau at Nice on 3/16 February 1900, and they settled in St Petersburg, but their marriage ended in divorce in 1908. Olga, now Countess Merenberg, had settled in Wiesbaden with her husband and children, George and Olga. Their younger sister Catherine, with her indifferent health, was a constant source of worry to her mother. With her congenital heart defect she suffered from frequent shortness of breath and a tendency to faint, and until adolescence she was particularly undersized. Ironically she would outlive the rest of her family by several decades. Her passions were animals and music; she was devoted to dogs, and during childhood she had a donkey which was supposed to live in the stables but was often smuggled into her nursery. She desperately wanted to learn to ride, but her mother feared she was not strong enough, and would only allow her to travel in a pony cart.

Learning the piano was considered a safer accomplishment, and she played well although she found it dull. One night when her mother was out, a maid took her to hear Dame Nellie Melba sing. Thereafter she was determined to be a concert singer herself. Fearing it would place undue strain on her heart, her mother initially resisted such demands. At length however she relented, and allowed her to train in Milan under the celebrated Polish tenor Jean de Reszke.

In October 1901 she married Prince Alexander Bariatinsky, heir to one of Russia's wealthiest families. A notorious playboy, he had already had a rather public affair with the opera singer Lina Cavalieri. Well aware of his past, Catherine accepted her as a friend, even copying Lina's hairstyle, and the three were regularly seen together in public. For a few carefree years life was an endless party, with opera, theatre and balls at Paris, and hunting, racing and bridge parties at Biarritz, or house parties on Alexander's estate at Lidenau in Bavaria. They had two sons, André, born in 1902, and Alexander, or 'Buddie' two years later.

Yet this extravagant lifestyle frequently exhausted their means. The Bariatinskys despaired of their son's spendthrift ways, and Princess Yourievsky was angry – yet forgiving enough – when her daughter turned up on her doorstep, clad in diamonds and furs which she wanted to save from their creditors. After a few weeks of scrimping the couple would return to their empty house and start again. Once this hollow existence became almost too much for Catherine, and in a mood of depression she made a half-hearted suicide attempt by cutting off the ends from a box of matches and swallowing them, but she did herself no lasting damage.

Her husband proved less robust. In March 1910 Alexander was recovering from a mild stroke when he collapsed at a bridge party in Florence and died soon afterwards. Though he had lived a rather aimless life, he had made no enemies. Nearly everybody with whom he came into contact agreed that he was a charming and thoroughly likeable personality.

Temporarily shattered by her loss, Catherine retired to Lidenau, finding relief in solitude, walking and riding in the hills. Later she resumed her singing, joined a local society, and decided to take her sons to the ancestral home of Ivanovskoie near Kiev, where she could teach them about estate management. She took over the running of Ivanovskoie on behalf on her sons and saved a considerable sum through careful management, according to her own account, though her more worldly-wise father-in-law was still living on the estate and very much in control.

Her health still continued to cause the family anxiety. Recurring spells of breathlessness sometimes made her faint while out riding, and on at least one occasion she was found unconscious some way from the house. On a visit to her aunt, the Dowager Duchess of Saxe-Coburg, both became so involved in doing a jigsaw puzzle that she suddenly passed out and it took a while to revive her.

Grand Duke Paul, the Tsar's only surviving uncle, was still in exile in Paris, and as one of the senior members of the family, it was only right that the hand of reconciliation and welcome back to his homeland should be extended to him and his wife as well. The marriage of his daughter Marie to Prince William of Sweden, brother of King Gustav V, did not long survive the birth of their son Lennart. Paul was anxious about the marital problems of the younger generation as well as the future of his weak, easily led son Dmitri. Olga's younger daughter was divorced in 1911, after a marriage lasting only three years; Marie was determined to dissolve a union into which she had been forced, and would obviously never be a success. Like his father King Gustav, Prince William was homosexual, and he offered no resistance to his wife's intention to leave him. In January 1912 after Dmitri had come of age and taken his oath of allegiance to the Tsar, the latter formally announced his decision to lift the sentence of banishment and therefore allow Paul, his wife and family to return and settle down in Russia. Paul, who had always owned a palace in St Petersburg, still cherished the idea of building his own house at Tsarskoe-Selo, similar to his Paris home, for his family and his art collection.

Their son Vladimir had already been sent to St Petersburg and enrolled in the military academy. His daughter Marie opened her heart to him, and he listened patiently. Initially he had been opposed to her idea of divorce. In his opinion, apart from all moral and political aspects of the case, she was too young to be alone in the world, and her stepmother strongly supported him. However, divorce was by no means an unfamiliar experience to them, or indeed to several members of the imperial family. Paul was distressed at the sight of his daughter, in a severe physical state, fainting regularly, unable to eat or sleep properly, and complaining about her kidneys. It was unthinkable that she could return to Sweden. When the marriage was annulled the following year he accepted the situation and gave her his wholehearted support, taking care of arrangements and correspondence as far as he could. The house was finished in May 1914, and with remarkably prescient timing they returned during the last few weeks of peace in Europe. That same month Marie also came home to Russia, her unhappy Swedish marriage behind her. Paul and his wife were living in the new house, and he was evidently glad to be back in Russia.

In view of the impending storm, it was fortunate that the Romanovs could at last put on a united front, particularly as tercentenary celebrations for the dynasty in 1913 had aroused little enthusiasm throughout Russia. The empire's first family failed to inspire the loyal but thin crowds who came out to cheer them on their public appearances in St Petersburg. Already there were furtive rumours that all was not well with the Tsarevich, though the severe attack of internal bleeding he suffered at his father's hunting lodge at Spala the previous year which he was lucky to survive remained as closely guarded a secret as that of Grigory Rasputin, the 'holy man' who, the Empress had become convinced, alone had the power to save his life. As for his four sisters, they were attractive lively girls, but very immature. Their mother had kept them living in a sheltered world at Tsarskoe-Selo, far from the excesses of St Petersburg, society and gay parties, and the decadence of the capital. Her own health had never been robust. As a girl she had suffered from sciatica; since marriage five difficult pregnancies, two miscarriages, and constant worry over her son had unbalanced her nervous system. She suffered from psychosomatic hysteria which produced dizziness and heart palpitations, and she lived the life of a semi-invalid, rising from bed late in the morning and spending much of the day reclining on a chaise-longue.

The Tsar was increasingly racked by anxiety for her health as well as that of their son. As his reign entered its twentieth year and Europe's Armageddon drew closer, he was to find the lengthening shadows comparable to those which had darkened the twilight days of his grandfather.

13

'Into the abyss'

On 15/28 June 1914 the heir to the throne of Austria-Hungary, Archduke Francis Ferdinand, and his morganatic wife were assassinated in the Bosnian capital of Sarajevo, and one month later to the day Austria declared war on Serbia. As statesmen throughout Europe had feared, the conflict proved impossible to localize. To prevent the annihilation of Serbia, Russia ordered partial mobilization of forces covering the Austrian front. A demand from the German ambassador that mobilization should be stopped within twelve hours was refused, and after an exchange of increasingly frantic telegrams between the Russian and German Emperors, Germany declared war on Russia on 19 July/1 August. Within three days Great Britain and France were also committed to the conflict alongside Russia, with Germany and the Habsburg empire ranged against them.

In Russia there was a tremendous surge of patriotic enthusiasm in favour of the war, but it did not long survive the knowledge that her woefully unprepared and inadequately armed troops were suffering one reverse after another. Despite fierce official censorship of the press, it was impossible to conceal from the people that there would be no quick or easy victory. By December 1916, of fifteen million men called to the colours, over eight million had been killed, wounded or taken prisoner.

As distressed by the bloodshed as everybody else, the Tsarina dedicated herself to hospital work as soon as the Tsar left for army headquarters. The war brought about something of a transformation in the woman who had recently been a semi-invalid who slept until midday and rarely left the couch in her boudoir. Now she rose to attend Mass at 7 a.m.; two hours later she and her two eldest daughters were at the hospital in their uniforms, sparing themselves nothing as they assisted in the most difficult operations and amputations. Ella was still committed to her nursing work in the Convent of Martha and Mary of which she was Abbess, and the other Grand Duchesses undertook similar roles in the war effort.

Now aged fifty-four, Grand Duke Paul and his wife were still busy organizing their new home. Within a few months it was almost fully furnished with their collections from Paris, glass cases containing valuable antique porcelain and silver, Chinese stone knick-knacks, and exquisite examples of cut glass, and walls hung with priceless pictures and portraits. His wife was still known as Countess of Hohenfelsen, the name conferred on her by the Prince Regent of Bavaria. It was impolitic for her to retain a German name, and as she could not be made a Grand Duchess, in 1915 the Tsar conferred on her and her children the style and name of Prince and Princesses Paley. The move came just in time, as their son Vladimir left for the front a few days later.

Before he went to war, initially in command of a corps of the imperial guard and then at army headquarters, Paul spent most of his leisure time reading, walking, playing with his younger daughters and taking them to the circus. Princess Paley excused herself from this treat as she was allergic to the smell of horses. Their daughter Irina disliked circuses herself, but she never had the heart to tell her father as he obviously enjoyed himself so much.

Soon after the outbreak of war they transformed their ballroom into a workshop where Princess Paley, the ladies of Tsarskoe-Selo and their children made comforts for wounded soldiers. No orchestra played there, but one evening they pushed back tables and sewing machines, and Paul invited Irina to waltz with him to *The Merry Widow* played on an old gramophone.

The divorced Grand Duchess Marie Paulovna felt her father had hardly aged at all. At fifty-five he still had a youthful figure, as well as the gift of reducing her to helpless laughter at stories and anecdotes 'which he told incomparably'.[1] His dressing room was still permeated by the scent of the perfume he had always used, and his clothes were laid out on the spare bed in the old way. Just as before, father and daughter went for a walk at eleven in the morning, and he took a nap between lunch and teatime. After dinner every evening they gathered in his study while he read aloud. For Marie it was a haven to return to this homely atmosphere, away from the stress of her hospital work.

The rest of the imperial family were becoming steadily less popular. As Rasputin's influence mounted, so did criticism of the Tsar and Tsarina. The latter and Grand Duchess Serge, those 'German women', or even 'Hessian witches', were easy targets for nationalist venom. As the Tsarina was blamed for much of what went wrong, and found herself treated with hostility by other members of the imperial family, Paul sprang gallantly to her defence. He remained ever supportive of her, consulted her regularly on day-to-day matters and kept her informed of his conversations with the French ambassador. According to his daughter he, if not the rest of the family, 'seemed to be sustained by courage, wisdom, and the power of abstract reasoning. The Crowd's moods left him untouched. He followed attentively, though not without agitation, the unfoldment of fanatical developments and the changed psychology at court.'[2]

Yet, almost unnoticed by the family, his health was declining, his determination to take a relatively active role in military affairs not matched by his physical strength. For some years before his return to Russia there had been concern about the state of his liver, and a tendency to suffer from stomach ulcers. During the winter of 1915–6 he was seriously ill with pleurisy, and his eldest daughter was horrified to see him so weak. He was losing weight, had a suspected gall bladder infection, and at one stage there was talk of operating on him in order to save his life. While the possibility of losing him suddenly seemed unbearable, she would later admit that she often had cause to regret that he did not die then.

During the four years between her husband's death and the outbreak of war, the younger Princess Catherine Yourievsky divided her time between Ivanovskoie, Lidenau, and her mother's homes in France and Russia. When hostilities began she was at Munich with her children, and returned to Russia under conditions of some difficulty. They settled at Ivanovskoie, where she ran an improvised hospital in one wing of the house. To help finance it she arranged concerts where she was inevitably the star attraction. Meanwhile her mother was reunited with the former wife of her late son George, and their son Alexander, whom she sent to school at her own expense. Both women became involved in running a military hospital in Paris.

While running a stall at a charity bazaar in Yalta in the spring of 1916 Catherine met an officer of the chevalier guard, Prince Serge Obolensky, whom she remembered as a small boy in Biarritz. A member of the Russian aristocracy, his father had been an aide-de-camp to Grand Duke Vladimir; in childhood he had known the family well, and he was also a close friend of Prince Felix Youssupov. Now aged twenty-six, and like the lonely Catherine he was at a low ebb himself, getting over a failed love affair, and recovering from the effects of exposure in East Prussia, suffering from pleurisy and suspected tuberculosis, the latter being disproved later by tests. Sent to Yalta on medical advice to convalesce, three days before his leave was up and he was due to return to the front, he wandered into the bazaar to look at items being sold for the benefit of a war relief organization. He and Catherine began to talk and remembered each other from earlier days. She invited him to a concert that afternoon at which she would be singing Russian ballads.

With a significant lack of enthusiasm he recalled some years later that he was 'deeply impressed' by her singing; 'that was all. In my boyhood she had appeared a glamorous figure to me as the daughter of Alexander II, and that day the extraordinary poignancy of her voice, and the mood I was in, touched me as I have been touched few times in my life.'[3] After the concert they went for a ride on horseback in the hills above Yalta, and he proposed to her. She promised to give him her answer in the autumn, and after a period of reflection she agreed to marry him.

With Tsar Nicholas II's blessing the wedding took place at the Russian Cathedral in Yalta on 6/19 October 1916, Serge's brother Vladimir acting as best man, and officers from his regiment as ushers holding the crowns over them at the ceremony. Also present were his half-brother Max de Reutern, Catherine's elder son André, and Count Fredericks representing the Tsar, who was commanding armies at the front but sent a present of aquamarines. After the ceremony they borrowed a car from Grand Duke Alexander Michaelovich to Simferopol on their way to St Petersburg for the honeymoon. Afterwards Serge continued to serve with his regiment until it was disbanded after the revolution, then he and Catherine returned to Yalta with her sons.

By September 1916 Tsar Nicholas II had aged considerably. He seemed to have lost all serious interest in anything as he went through his daily routine like an automaton, paying more attention to the hours for his meals or walks in the garden than to affairs of state. With the Tsarina's increasing influence over government appointments, made largely on the whims of 'our friend' Rasputin, he was becoming increasingly isolated from the rest of his own family.

Meanwhile the atmosphere was heavy with plots and rumours of plots, mainly designed to remove the Tsarina and Rasputin. The Dowager Empress was said to have given her son an ultimatum that if he did not send Rasputin away she would leave the capital. He did nothing, and his mother took up residence in Kiev, where it was whispered that she was involved in a conspiracy to overthrow her son. That she would have encouraged such an idea, let alone taken steps herself to destabilize the dynasty by plotting against the Lord's anointed imperial sovereign who was also her eldest son, beggared belief; but she would hardly have been human if she did not at least privately curse the daughter-in-law who she was convinced, as her private utterances would later confirm, was leading them headlong into disaster. This did not prevent rumours that either Grand Duke Paul, the sole surviving brother-in-law, would seize power in the name of the Dowager Empress, and she would take the throne in her own right; or that she and Paul would seize the throne together as co-regents for the haemophiliac Tsarevich, Grand Duke Alexis Nicolaievich, until he attained his majority – if he lived that long. It was also said that the Tsarina heard of it and asked the Tsar to send his mother into exile.

The widowed Grand Duchess Vladimir, still thirsting for power for her sons, especially Cyril, despised the Tsar and Tsarina, but disliked the Dowager Empress almost as much. Paul tried to stay out of the plotting, but he found it impossible to distance himself completely from what his relations were saying.

Grand Duchess Vladimir was allegedly responsible for many of the most exaggerated stories about the Tsarina, especially one that she kept her husband plied with drink to make him more amenable to her requests. According to Michael Rodzianko, president of the *Duma*, she said that she hoped the Tsarina 'would soon be eliminated or shut up'. Her son Boris shared his parents'

Anglophobia, and at a regimental dinner attended by British troops the previous June he had burst out drunkenly that a war was certain to break out soon between Britain and Russia, and that the British were sitting tight in their trenches doing nothing while the French were being massacred in their thousands.

In November Grand Duke Alexander, on behalf of the rest of the family, asked Paul on his return to Petrograd to summon a family conference with his brothers and the Vladimirovichi, and then 'see their Majesties and speak to them with all possible frankness and from your heart . . . for things will begin to happen suddenly very soon, and will drag us all down into the abyss'.[4] They all depended on him, as the Tsar's 'nearest and dearest relative' as well as his only surviving uncle. When the imperial family returned to Tsarskoe-Selo on 3/16 December the Grand Duke asked for an audience and was received that same afternoon. He had no illusions as to the magnitude of his 'arduous and ungrateful' task.

After they had finished tea, Paul began to tell the Tsar how bad the situation was; of German propaganda, becoming bolder and more insolent by the day, and its demoralizing effect on the Russian army; and the increasing discontent of people in Petrograd and Moscow, especially those who had to queue for bread, the price of which had recently increased threefold. Finally he raised the most contentious issue of all. As a true patriot he wished only for the welfare of Russia and was sacrificing his traditional feelings and personal convictions; at a family gathering he had been charged respectfully to press for the granting of a constitution while there was yet time, as proof that the sovereign was anticipating the desire of his people. A perfect opportunity was at hand, as in three days' time it would the the Feast of St Nicholas. If His Majesty chose that day to announce that the constitution of 1905 was to be granted and honoured in full, he would be acclaimed by his people.

At this the Tsarina shook her head, while the Tsar thought a moment and then replied wearily that it would be impossible. On the day of his coronation he had taken his oath to the Absolute Power, and nothing could absolve him from leaving this oath intact to his son.

Realizing that he had failed, Paul tried to salvage what he could by asking that at least a Ministry of Confidence could be granted, and that Stürmer and Protopopov, two particularly incompetent ministers, should be dismissed. That they had been nominations of the *staretz* was criticized; Rasputin's meddling in state matters and influence in the Palace horrified people throughout Russia. Though he had never even met or seen Rasputin, his knowledge of the man from unimpeachable sources told him all he needed to know. The Tsar said nothing, but the Tsarina broke in with a passionate defence of Rasputin. He was merely a victim of the calumny and envy of those who wished they were in his place, she insisted; he was a devoted friend who prayed for the Tsar, the Tsarina and their children; he recognized the needs of the Empire; and that to sacrifice ministers to the whim of a minority was out of the question.

With a heavy heart Paul took his leave. Three days later, on the Feast of St Nicholas, he was received at the Palace as if no conversation had taken place.

Later that month the Tsarina and her elder sister Ella had what turned out to be their last meeting. Whether it took place at the request of ministers who thought it was their last chance to find somebody level-headed enough to tell her the truth about Rasputin, whether the Tsarina summoned her sister herself, or whether Ella took the initiative as a final attempt to persuade her to see reason, is anybody's guess. Likewise the conversation that passed between them is shrouded in mystery. All that is known for certain is that it was a short meeting, as Ella had to return urgently to Moscow. It took place in private, but the memoirs of Pierre Gilliard, tutor to the Tsar's children, are probably closer to the truth than the account of anybody else. According to him Ella pleaded with her to listen to her warnings for the sake of family and country. Others have suggested, with doubtless a certain amount of artistic licence, that she tried to persuade her sister to send Rasputin away, reminding her of the fate of King Louis XVI and Queen Marie Antoinette, and that the Tsarina cut matters short by promptly picking up the telephone and ordering a carriage to take her sister back to the train, with Ella saying sadly that it might have been better if she had not come. Nevertheless the Tsarina asked her never to bring up the subject of Rasputin again, and when Ella persisted, the Tsarina broke off the conversation. A few hours later they parted at the Moscow railway station, more in sorrow than in anger. Felix Youssupov put his own rather melodramatic construction on the course of events, asserting that Ella was in tears, saying that 'she drove me away like a dog!' The

Tsarina did not dismiss her, but she was left in no doubt that on the subject of the *staretz* there was an irreconciliable gulf between them.

Unknown to them a few individuals had decided to remove the man for once and for all. The night of 17/30 December 1916 saw the culmination of a conspiracy by Vladimir Purishkevich, an extreme right-wing deputy in the *Duma* described by Paléologue as the self-made 'champion of orthodox absolutism', Prince Felix Youssupov, and Paul's son Dmitri. Rasputin's death came only after several hours of black farce. Lured to Youssupov's Moika Palace on the pretext of a party, he was given poisoned cakes and wine which failed to kill him. Youssupov shot him in the back, and was congratulating himself on having despatched the scourge of Russia when the body twitched, opened its eyes and confronted him with a perfectly understandable look of demonic hatred. Youssupov was rooted to the floor in terror as Rasputin leapt to his feet, grabbed him by the throat, and chased him up the stairs of the cellar as he broke free, running outside, shouting he would tell the Empress everything. A few further shots as he fled and a well-aimed boot rendered him unconscious, but his murderers were taking no chances. His body was rolled up in a curtain, bound firmly with rope and pushed through a hole in the ice on the River Neva where it was found three days later. He had survived bullets and physical force, only to die by drowning.

When the news broke Paul was with the Tsar at headquarters, and the Grand Duke was astonished by his composure. An expression of serenity, not to say happiness, played around his face when uncle and nephew had tea that afternoon. The *staretz*'s elimination, it was not hard to surmise, had given him a sense of relief. While he had found it impossible to go against the wishes of the wife whom he loved so much, he seemed glad that the fates had delivered him from the nightmare which had weighed on him so heavily.[5] On the other hand Anna Vyrubova believed that his disgust with the behaviour of the Grand Dukes reached a crescendo with Rasputin's murder, and that he was now 'entirely through with them all'; but as one of the Tsarina's most loyal friends and a fervent disciple of the *staretz*, her words have to be regarded with scepticism.

Nonetheless the knowledge that his own son had been involved in the murder shook Paul, and he did not share his daughter's optimistic belief that as he was of imperial blood Dmitri was probably immune from prosecution. Even so he and Youssupov had become temporary heroes of all classes throughout Russia. To prosecute them would fly in the face of the opinion of almost everyone but the Tsarina and the few incompetent politicians who had benefited so handsomely from Rasputin's patronage.

Paul wanted to go to Dmitri immediately in Petrograd but Princess Paley, fearing for his health, dissuaded him from leaving. He asked Dmitri to come to see him at Tsarskoe-Selo, but he had already been placed under arrest and was to be exiled to the Persian front by order of the Tsar for his part in Rasputin's murder. Further distressed by the sentence, Paul spoke to his son on the phone and asked whether he wanted to come and see him. Dmitri admitted sadly to his sister that he had caused his father enough sorrow, and that saying goodbye would be too hard. Notwithstanding the sentence of exile, Paul accepted that his son must take the punishment like a man. The Tsar bore his nephew no ill will.

Even so he was angry that the Tsarina had apparently assumed her husband's prerogative by ordering Dmitri's arrest and asked the Tsar 'by what right' she had to do this herself.[6] A little unconvincingly the Tsar told him that the order had been his. Next day Paul went to see Dmitri, and asked him if he could swear that there was no blood on his hands. Dmitri crossed himself in front of an ikon hanging in the corner and swore faithfully by the name of his mother.

Two days later it was rumoured that the Tsarina was demanding a court martial for Dmitri and Youssupov. Dmitri gave Paul a letter which he begged him to pass to the Tsar. In it he said that he would be asked for his motive in lifting his hand against Rasputin, and as they had taken an oath not to give any explanations he would not give any answer, but instead he would shoot himself. By such an act he felt he would justify himself in the eyes of the Tsar, but whether this letter ever reached the sovereign is doubtful.

As the elder statesman of the Romanovs, Paul saw that the deed had been carried out from patriotic motives, but it had been a dangerous act with scant regard for the consequences, and a stain on the family name, and he was angry that Youssupov should have involved his easily led son. He also saw that it would make the Tsarina even more obstinate and reactionary in her views, and would oppose more rigidly than before the slightest concession to public opinion. No advice, he knew sadly, would have any effect. She and the Tsar were completely estranged from everyone except Rasputin's partisans.

Grand Duchess Vladimir, third lady of the empire after the Tsarina and Dowager Empress, was the undisputed leader of society, still gathering round her the local elite who liked and respected her, as well as diplomats and foreigners coming to Petrograd. More at odds with the Tsarina than ever before, she was furious that Dmitri, the least guilty, had apparently been singled out for the most savage treatment of all. Youssupov, the chief perpetrator, had been exiled to his estate, in effect no punishment at all. Grand Duke and Duchess Cyril were also disgusted by the sentences. As none of them could visit the palace in person, they decided to draw up a family petition asking the Tsar to pardon Dmitri or at least reduce the sentence. Signatures were collected, headed by that of Olga, Dowager Queen of the Hellenes, mother of Paul's late first wife. The petition was taken to the Tsar at the Alexander Palace, and returned to Paul with a handwritten note in the margin signed by the Tsar: 'No one has the right to kill, and I am astonished that the family should address itself to me with such requests.'[7] Grand Duchess Vladimir was so angry that she showed it to everyone. It was further proof of dissension within the imperial family's ranks and of the isolation of the Tsar and Tsarina.

The Dowager Empress added her voice to those of the critics, writing from Kiev to the Tsar that he must realize how deeply he had offended all the family by his brusque reply, throwing at their heads an entirely unjustified accusation. 'I hope also with all your heart that you will alleviate the fate of Dmitri Pavlovich by not leaving him in Persia where the climate is so dreadful that with his poor health he will never be able to stand it. Poor Uncle Paul wrote to me in despair that he had not even been given a chance to say goodbye to him or bless him, as he was whisked away so unexpectedly in the middle of the night. It is not like you with your kind heart to behave in this way; it upsets me very much.'[8] Ironically Dmitri's banishment would save his life, for within two years any member of the house of Romanov still on Russian soil would have a price on his or her head.

The Tsar's brother-in-law Grand Duke Alexander begged him to grant a government acceptable to the *Duma*, and for the Tsarina to withdraw from politics. When the Tsarina, lying in bed while her husband sat on the other side of it, told him brusquely that it was impossible for an autocrat to share his powers with a parliament, he retorted that he had ceased to be an autocrat in October 1905. The conversation ended when Alexander lost his temper, insisting that she had no right to drag her relatives with her down a precipice, and stormed out.

Those who had hoped that the elimination of Rasputin would prove in itself to be the salvation of the dynasty soon realized that their hopes were in vain. The Empress seemed more determined to be guided by what she thought he would have advised, and within a few days it was common knowledge that several of the family were talking openly about saving the throne by a change of sovereign. Paléologue recorded that the sons of Grand Duchess Vladimir were advocating the enlistment of four regiments of the guard, whose loyalty to Tsar Nicholas was already in doubt, in order to lead a night march of Tsarskoe-Selo and seize the sovereigns. The Tsar's abdication would be formally demanded, while the Empress would be confined in a nunnery, and the accession of the Tsarevich would be proclaimed under the regency of the popular and eminently more capable Grand Duke Nicholas Nicolaievich.

In January 1917 Grand Duchess Vladimir invited Rodzianko to lunch at the Vladimir Palace. After they had eaten she talked of the general state of affairs, of the incompetence of the government, ministers and above all the Empress, who was leading the country to destruction. Things must be changed, something done, removed, destroyed. When Rodzianko asked her to explain precisely what or whom, she replied bluntly that the *Duma* must do something, and the Tsarina must be annihilated. He very properly asked her to allow him to treat the conversation as if it had never taken place, because if she was addressing him as President of the *Duma*, his oath of allegiance compelled him to report at once to His Imperial Majesty and repeat her threat.

Meanwhile in the capital events were moving beyond all control from the forces of law and order. On 23 February/8 March one of the queues for bread in Petrograd broke ranks and ransacked a baker's shop. It was the start of what ministers blandly informed the Tsar, then at army headquarters, were 'street disorders'. Within three days the situation had escalated, troops were called out and fired into the crowds, leaving over two hundred dead. When reinforcements were sent to the city, some of the garrisons mutinied and began to fraternize with the rebels.

That same week, on 28 February/13 March, the Tsarina summoned Paul. He was surprised, as all relations between his family and the Alexander Palace had been broken off after the murder of Rasputin. Giving him a predictably chilly reception, she asked him for details of what was happening in Petrograd. Next she accused all the imperial family, headed by him, of trying wrongly to influence the Tsar and of being insufficiently devoted to the throne. More than ever before she opposed the idea of concessions. She was certain, and said she had proof, that throughout Russia people were on the side of the Tsar. He replied that neither the Tsar nor she had any right to doubt his fidelity and loyalty to them, that there was no time to discuss old disputes, but at the same time he had to remind her that all he had personally undertaken had been with the purpose of dispelling illusions which constituted, in effect, a fool's paradise. It was essential that the Tsar should return as quickly as possible, whereupon she assured him that the Tsar was expected back the following morning, and he promised to go and meet him at the station.

Paul arose early next morning for the rendezvous but the train did not arrive. After waiting a long time he returned home, deeply concerned. Later that day a report came through that the train had not been allowed to come through to Tsarskoe-Selo.

It was a time for desperate measures, and on the next day, 1/14 March, Paul hastily drafted a manifesto for the Tsar to sign, granting a Constitution. It was taken to the Alexander Palace at Tsarskoe-Selo for the Tsarina to ratify in her husband's absence. As she inevitably refused to do any such thing, Paul signed it himself and the signatures of Michael, the Tsar's brother, and Cyril were also appended. With the manifesto he sent a private letter to Rodzianko, asking him to do everything in his power to protect the person of the Emperor. It was taken at once to the *Duma* and handed to Paul Miliukov, minister of foreign affairs, who put it in his portfolio with the remark that 'this is an interesting document'.[9]

Paul was adamant that something had to be done to force the Tsar's hand. He was aware of gossip suggesting that Rodzianko and

Michael's morganatic wife were leading a movement for the Tsar to abdicate in order to promote their own interests, Rodzianko to become premier and Michael to become regent or even Tsar.

That same day he wrote to Cyril to express his concern at rumours over the prospect of a Grand Duke Michael regency, which he called 'inadmissible'. Maybe it was just idle gossip or possibly an intrigue on the part of his morganatic wife Madame Brassova and her family; 'Nevertheless we must be on our guard and do all that is in our power to preserve the Throne for Nicky. If Nicky signs the Constitution Manifesto which we have sanctioned, the demand of the people and of the Provisional Government will have been satisfied thereby.'[10]

At 4.15 on the morning of 3/16 March, Paul's valet came knocking at his door to say that an officer belonging to the Tsar's escort wanted to speak to him urgently. In their dressing gowns they received the officer, who was as white as a sheet. He said that General Ressine, in command of one of the Tsar's regiments, had sent him to the Grand Duke to announce that the new commandant at Tsarskoe-Selo had tried to telephone him, but without success, and needed to see him at once. Without any further words, they all knew what that meant. Having gone pale with shock himself, Paul said that he was ready to see the commandant.

Five minutes later a colonel of artillery and his orderly made their way in. After saluting in military fashion and apologizing for the early hour of 4.30 a.m., the colonel proceeded to read a manifesto from the Tsar signed the previous afternoon, at 3 p.m., in which he announced that he would 'abdicate the Crown of the State and to lay down the supreme power'. Initially he had said that he would step aside in favour of his son, but when he asked the advice of a doctor who warned him that Grand Duke Alexis would always be at the mercy of an accident, and that once he himself had abdicated he and his wife would almost certainly be exiled from Russia, Nicholas decided that they could not be parted from their child. He therefore nominated his brother Grand Duke Michael to succeed him.

Paul and Princess Paley were thunderstruck. In their view Michael was too feeble to continue the honourable tradition, by wearing the crown, and feared the 'pernicious influence' that Madame Brassova would undoubtedly exert over him. They both loved 'their' Tsar, the anointed of the Lord, and maintained that they would have no other. Only loyalty to the Lord's anointed, one must assume, prevented them from admitting that the man who had just laid down the crown after twenty-two years had hardly been a model of strength himself and that his wife's influence, if not pernicious, had done much to lead them all to catastrophe.

The grand matriarch of the family had no such qualms. After her son's abdication the Dowager Empress, her daughter Olga observed, was more angry than miserable, and held her daughter-in-law responsible. 'She understood nothing of what had happened. She blamed poor Alicky for just everything.'[11]

At 11 a.m. Paul went to see the Tsarina. Though some of her entourage may have already been acquainted with the knowledge that she was no longer Empress, none of them – as her uncle had foreseen – had the courage to inform her. When he told her that he wanted to be with her at 'this painful moment', she looked him in the eyes, as if fearing the worst. At once he reassured her that 'Nicky' was well, but that at 1 a.m. he had signed a deed of abdication for himself and for Grand Duke Alexis. Drawing herself up to her full height, but with tears rolling down her cheeks, she said that if he had done so, it was because he had to, but 'God will not abandon us'. As she was no longer Empress, she would remain a Sister of Charity, and look after her children – all of whom were recovering from measles – and her hospital. He stayed with her for another hour and a half, giving her details of everything that had happened at the *Duma*.

Later that same day Grand Duke Michael declined the poisoned chalice. After three centuries and four years, the Romanovs no longer reigned in Russia.

14

'God forgive them'

After the fall of the monarchy, the military command realized that it would be almost impossible to keep the troops in order and enforce discipline and obedience on the fractious and resentful, if not openly rebellious, men who were now answerable to them only in theory. A provisional government was formed in Russia, and at Paul's request the Grand Dukes unanimously agreed to follow the former Tsar's instructions – as announced in his abdication manifesto, 'to facilitate a close union for our people and the organisation of all its forces for the rapid realisation of victory'[1] – to submit to the new government, to help it in everything and to have only one purpose, of bringing the war to a satisfactory conclusion.

Later that evening Paul went to visit the Tsarina again, and was glad to find her calm and resigned. Already the Palace courtyard was full of soldiers, sent there by the government ostensibly for the security of her and her children, but really to prevent sympathetic elements from helping them to escape. When Paul left he tactfully addressed the soldiers as 'brothers', telling them that there was no Empress or heir to the throne, only a woman, a nurse looking after her own sick children. He ended up by asking for their cooperation in ensuring there would be no noise or disturbance, and they promised him good-naturedly that there would be none. The effect of his words was shortlived, for once he had gone they threw decorum to the four winds and wandered around under the palace windows, shouting insults loudly enough to ensure that they were overheard.

On the next day the former Empress was told by General Kornilov, the new commander-in-chief of the Petrograd district, that she and the children were under arrest. In the evening she invited Paul to the Alexander Palace again as Kornilov and

Alexander Guchkov, minister of war in the provisional government, had asked her to receive them. She knew it would be unwise to refuse, but she dreaded being on her own at such an ordeal, so she asked Paul to come and provide her with moral support. He arrived to find her alone, wearing her nurse's uniform, absolutely calm. They arrived two hours late, probably keeping her waiting in order to humiliate her. Paul was disconcerted by their shifty appearance and their ill-at-ease demeanour. For herself she wanted nothing, but she requested freedom for her arrested attendants who were only guilty of devotion to her; and that the new government would continue to supply the hospitals she had organized in Tsarskoe-Selo with all necessary equipment and sundries. To this they raised no objection. As they were leaving, Paul asked them if they would remonstrate with the soldiers appointed to guard her, as their conduct left much to be desired; for forty-eight hours they had been shouting, singing, and invading her privacy by opening doors and looking inside. They both promised to lecture the guard, but as the provisional government had no legal powers it could only proceed by persuasion, so little hope could be entertained. Nobody dared to give the soldiers orders.

On the following day Paul sent Guchkov his resignation as inspector-general of the guard, as he could hardly reconcile loyalty to his former sovereign with serving under the provisional government. Later that week General Alexeev, the Tsar's former aide-de-camp and chief of his general staff, who had now nailed his colours to the mast of the new government, belatedly sent him a telegram announcing that he was relieved of his functions, a message to which the Grand Duke replied cheerfully that he had already resigned. Before taking his leave of the Tsarina, he offered her the use of his house in Paris if she should be forced into exile. Neither of them could know that such a stroke of good luck would be denied her, nor that they would never meet again.

At Paul's home at Tsarskoe-Selo his eldest daughter Marie still found 'a certain atmosphere of inward warmth and comfort that made it seem doubly a refuge from surrounding chaos and uncertainty'.[2] Paul met material deprivations with patience and resignation, almost as if he had foreseen and prepared himself for the collapse of Romanov rule and it was a relief when the uncertainty was over. Anybody who openly admitted to friendship with the Grand Duke and his family would inevitably compromise themselves in the eyes of the new regime, and he preferred not to place his friends in jeopardy, so their circle of acquaintances narrowed accordingly.

Otherwise at first everyday life went on much as before. Paul continued to enjoy his reading, and in the evenings he would read aloud to his wife while she did her embroidery. During the day he went walking, always with a stick in hand. When his younger daughters asked him about his childhood, he told them fondly about the games he and Serge played together when they were small, and how whenever one of them was unwell and in quarantine they would exchange letters. Memories of carefree days flooded back – of life at the palaces, their toys, the miniature port built for them on a small canal in the park, and more. Then he fell silent, suddenly haunted by the ghosts of their estrangement and Serge's assassination. After that they could not bring themselves to question him again.

Later that year Marie became friendly with Alexander Putiatin, son of the commander of the palaces at Tsarskoe-Selo. Paul warned her that nobody could possibly know what would happen to them, as they might be obliged to part or be separated by force. He would feel happier about her if she had the protection of a husband in such uncertain times, and that she ought to consider remarriage. By August Marie and Putiatin were engaged.

These paternal warnings were just in time, for the revolutionary ratchet was about to turn. After five months under arrest in their own palace, the former Tsar and his family were moved to Tobolsk in Siberia. At around the same time, 27 August/9 September, Paul and his family were placed under arrest in their own home by order of Alexander Kerensky, leader of the provisional government. When they asked the commandant who came to tell them why, he shrugged his shoulders and said he did not know. All he knew was that orders had been given for their telephone to be cut off, and for a squad of soldiers to arrive that night to guard all exits from their palace. Privately, though, they believed that the reason was that Princess Paley was said to have spoken disrespectfully about the government, and to have circulated satirical verses about Kerensky, written by Vladimir Paley.

Paul was forbidden to attend his daughter Marie's wedding at Pavlovsk ten days later, but he was relieved that she was no longer alone, and that she could relinquish her title of Grand Duchess as well as the name of Romanov. After the wedding ceremony there was no question of a honeymoon, but Prince and Princess Putiatin were allowed to go and see Paul unhindered by guards as they had a permit. A few days after the wedding the guards were removed from his home, and his daughter felt less anxious.

It was a false dawn, for shortly afterwards came the revolution in which Lenin and his hardline Bolshevik supporters seized power from Kerensky and took control of Russia. On 31 October/13 November Paul's palace was searched. When the soldiers had ransacked and taken away most of his firearms collection, including revolvers and swords, now prohibited in private houses, the officer in charge told him that he had orders to take him to the Smolny Institute, Petrograd, where the Soviet was sitting. The Bolsheviks had vowed death to the whole aristocracy, and everybody feared the worst.

When Princess Paley went to visit him the following day a self-styled *chargé d'affaires* of the Soviet of the people's commissaries assured the Grand Duke that he had been arrested through a misunderstanding. Although he would not be sent to the fortress of Peter and Paul, he could not be set free that day, but probably on the next, on condition that he would not leave Petrograd until he had received special permission to do so. After spending three days at Smolny he was told that he would be transferred to the fortress after all, and he understood perfectly how such an imprisonment might end. Yet for the time being he was allowed out on parole with his family in Petrograd, and later they received permission to return to Tsarskoe-Selo, accompanied by a sailor, a member of the Petrograd Soviet. His home was repeatedly searched by members of the local Soviet, and when they found his extensive collection of fine wines, including a cellar begun and bequeathed to him by his brother Alexis they removed every bottle overnight, drinking what they wanted and smashing the rest, by which time they were too drunk to do any further damage.

In March 1918 a decree was published making it obligatory for all the Romanovs and all those who belonged to the family by marriage to present themselves on the following day, without fail, to be registered by the *Tché-Ka*, or Petrograd Extraordinary

Commission. Princess Paley managed to save Paul from the ordeal by obtaining a certificate of ill-health signed by his physician, Dr Obnissky, which she personally presented to the commission. The suspicious Bolsheviks had him examined by two of their doctors in turn, but when both independently confirmed that he was too unwell to travel, they reluctantly released him from the registration. His son Vladimir was given a chance to disown his father and all the Romanovs. He refused, and was taken to Viatka with some of his relations, including John, Constantine and Igor, sons of the late Grand Duke Constantine Constantinovich. At the end of April they were removed to Ekaterinburg, and then north to Alapaevsk, where they were joined by Ella.

Now aged fifty-three, the woman whom everyone had remembered as the charming, immaculately dressed and bejewelled Grand Duchess Serge had long since sold or given away her earthly possessions and founded the Convent of Martha and Mary in Moscow. Here she lived in a simple little room, unfurnished except for a single chair and a hard bed, dressed in grey robes she had designed herself, with her only personal ornament a wooden cross around her neck. She looked after the sick, the orphaned, the needy and helpless, with only a small but dedicated team of nursing sisters to help. Not even Lenin and the Bolsheviks dared to liquidate her for fear of disturbances, yet the fact that she was a Romanov – and still a popular one – meant that she represented a threat to the revolution. They decided to remove her from Moscow by playing on her affection for her sister. In the spring of 1918 a man was sent to the convent to tell her that the Tsar and his family had been removed from Tobolsk for greater safety, and that she might like to join them. She replied that she believed her duty was to stay with her nursing sisters in Moscow, but she was ready to go whenever and wherever God wished her to go.

A few days later an armoured car drew up to take her away, since the government could no longer be held responsible for her safety in Moscow. She asked for two hours to get her belongings together and to say goodbye to everyone under her care and to the other sisters, only to be told brusquely that she could have half an hour. When she asked if one of the sisters could accompany her permission was given, and her closest confidante Sister Barbara asked to be allowed to join her. First they were driven to a convent at Perm, then to Ekaterinburg where her sister, the former Tsar and their children were imprisoned at the Ipatiev House, although she and Sister Barbara were guarded so closely that they were almost certainly unaware of the fact. Next they were transferred to a disused school at Alapaevsk with the other imperial captives.

On the evening of 18 July they were collected by a group of soldiers, ordered into a lorry, and driven into the countryside where they were all thrown down a disused mine shaft. A couple of hand grenades were pitched in after them. When the White Army reached Alapaevsk some ten days later, hoping to rescue the prisoners from the school building, they were directed by local peasants to the mine shaft. When the bodies were brought up to the surface, it was found that only Grand Duke Serge Michaelovich had gunshot wounds. The rest had perished from starvation.

Grand Duke Paul was unaware of their fate. He and Princess Paley were distraught at the separation from their son, and she blamed herself bitterly for not having encouraged him to go abroad while it was still possible. Meanwhile, matters at the house gradually changed for the worse. As winter drew near it was evident that the family did not have enough fuel for central heating, and several rooms were closed. Still suffering from his stomach ulcer, Paul was kept on a strict diet, and only with difficulty were the necessary provisions procured. In January 1918 their fuel ran out completely and they had to move into the house of his nephew Boris, also at Tsarskoe-Selo, where stoves could be heated by wood fires. Marie and Prince Putiatin moved to a cottage in Pavlovsk to be near him. She was pregnant, and gave birth to a son, named Roman, in July 1918. Ten days later he was christened, with his grandfather Paul one of the godparents. His daughter later recalled that the baby's arrival was his last joy, and she had never seen him so happy as he was on that day of the christening. Ironically, that same day, perhaps almost that same hour, in Alapaevsk several of their family were being murdered.

Shortly afterwards came unconfirmed reports in Bolshevist newspapers of the Tsar's death, and of the escape of the prisoners at Alapaevsk. On 19 July Paul and Princess Paley read with horror that 'Nicholas Romanov' had made an effort to escape from prison, and had been killed by the Red Guard. No mention was made of the fate of his wife or children. Not for some weeks was it revealed to a horrified world that the former Tsar, Tsarina, their children and remaining servants at Ipatiev House had been roused from their sleep one night, ushered into a small room downstairs and shot dead by a small group of Bolshevik guards. Grand Duchess Cyril echoed the views of the whole family when she wrote to Xenia a few days later to say that they were 'living with such a profound & overwhelming despair in our hearts that life itself seems to be over.' Nicky's martyrdom was over at last, and maybe they could take solace in religion. Perhaps God thought that 'Nicky had suffered enough and that for a kind & pure heart like his, eternal rest might be granted sooner. Perhaps he knew that that poor heart had born it's [sic] trials to breaking point.'[3]

At the time Paul and his wife did not know what to believe, but for a long time they hoped that it was only a ploy by the Bolshevists to conceal from the world their dismay at their former Tsar having made good his escape. Two days later they opened their papers again to read a report of the escape of ex-princes Serge Michaelovich, Constantine, Igor Constantinovich and Paley, from Alapaevsk. Some other men were killed or wounded in the struggle, and soldiers had been sent in pursuit of them. Convinced that their son would make his way by Siberia to Japan and then to France, they were profoundly grateful. Paul was thus spared the knowledge of his son's death.

On 31 July/13 August he was arrested. The Bolsheviks were determined to round up the last few Grand Dukes remaining on Russian soil, and at 3 a.m. a group of soldiers came to take him away. Dawn was breaking as he took leave of his wife. Resigned to his fate, he told her in a voice trembling with emotion that their happiness was at at end. 'I don't know how much longer I have to live, but I thank you with all my whole soul, with all the strength of my heart which loves you, which has never loved anyone save you, for these twenty-five years of happiness. Take good care of the little daughters.'[3]

He was held in Schpalernaia prison for six months, partly in the prison itself and partly, because of ill-health, in the infirmary. Princess Paley was given a pass by the director, a lenient man who had every sympathy with them, to visit him twice a week, staying from 1 p.m. to 6 p.m. She tried to secure his release, and for a while it seemed that the Bolsheviks would spare him. Like Grand

Duchess Serge, he was no threat. Wearing a rough cape over his shoulders and a felt hat, he walked down the stairs with the same style and the same dignity that he would have shown at home. The guards were notoriously rough, but he never lost his calm manner or his dignity and pretended not to hear them, so great was his joy in seeing the family again. He had several chances to escape but he knew that if he gave in to temptation he would put the lives of his cousins in danger, and he could never have lived with that on his conscience. One night at midnight a Red Guard came into his cell, and at first he thought that his final hour had come, until the man removed the five-pointed Bolshevist star from his uniform and revealed a carefully thought out plan of escape. Suspecting that the man could be an *agent provocateur*, he diplomatically declined to have any part in it.

The last time Countess Kleinmichel saw him, in the autumn of 1918, she found him as pleasant and affectionate as of old, but his face was thinner, almost emaciated. Yet he seemed content, almost happy in spite of everything that had happened; 'he never seemed to need anything more than the near presence of his beloved wife; she was the centre of his world'.[4] Their daughters, she noted, no longer had a governess, and were not accompanied by a servant; 'their minds had quickly matured in adversity'.

On Christmas Day 1918 the final blow came. Princess Paley arrived at the hospital to be greeted by signs of excitement and anguished faces. The Director told her with regret that he had been relieved of his functions, as the commission found him too indulgent towards the prisoners. He was to be replaced with three commissaries from another prison, and she would soon 'see how things are'. Paul had already seen for himself. Before her arrival his door had opened and a man entered, staring at him. He recognized a clean-shaven man with elegantly done hair, fingers laden with stolen rings. Only a year or two previously he had been Deverenko, the kindly sailor who had tenderly looked after the haemophiliac Tsarevich, but joined the Bolsheviks when the revolution came. When Paul greeted him in friendly fashion, the embarrassed man backed out of the room without saying anything.

Princess Paley had been with her husband barely quarter of an hour when an officer and two soldiers walked in without knocking. The first of them asked her brutally what she was doing. When she told him and produced her permit, he snapped back that the permit no longer had any value, as they now had to be renewed every week. He tried to order her out, deaf to her entreaties that she was tired, ill and that it was Christmas Day – to him Christmas was 'rubbish', as all festivals had been abolished except for the anniversary of the revolution and May day, 'that of the Proletariat'. Only when she began to weep did he grudgingly let her stay for twenty minutes, as long as a Red Guard was present. The soldier he left to watch them was kind enough to wait until the officer was out of earshot, told them with sympathy that the gaolers were mad, and that he would wait for them outside the door. Unhappily the officer came back five minutes later and was furious at his orders being disobeyed. He ordered the Princess out brusquely, 'and you'll see whether you'll come so soon again to your darling'.[5] She and her husband embraced each other lingeringly for what they sensed was the last time.

Despite her efforts she was unable to obtain a new permit. On 28 January 1919 she learnt that he was to be taken to another prison, the Gorochovaïa. A nurse at the hospital told her, adding in apparent good faith that perhaps it was with a view to releasing him. The same rumour had reached the ears of others. According to Countess Kleinmichel, it was rumoured that Lenin had already agreed to set Grand Duke Paul free and intended to sign the order early in the new year of 1919. Other sources suggested that the writer Maxim Gorky, a close friend of Lenin, had asked him that the lives of all four Grand Dukes should be spared as they were innocent of any political associations. Whether Lenin disagreed or agreed yet merely failed to prevent matters from taking their course; whether he had any intention of sparing any of the Romanovs, even the most harmless, is highly debatable. All that is known is that one of the Bolshevik deputies telegraphed to La Yakovleva, head of the commission for the fight against counter-revolution, 'The order to release the Grand Duke is signed; take action accordingly'.[6]

This highly ambiguous message was construed, or misconstrued, as a death sentence. On 29 January Princess Paley went to the island of Golodaï in the hope of seeing one of the commissaries and finding out what had happened. He told her rudely not to come back any more, as her husband was no longer there. With a heavy heart she went to the Gorochovaïa next day with the usual baskets of food for him, only to be treated with a similar display of rudeness and ignorance from another officer. At length she walked down the street to a hairdresser whom they had both known well. He let her use his telephone, and after waiting for an hour she was put through to the *Tché-Ka* where a voice told her that her husband was not there. If she returned the next morning, a permit would be ready for her at the entrance, and she would be told everything then.

Fearing the worst, she returned home to a restless night. Waking in the small hours with a start, she felt she distinctly heard a voice in the darkness saying in Russian, 'I am killed'. Her premonitions were confirmed later that morning when, leaving no stone unturned to find out what was happening, her attention was drawn by friends to a report in the newspaper. His sufferings were over.

The full story in all its horror was given her some weeks later in Finland by a Dr Maltzov, who had been imprisoned in the hospital but was later released. On 28 January the doctor was present when one of the commissaries entered Grand Duke Paul's cell and ordered him to pack and get dressed as he was leaving for the Gorochovaïa. When a colonel suggested that it was probably to set him free, Paul shook his head sadly. He said he knew it was all over, and he asked the doctor to convey his love to his wife and children, and that before dying, 'I ask pardon of all those to whom I may have given offence during my life'.[7] The following evening, at the *Tché-Ka*, he asked a Georgian prisoner who was being set free if he would telephone his wife to inform her what was happening. The Georgian declined, either out of fear or because he could not get through to her. He was then taken alone to the Gorochovaïa and kept there until 10 p.m., when he was driven to the fortress of St Peter and St Paul; the other three Grand Dukes (Nicholas Michaelovich, Dmitri Constantinovich and George Michaelovich) were taken there direct from the Schpalernaia, and all were locked up in the dungeons of Troubetzkoy Bastion.

At 3 a.m. the next day all four were ordered outside, stripped to the waist, and led in front of the Cathedral. They saw a vast common grave in which there were already thirteen bodies. The soldiers of the Red Guard made them stand in line near the grave, and without further torture summarily drew their pistols and shot them dead. Just before the shots rang out, one observer who had been with the doctor heard Paul say out loud, in Russian: 'God forgive them, they know not what they do.'

Grand Duke Alexander pondered with incredulity 'the destruction of these men who had always kept aloof from the political turmoil of Russia and who could not have presented any danger whatever to the triumphant march of the revolution'. In particular Grand Duke Paul, 'handsome, kind-hearted, supremely happy in his morganatic marriage, not caring a snap about monarchy or power',[8] was surely no threat. Even so, none of the Romanovs still on Russian soil were free from the reign of terror which the Bolsheviks had unleashed.

At least Paul knew nothing of the murder of his son Vladimir. The full blow fell on his widow, who did not give up hope until she had a letter in March 1919 from Grand Duchess Constantine, whose three sons had also perished in the mineshaft at Alapaevsk, giving her every detail of the atrocity.

Only one of the children of Tsar Alexander II and Empress Marie was still alive. The woman who had lived a privileged sheltered childhood as a Grand Duchess of Russia, become Duchess of Edinburgh at the age of twenty, and later Duchess of Saxe-Coburg Gotha, was now homeless. She had seen the defeat of her beloved Russia and Germany and the violent deaths of so many of her family. Banished from Bolshevik Russia and from her late husband's duchy, and with no inclination to return to England where she had never been happy, there was only one country in Europe left for her to go. Grand Duke and Duchess Cyril gallantly came to her rescue. While they had little material wealth apart from the jewels they had managed to take out of Russia, there were sufficient funds to accommodate her in the Waldhaus, a rather down-at-heel annex of the Dolder Grand Hotel in Switzerland. The Grand Duchess had lost a good deal of weight, her once plump hands were thin and trembling, and she walked with difficulty, but she had lost none of her indomitable Romanov spirit. Grand Duchess Cyril, 'Ducky', was now a kindred soul, having suffered similar tragedy and also become an exile from their beloved Russia. Her eldest daughter 'Missy', Queen of Roumania, felt the full wrath of her bitter tongue. It was the Queen's misfortune to have been on the winning side; unequivocally pro-English, she was accused of rejoicing over 'devastating peace terms' imposed on Germany by the victorious allies.

In Germany the Duchess's last true surviving friend was the former German Emperor William's eldest sister Charlotte, the sharp-tongued Princess of Saxe-Meiningen. Yet Charlotte was in poor health, suffering from the cancer which had killed her parents and would claim her life in October 1919. During the summer of 1920 Marie received a visit from her sister-in-law Grand Duchess Vladimir. The fates of each had proved complementary; one, born in Russia, had married an English prince who became a German Duke, while the other, German born, had married into the Russian imperial family. Both had been on opposite sides in the war, and now they were exiles. Neither was in good health, and neither had much to live for.

Grand Duchess Vladimir survived long enough to move to her villa at Contrexeville in France, where she became seriously ill and died on 6 September. The Dowager Duchess of Coburg lingered for another six weeks. On 25 October 1920, eight days after her sixty-seventh birthday, she died in her sleep of a heart attack. Gossip had it that her end was hastened by receiving a letter addressed to 'Frau Coburg'. To her eldest daughter Marie, Queen of Roumania, it was a release; 'I hope God will not disappoint her as most things & beings did in this life.'[9]

Princess Paley escaped to Finland and eventually to France with her daughters, who were married within a few years. Their mother divided her last years between Paris and Biarritz, and she published her reminiscences, *Memories of Russia 1916–1919* in 1924. The last chapter concluded with the words: 'May God have pity on me and not prolong my torment on earth! May the Lord permit my tortured soul to discard the mortal covering which burdens it, and may He allow it to take wings towards THEM whom it so loved here below!'[10] Her wish was granted five years later when she passed away in Paris in November 1929, aged sixty-four.

Of the three children of Tsar Alexander II and his second wife Princess Yourievsky who had reached maturity, both daughters were still living, but their hapless brother George had long since passed away. He had already been in failing health by the time his marriage was dissolved in 1908. Suffering from kidney disease, he endured five years of constant pain and moods of depression, from which he found release at Marburg in September 1913.

His eldest sister Olga was in Germany with her husband and children at the outbreak of war. Her husband was attached to a Red Cross unit, while their son George was fighting on the western front, and taken prisoner near Verdun. She died at Wiesbaden in August 1925.

After their wedding Serge and Catherine Obolensky set up home at Mordvinov Palace in the hills above Yalta. The Crimea was relatively peaceful until the revolution of October/November 1917, but when the Bolsheviks seized power in the capital, Serge told her he was going to join a rebel force of Tartars and former guards officers, deaf to her forebodings that it would end in disaster. A few hours after his departure Yalta was bombarded from the sea, and she immediately sent her sons down to the cellar for safety. Soldiers burst in and took possession of the Palace, and she feared that on his return Serge would be put to death. Their boys were allowed to leave the following morning with an English governess.

As a daughter of a Tsar of Russia there was a price on her head, and she would have almost certainly been captured to meet her death in front of a firing squad had one of Serge's friends not bribed a guard. Leaving the boys in the care of a friend she was hurried away, carrying her dog in her arms. Under shellfire she and her protector found safety in the house of another friend.

When Serge returned to Yalta he found the Palace ransacked, but he learnt what had happened to his wife. She was still sheltering in their friend's house and he persuaded her to join him, but they were still under constant fire from the soldiers, and as a resistance fighter he too was under sentence of death if captured. In their ensuing adventures they lost contact with each other for a time, and she found shelter in another house, until the family realized that they faced danger by harbouring her, and she agreed to go when they promised to look after the dog for her. Next she was given refuge on a farm in the country owned by a former gardener of Serge, and posed as one of the family, looking after the baby and helping around the house and farm. There were rumours that Serge had been killed, but friends told her that he had been smuggled away safely to Moscow. Her relief at knowing he was still alive was tempered by fear of discovery.

The friends who had arranged Serge's escape sent her off to a boarding house where she assumed the identity of Mlle Helene, a French governess stranded in Yalta. Bolshevik forces were still nearby and she was concerned about the possibility of being unmasked. One soldier was keen to learn French and she taught him, while continuing to help cook and clean. Within a few months she left discreetly in her nursing uniform with a bribed soldier for Moscow by train, perching on the luggage rack of a carriage full of soldiers.

Once she and Serge were reunited they still had to pretend they were strangers. Some months later their host found them places with a trade delegation en route for the Ukraine, then in German hands. Another hazardous train journey fraught with dangerous checkpoints followed, before they were reunited at Kiev with Prince Anatole Bariatinsky, brother of Catherine's first husband. At last they could resume their genuine identities and go to fetch her sons André and Alexander, still in Yalta. Serge had to seek permission from the German authorities, who controlled the Crimea as well, before he could bring the boys to join them. They arrived safely with their mother's dog but the governess, Miss Picken, and the coachman, Albert Stannard, who had protected them during the last few months, were forbidden by the Germans to enter the city as they were English and therefore technically enemy aliens. They were smuggled back to French-controlled Odessa, and put on board ship back to England.

Serge's greatest fear was that Kiev would fall to the Red Army. He sought permission to go to Vienna, and they left Kiev just before the fall of the Ukraine. They reached the city safely, but one look at mobs wandering around the streets evoked painful comparisons with St Petersburg at the time of the revolution. As soon as possible they left for Switzerland by train, entering the country just as revolution was breaking out in Austria.

Relieved to be in a country at last which was at peace, they stayed in Berne for a while before going on to Lausanne and meeting old friends. Among them were Prince and Princess Nicholas of Greece, and the Dowager Duchess of Mecklenburg-Schwerin, whose world had been turned upside down by

Germany's declaration of war on her native Russia. Their immediate priority was the boys' education, and they were sent to school in Lausanne.

After spending Christmas 1918 skiing at Gstaad, they went to Nice where they were reunited with Princess Yourievsky, who had heard rumours that they were both killed, and was overjoyed to find them safe and well. It was the first time she had seen Serge since he was a boy of ten. Her last journey had been to St Petersburg six years earlier, and some said it was solely to ask the Tsar to double her allowance. Returning to France just before the outbreak of war in 1914, she had offered to maintain and finance a hospital for wounded allied soldiers. However her substantial investment in Russian imperial bonds came to nothing, and her allowance ceased on the Tsar's abdication. All she had apart from her memories of ages past were her property in Nice and her remaining jewellery. Aged seventy-one by the time war was over, she lived increasingly in the past, and her health was declining. Yet every day she drove to a small villa in the hills where her pet dogs were buried. As she was plagued by insomnia, her son-in-law and daughter used to come into her room every evening and talk about happier times in days gone by until late into the night.

Money was scarce, and most of their remaining funds had gone on the boys' education. Occasionally Serge would have a lucky streak at the casino and on one occasion he was able to buy a new car. Yet adjustment to the post-war world, with no ready fortune to fall back on, was hard for them both. Catherine revived her old ambition of becoming a professional singer and began to train with Madame Litvin, the most famous Russian concert performer of her day, and Dame Nellie Melba. While she practised conscientiously and became ever more absorbed in her art, Serge became increasingly restless and longed to work. Any future for her as a singer meant nothing to him. He sold the car purchased with his casino winnings, and moved to Paris.

In April 1919 his contacts in London helped him to acquire a visa for England. Initially the Home Office rejected his application, ostensibly on the grounds that there was insufficient reason for admitting him, but more probably as a result of confusion between him and another, unconnected, Prince Obolensky who had been a notoriously pro-German governor-general of Finland during the war. The objection was withdrawn in May, by which time he had already purchased a travel ticket for London and arranged to stay at the Ritz while he looked for somewhere to live. As a student at Oxford in pre-war days he felt at home in England, and with the help of long-standing friends found a job with a subsidiary of the Vickers company, selling grain elevator machinery, and later as a half-commission broker in the City. He leased a house at London for himself and Catherine in Hill Street, near Hyde Park, and went to Nice to bring her back.

Once they were settled she began to hold informal concerts and gatherings, accompanied on the piano either by the exiled former King Manuel of Portugal, or the Russian expatriate Dmitri Tiomkin, who later went to Hollywood and became a successful composer of film scores. Her first professional performance in England was held in December 1919 at the home of Mrs William Corey in Connaught Place. Yet not everybody took her seriously in her new role, finding something strange about an Emperor's daughter determined to earn her living as an entertainer. Trying to manage mundane activities like housekeeping and shopping was more difficult than it had been while she was in hiding, and on her first nervous visit to Selfridges she ran away in confusion. As Serge would later recall, her temperament 'was magnificent in adversity', but everyday life in peacetime London was a different matter.

In 1920 they moved into a house in Sussex Place which they shared with another royal friend, Prince Paul of Yugoslavia. Catherine's career was progressing, with concerts at the major London venues including the Queen's Hall and London Coliseum. Increasingly restless and tired of his wife's complaints that she 'made' him meet her friends, he realized that they no longer had anything in common, and he persuaded his company to transfer him to Australia. By the end of the year he had gone, though they continued to write to each other.

She had had to sell much of her possessions and property, and anything that would have gone to her was claimed by French law as she was still liable for her first husband's debts. Her problems were exacerbated by news that a former secretary of her mother, if not her mother herself, intended to publish private papers belonging to her father, including sensitive information which supposedly proved allegations regarding the suicide of Tsar

Nicholas I, as well as some of her own letters and diaries. She and her sister Olga took out a court action to prevent publication, but though they failed nothing more was heard of the plan.* By now Princess Yourievsky's health was failing, and Catherine went to Nice to spend as much time with her as possible. She died peacefully on 4 February 1922, aged seventy-four.

Moving to a house in Kensington and taking criticism of her inexperience on the concert stage to heart, she hired a professional teacher, Signorina Carlotta de Féo, and practised until she had a repertoire of two hundred songs in five languages. She threw herself with zeal into more concerts, but the need to travel home each night to avoid the cost of hotels restricted her venues to the London area. She was well aware that some of her bookers were treating her more as a name or a historical novelty than as a serious artiste, especially when sometimes promotional posters and handbills did not even mention her singing, only her name. However, she steeled herself for what often proved an ordeal, and found it all worth the effort when audiences genuinely appreciated her singing.

Serge had returned to London, but it was too late to entertain any hope of reconciliation. While she was reluctant to face the fact that their marriage had failed, Catherine blamed his companions for everything that had gone wrong. He was more philosophical, seeing their union as 'one of wartime delusion, of a short, sharp, romantic attachment sought by both of us in a tiny moment of desperate calm'.[11] In his view the main obstacle to their happiness was the fact that their friends were so different. Most of hers were older than his, hardly surprising in view of the twelve years between them. English people, his friends, were generally interested in sport, while her musical circles contained

* Tsar Alexander II and Princess Yourievsky had been prolific correspondents since the early days of their liaison, and their private papers regularly came on the open market after her death. In 1931 and 1941 substantial collections of Princess Yourievsky's letters and photographs were auctioned, some going to the USA where they formed the basis of a biography of her by Alexandre Tarsaidze, published in 1970. Another, containing 965 letters written between 1868 and 1872, was sold at Christie's, London, in September 1984; yet another, containing over 530 covering the years 1866 to 1880, realized $79,200 at Sotheby's in May 1990.

no sporting people. He could still regard her as a friend, but no longer felt any affection for her. A Roman Catholic priest persuaded her to seek divorce, which became absolute in June 1924. Her autobiography published that year revealed her bitterness, referring to 'my late husband (I ought to put "ex", but put "late", for to me he is now dead)'.[12] Friends of hers, she believed, abandoned her after the divorce, staying loyal to him because they found him more amusing.

Now a Roman Catholic, Her Serene Highness Catherine Yourievsky was now alone except for the ever-devoted Miss Picken and her dog Bobby. With her sister Olga's death in 1925, she was the sole survivor of her generation. Continuing to sing, she built up a social life of her own, with a few close friends from society, despite her distrust of 'society people' whom she felt had soured her marriage, and her claims that only the middle and lower classes could give true genuine friendship.

Meanwhile the last embers of the Russian empire were slowly dying away. In 1924 Grand Duke Cyril Vladimirovich proclaimed himself Tsar, or more precisely issued a 4,000 word manifesto from his home in St Briac, northern France, proclaiming his assumption of the title. One of his reasons for doing so was that Tsar Nicholas II, his wife, their children, and the next in line, his brother Michael, had all been killed, and Russian laws of succession did not permit the imperial throne to remain vacant. For his bold initiative he was angrily criticized by most of the other surviving Romanovs, especially as he had been the first Grand Duke to declare his allegiance and that of his wife to the provisional government in 1917, and was consequently regarded as a turncoat ever since.

Nobody deplored his behaviour more fiercely than the Dowager Empress. Now in her late seventies, the widow of Tsar Alexander III, her daughters and their children had been rescued from Russia and brought to England on a British warship in 1919. after an unhappy spell in England living with the widowed and increasingly senile Queen Alexandra, the Dowager Empress returned to her native Denmark and her retirement home, Hvidøre, purchased jointly with the Queen after the death of their father King Christian IX. At first she had declared publicly that there was nosuch dynastic issue to consider as her sons, daughter-in-law and grandchildren were still alive. However, after hearing of Cyril's actions, she wrote to him of her fears that his manifesto would 'create a schism and in doing so will not improve but on the contrary will worsen the position in Russia which is already sufficiently tormented.' That it had been 'the Lord God's will according to his unknowable ways to call to Himself by beloved sons and grandson'[13] made no difference to her views.

After a short illness she died in October 1928 at the age of eighty. Shortly before her death she let it be known to her immediate surviving relatives that the future of the dynasty should be left in the hands of the Russian people, and that none of them should force the issue by laying claim to the throne. In one final flowering of the glittering pageantry that had characterized imperial Russia she was accorded a magnificent state funeral at Roskilde Cathedral, the traditional burial place of the Danish royal family. All the remaining royal houses of Europe were represented, among them many of the surviving Romanovs, even the self-appointed Tsar Cyril. In the words of his cousin Olga, now married to her second husband Colonel Nicholas Koulikovsky, he 'should have had the sense to stay away.'[13]

One who did stay away was the only surviving child of Tsar Alexander II. For the woman born Catherine Dolgorouky, now aged fifty, such pomp and pageantry must have seemed like the death throes of a past which she had been more than glad to put behind her. Whatever her thoughts, her world was shrinking. Asthma and heart trouble caused increasing attacks of breathlessness, and to her regret she had to give up her cherished singing career. Hayling Island, Hampshire, had been recommended to her as a good place for asthma sufferers and in 1932 she bought The Haven, a bungalow with a large plot of land at Park Road in the West Town area. As she lost money on her savings because of inflation and the slump, she was lucky to sell the house for a substantial profit two years later and move to another property a mile north, a bungalow consisting of two former almshouses which she named Naini, Indian for princess.

Despite their divorce Serge still cared about her as a deeply beloved friend, and paid her occasional visits. Her bitterness against him had healed with time, and she took some pride in his achievements. During the war she told local friends that he had become the special Russian adviser to General Eisenhower, although he never achieved this exalted role. He did however take part in undercover operations with the American forces, notably a parachuting operation in Sardinia culminating in the surrender of 270,000 Italian troops. She had lost touch with her elder son André, who died in 1931. Alexander also joined the American army during the war, rising to the rank of sergeant.

Another close friend Sir Henry 'Chips' Channon, Conservative Member of Parliament for Southend, provided Catherine with £300 a year. He visited her at Naini in February 1942, and was shocked by the squalor and poverty in which she lived, but at the same time reassured that a certain pride in her imperial heritage evidently gave her the spirit to keep her head held high in the face of adversity. In his diary he wrote of her 'horrible little house', her lack of servants, and loneliness.

> But somehow she still exudes a certain atmosphere of grandeur, and still has her pearl ear-rings, the only tangible touch of the past. She chatted of her royal relatives, her various nephews and nieces, reigning still or in exile. . . . It was a depressing visit, but she was so cheerful that she has obviously achieved a certain philosophy of life. As we left her to her loneliness and drove away, I remarked that she is one of those people to whom every misfortune falls. She even found her last servant dead in bed a few weeks ago; and her three beloved Pekinese all have died recently.[14]

She lived at Hayling for twenty-seven years, and with time she became rather a recluse. Her broken accent and asthma made her conversation difficult to understand. All the same she was popular with the islanders, though how many of them genuinely wished to be friends or were drawn to her simply for the distinction of saying they were friends with the daughter of an Emperor, one may wonder.

When she had no servants left a neighbour, a retired Southsea café owner, volunteered out of pity to act as an unpaid handyman around the house. Other hangers-on would sit around with her drinking gin. She loved children, and one local person recalled that while he was a child in West London and she lived in Kensington, he had been invited to attend one of her children's parties. Her hairdresser remembered that she was 'full of breeding', but could be 'hot or cold', and very short with anybody who tried to be too familiar.

Her connections with British royalty, such as they may have been, were extremely discreet, particularly as Britain's alliance with Stalin's Russia and any connections with the Tsarist regime called for caution. Nevertheless with her retiring nature she was grateful for a secluded life out of the public eye. Rumour and legend were inextricably combined. It was said that she attended the wedding of King George V's youngest surviving son George, Duke of Kent, to Princess Marina of Greece and Denmark – a granddaughter of the late Grand Duke and Duchess Vladimir through their only daughter Helen – in November 1934, and returned to Hayling with a certain amount of wedding cake which she generously shared with some schoolchildren in the area.*

Though she lived in poverty, there was usually money from somewhere. Serge probably paid her an allowance, as it was unlikely he would have left her in poverty if he could have prevented it. According to rumour she used to receive a quarterly cheque from an unnamed member of the royal family, believed by people in Hayling to be Queen Mary, which however ceased on the latter's death in 1953. One day she had to come to her hairdresser on Hayling seafront by bus instead of taxi. She had a weekly standing order for gin and sherry at an off-licence in Havant, and it was said that near the end she sold her last piece of jewellery for £40 and a bottle of gin. In her last days she was an eccentric-looking figure shuffling around the streets, mocked by children.

Some tradesmen found it difficult to persuade her to settle her bills. Those who could afford to readily made allowances, did not press her unduly, and often gave her food as well. At Christmas she was usually invited to Hayling's three star Royal Hotel for dinner. She

* A rumour persists that Philip, Duke of Edinburgh (by birth a first cousin of Marina, Duchess of Kent) paid at least one social visit to Princess Catherine Yourievsky at Hayling, although a recent enquiry to His Royal Highness The Duke of Edinburgh's office elicited the reply that the Duke and Princess Yourievsky probably never met each other.

would arrive in a magnificent gown, always ravenously hungry, and no food was ever left on the table afterwards. When a telephone engineer called at her bungalow, he was treated to a glass of sherry after he had finished his work, and asked to drink a toast with her to 'The Prince in Canada'. In her confused mind she may have meant Colonel Koulikovsky, who had settled with Olga in Toronto and whom she may have regarded as the *de jure* Tsar. When the engineer had to leave he told her it was his small daughter's birthday. At once she found a photograph of herself in her singing days, and autographed it on the back with the words, 'from a new friend'.

When she could no longer look after herself she went into a nursing home, where she died on 22 December 1959, alone and penniless, aged eighty-one. A brief paragraph in *The Times* two days later gave her age as eighty-four. Her funeral was held on 29 December at St Peter's Church, North Hayling. Eight mourners were present to see her laid to rest including her doctor, a matron from the nursing home and ladies from the North Hayling community, but the only representatives of her family were Serge, her former husband – who outlived her by almost nineteen years – and her nephew Prince Alexander Yourievsky. The gravestone recorded that she was born in 1880. Perhaps the stigma of birth before her parents' marriage rankled to the end.

The sun was setting on the lives of the last three daughters of the Tsars of Russia, all of whom died within twelve months of each other. At Wilderness House, Hampton Court, Grand Duchess Xenia had but four months to live, and her sister Grand Duchess Olga, long since settled in Toronto, would pass away eleven months later, in November 1960.

In August 1880 Tsar Alexander II had written to his eldest surviving daughter Marie, Duchess of Edinburgh, of the feelings they shared for England; 'you yourself know how unfriendly she is to us'.[15] How ironic it was that within less than half a century nearly all his relations unfortunate enough to be remaining in Russia would have been executed, and that his granddaughter and youngest daughter would both find a safe haven in this 'unfriendly' country.

Almost a century and a half had elapsed since the marriage of Grand Duke Nicholas and Princess Charlotte of Prussia and the birth of their first child Alexander, 'the poor helpless little thing', while the defeated Napoleon Bonaparte lived out his last years in exile on St Helena, and the blind deranged King George III of England wandered around the corridors of Windsor Castle. Now Alexander's youngest child breathed her last on an island off the south coast of England. A continent which had changed out of all recognition separated her from the land of her birth, which she had known but briefly as her father's empire, now the Union of Soviet Socialist Republics – a world he would never have recognized.

Postscript
The Reburial of the Romanovs

On their deaths in 1881 and 1894 the bodies of Tsar Alexander II and III were laid to rest in the Romanov family vault in the fortress church of St Peter and St Paul, St Petersburg. For years the remains of the last Tsar and his family had lain where they were buried ignominiously by the Bolsheviks, close to Ekaterinburg where they were shot in July 1918. In 1991 bones were exhumed from an unmarked grave in the area. They had been burnt and doused in acid to try and make identification impossible, but DNA testing using blood from relatives of the family, including Philip, Duke of Edinburgh, the Empress Alexandra's great-nephew, and the bones of Tsar Nicholas's brother Grand Duke George, who had died in 1899, led specialists to affirm with, in their words, '99.99 per cent certainty' that the bones were indeed those of some of the victims at Ekaterinburg, family and servants. Those of the Tsarevich and Grand Duchess Marie, the third daughter, were not found. According to some authorities they were buried separately, while others maintain that they were burnt, the bones crushed to dust and scattered.

In February 1998 the first deputy prime minister of Russia, Boris Nemtsov, confirmed that the bones would be buried in the family vault five months later on 17 July, the eightieth anniversary of their murder. The Russian Orthodox Church, which had long been keen to recognize the family as holy martyrs, cast doubts on the findings of the scientific tests. A Metropolitan excused their hesitation by saying that if they were to worship false remains they would be committing sacrilege; 'the church does not have the right to make a mistake'. Few others shared their uncertainty. Eduard Radzinsky, one of Tsar Nicholas II's most recent biographers and a member of the burial commission, asked that if the bones were not genuine, 'will someone please tell me which other relatives of Prince Philip were buried in a mass grave in the Urals?'

Representatives of reigning European dynasties were invited to attend the ceremony, and Prince Michael of Kent appeared on behalf of Queen Elizabeth II of Britain.

The reburial marked a squaring of the circle, a symbolic gesture of reconciliation from a modern Russia coming to terms with her oft-maligned imperial past in a manner which the Bolsheviks and the USSR naturally never deigned to consider. It also drew a line under a troubled family chapter left in suspended animation for too long.

THE DESCENDANTS OF CATHERINE THE GREAT

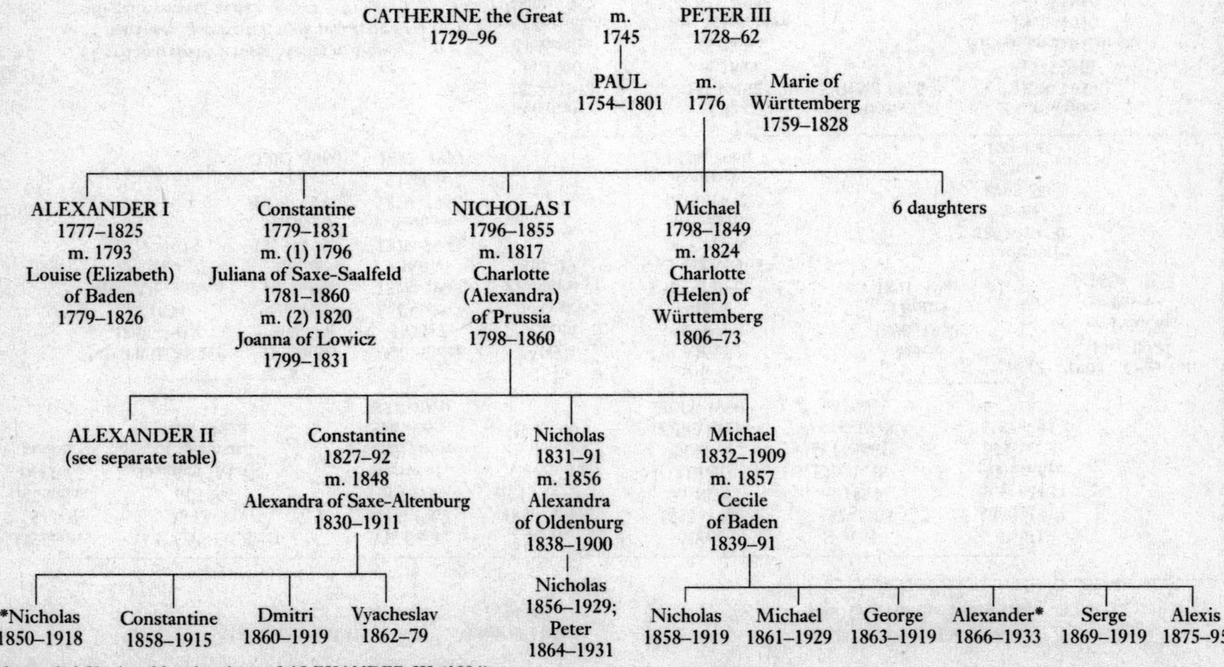

* married Xenia, elder daughter of ALEXANDER III (1894); author of *Once a Grand Duke and Always a Grand Duke*

THE DESCENDANTS OF TSAR ALEXANDER II

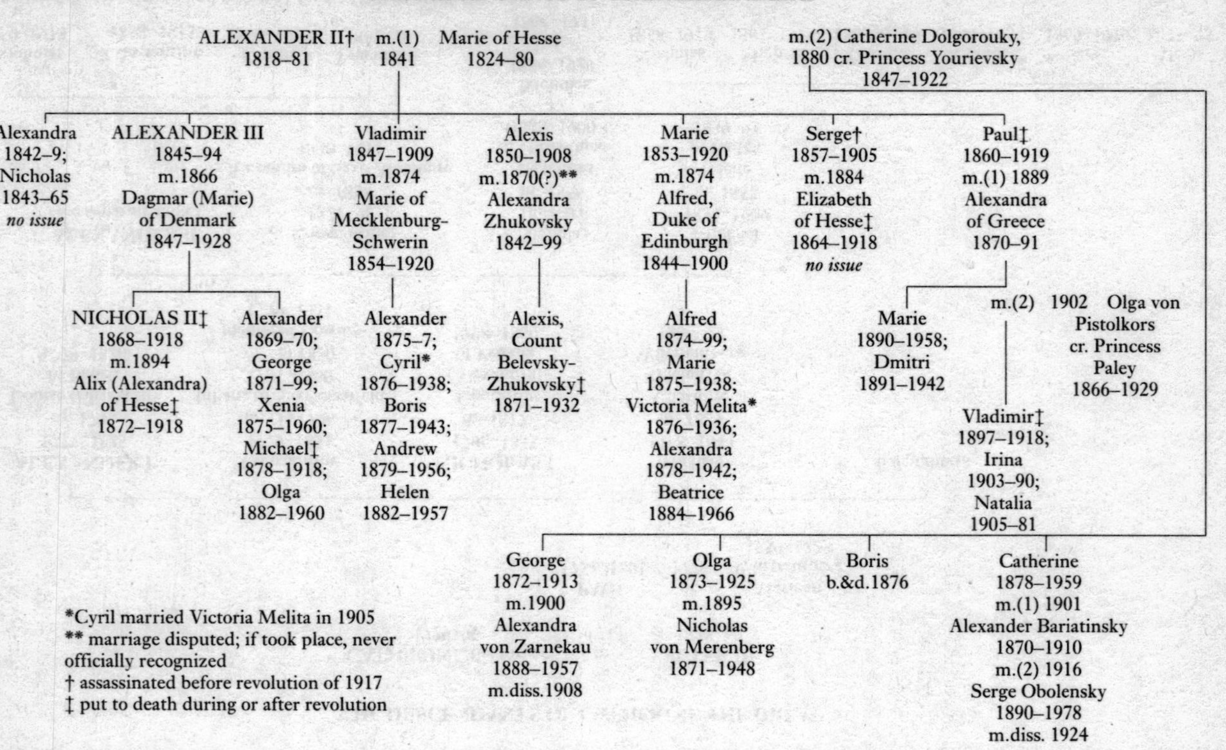

Tsar Alexander II's Children and Grandchildren

Grand Duke ALEXANDER Nicolaievich, b. 17/29 April 1818; m. (1) 16/28 April 1841 Princess Marie of Hesse and the Rhine (8 August 1824–22 May/3 June 1880); succeeded father, NICHOLAS I, as Tsar ALEXANDER II, 18 February/2 March 1855; crowned 1856; m. (2) 6/18 July 1880 Princess Catherine Dolgorouky, created Princess Yourievsky (21 October/2 November 1847–15 February 1922); d. (assassinated) 1/13 March 1881. Issue by 1st marriage:

1. ALEXANDRA, b. 18/30 August 1842, d. 16/28 June 1849

2. NICHOLAS, b. 8/20 September 1843; engaged 1865 to Princess Dagmar of Denmark (1847–1928); d. 12/24 April 1865

3. ALEXANDER, b. 26 February/10 March 1845; m. 1866 Princess Dagmar of Denmark, prev. eng. to Nicholas Alexandrovich [*above*]; s. Alexander II as Tsar ALEXANDER III, 1/13 March 1881; d. 20 October/1 November 1894. Issue:
i. Nicholas, later Tsar NICHOLAS II (1868–1918), m. 1894 Princess Alix of Hesse and the Rhine (1872–1918)
ii. Alexander (1869–70)
iii. George (1871–99)
iv. Xenia (1875–1960), m. 1894 Alexander Michaelovich (1866–1933)
v. Michael (1878–1918), m. 1911 Natalie, Countess Brassova (1880–1952)
vi. Olga (1882–1960), m. (1) 1901 Prince Peter of Oldenburg (1868–1924), divorced 1916; m. (2) 1916 Colonel Nicholas Koulikovsky (1881–1958)

4. VLADIMIR, b. 10/22 April 1847; m. 1874 Princess Marie of Mecklenburg-Schwerin (1854–1920); d. 4/17 February 1909. Issue:
i. Alexander (1875–7)
ii. Cyril (1876–1938), m. 1905 Victoria Melita, divorced wife of Ernest, Grand Duke of Hesse and the Rhine [*see 6. iii. below*]
iii. Boris (1877–1943), m. 1919 Zenaida Rashevska (1898–1963)
iv. Andrew (1879–1956), m. 1921 Maria Kchessinkska (1872–1971)
v. Helen (1882–1957), m. 1902 Prince Nicholas of Greece (1872–1938)
5. ALEXIS, b. 2/14 January 1850; m. (?) 1870 Alexandra Zhukovsky (1842–99); d. 14/27 November 1908. Issue of marriage or partnership:

i. Count Alexis Alexeievich Belevsky-Zhukovsky (1871–1932), m. (1) Marie Petrovna, Princess Troubetskoy (1872–1954), divorced; m. (2) Natalie Vladimirovna, Baroness Schoeppiegk

6. MARIE, b. 5/17 October 1853; m. 1874 Alfred, Duke of Edinburgh, later reigning Duke of Saxe–Coburg Gotha (1844–1900); d. 25 October 1920. Issue:
i. Alfred (1874–99)
ii. Marie (1875–1938), m. 1893 Ferdinand, Crown Prince, later King, of Roumania (1865–1927)
iii. Victoria Melita (1876–1936), m. (1) 1894 Ernest, Grand Duke of Hesse and the Rhine (1868–1937), divorced 1901; m. (2) 1905 Cyril, Grand Duke of Russia (1876–1938) [*see 4. ii. above*]
iv. Alexandra (1878–1942), m. 1896 Ernest of Hohenlohe–Langenburg (1863–1950)
v. Beatrice (1884–1966), m. 1909 Don Alfonso, Infante de Orleans y Bourbon (1886–1975)

7. SERGE, b. 30 April/11 May 1857; m. Princess Elizabeth of Hesse and the Rhine (1864–1918), 1884; d. 4/17 February 1905 (assassinated). No issue

8. PAUL, b. 21 September/3 October 1860; m. (1) 1889 Alexandra, Princess of Greece and Denmark (1870–91); m. (2) 1902 Olga von Pistolkors, later created Princess Paley (1866–1929); d. 30 January 1919 (executed). Issue by 1st marriage:
i. Marie (1890–1958), m. (1) 1908 Prince William of Sweden (1884–1965), divorced 1914; m. (2) 1914 Serge Putiatin (1893–1966)
ii. Dmitri (1891–1942), m. 1926 Audrey Emery (1904–71), divorced 1937
Issue by 2nd wife, firstborn before marriage:
i. Vladimir (1897–1918)
ii. Irina (1903–90)
iii. Natalie (1905–81)

Issue by 2nd wife, all before marriage:

1. GEORGE, b. 29 April/12 May 1872; m. 1900 Countess Alexandra Zarnekau (1883–1957), divorced 1908; d. 30 August/13 September 1913. Issue:
i. Alexander (1900–)

2. OLGA, b. 27 October/9 November 1873; m. 1895 Count George von Merenberg (1871–1948); d. 10 August 1925. Issue:
i. George (1897–)
ii. Olga (1898–)

3. BORIS, b. and d. 1876

4. CATHERINE, b. 9/21 September 1878; m. 1901 (1) Prince Alexander Bariatinsky (1870–1910); m. 1916 (2) Prince Serge Obolensky (1890–1978), divorced 1924; d. 22 December 1959. Issue by first marriage:
i. Andrei (1902–31)
ii. Alexander (1905–)

Reference Notes

All references to Almedingen indicate *Emperor Alexander II* unless given otherwise
LP – Letter in private possession, dated according to Old Style calendar
RA – Royal Archives, Windsor

Chapter 1 (pp.3–24)

1 Almedingen, 14
2 *ibid.*, 18
3 Cowles, 153
4 Almedingen, 29
5 *ibid.*, 26
6 *ibid.*, 34
7 *ibid.*, 38–9
8 *ibid.*, 49
9 Mosse, 33
10 Graham, 18
11 Almedingen, 57
12 Jackman, 285
13 Victoria, *Girlhood* II, 156
14 Almedingen, 61–2
15 LP 17.6.1849 (translated from French)
16 Almedingen, 65
17 Crankshaw, *Shadow*, 166
18 Almedingen, 85
19 Harcave, 145

Chapter 2 (pp. 25–39)

1 Almedingen, 108
2 Kochan & Abraham, 180
3 Harcave, 163
4 Graham, 110
5 Victoria, *Letters 1837–61*, III, 111
6 Redlich, 159
7 Victoria, *Letters 1837–61*, III, 203–4
8 Martin, Theodore, III, 504–5
9 Almedingen, 129
10 *ibid.*, 145
11 Harcave, 172
12 Corti, 103
13 Almedingen, 163
14 *The Times*, 19.2.1861

Chapter 3 (pp. 40–56)

1 Kleinmichel, 26
2 Paléologue, 47–8
3 Hamilton, 407–8
4 Graham, 65
5 Victoria, *Dearest Mama*, 345
6 LP 26.11.1864 (translated from Russian)
7 LP 11–12.4.1865 (translated from French)
8 LP 6–7.4.1865 (translated from French)
9 Almedingen, 206
10 LP, undated, April 1865 (translated from French)
11 Alexander, *Always a Grand Duke*, 199
12 Lowe, 17
13 *ibid.*, 17
14 *ibid.*, 19
15 Poznansky, 367

Chapter 4 (pp. 57–78)

1 Crankshaw, 202
2 Harcave, 181
3 Lieven, 142

4 Kornilov, 112–3
5 Almedingen, 238
6 Victoria, *Letters 1862–85*, I, 428
7 Paléologue, 67
8 Lowe, 27
9 Alexander, *Once a Grand Duke*, 165
10 Poliakoff, 86
11 Abrash, *Slavonic Review*
12 RA Queen Victoria's Journal, 21.6.1873
13 Lowe, 31
14 Victoria, *Darling Child*, 97
15 Victoria, *Letters 1862–85*, II, 296–7
16 Loftus, II, 87
17 Stanley, 218
18 *ibid.*, 204
19 Loftus, II, 87–8
20 McClintock, 172
21 Buchanan, 115
22 Stanley, 204–5
23 *Punch*, 16.5.1874
24 Buckle, V, 415–6
25 Morley, II, 490
26 *Royalty Digest*, Jan, 1997
27 Victoria, *Letters 1862–85*, II, 337
28 RA H41/158 (translated from French)
29 RA H41/159 (translated from French)
30 RA H42/25

Chapter 5 (pp. 79–88)

1 Graham, 203
2 Loftus, II, 184–5
3 Victoria, *Letters 1862–85*, II, 473
4 Abrash, *Slavonic Review*
5 Ponsonby, Arthur, 345
6 Almedingen, 289
7 Vorres, 22
8 Almedingen, 288–9
9 *ibid.*, 295
10 Lowe, 39–40
11 *ibid.*, 40n

Chapter 6 (pp. 89–108)

1 Mosse, 167
2 Harcave, 232
3 Almedingen, 329
4 Corti, 272
5 Victoria, *Letters of the Empress Frederick*, 182
6 Alexander, *Once a Grand Duke*, 50–1
7 *ibid.*, 51–2
8 Almedingen, 341
9 Alexander, *Once a Grand Duke*, 56
10 *ibid.*, 57
11 Hamilton, 446
12 Mosse, 176
13 Crankshaw, 178
14 *ibid.*, 198
15 Almedingen, 345
16 Orlova, 197
17 *ibid.*, 389
18 Buckle, VI, 608
19 Alexander, *Once a Grand Duke*, 63
20 Graham, 302

Chapter 7 (pp. 111–130)

1 Maude, II, 69–70
2 Lowe, 53–4
3 Hamilton, 227
4 Lieven, 89
5 Lowe, 312
6 Almedingen, 337
7 Yourievsky, 6
8 Alexander, *Once a Grand Duke*, 63
9 Lowe, 207–8
10 *ibid.*, 211
11 *ibid.*, 209
12 Ponsonby, Magdalen, 167
13 Lowe, 245
14 Ponsonby, Magdalen, 167

Chapter 8 (pp. 131–150)

1 Vorres, 41
2 Lowe, 332
3 Volkoff, 158
4 *ibid.*, 158
5 Poznansky, 481
6 Maylunas & Mironenko, 15
7 Lieven, 109
8 Alexander, *Once a Grand Duke*, 137–8
9 Vorres, 54
10 Alexander, *Once a Grand Duke*, 139
11 *ibid.*, 188
12 Victoria, *Beloved Mama*, 153
13 Almedingen, *Unbroken unity*, 19
14 Hough, 55
15 RA Add A20/1625
16 Almedingen, *Unbroken unity*, 32

Chapter 9 (pp. 151–170)

1 Vorres, 52
2 Morley, II, 267
3 Aronson, 82
4 Bing, 33
5 Vorres, 58
6 Lowe, 146
7 Alexander, *Once a Grand Duke*, 67
8 Martin, Ralph, 203
9 Victoria, *Letters 1886–1901*, I, 369
10 Vorres, 54
11 Nowak, 238–9
12 Lowe, 102
13 Lieven, 109
14 Rogger, 17
15 Poznansky, 483
16 Marie, Queen of Roumania I, 93
17 William II, 320
18 Almedingen, *Unbroken unity*, 81
19 Alexander, *Once a Grand Duke*, 139
20 Nicholas of Greece, 89
21 Marie, Queen of Roumania I, 214–5
22 Nicholas of Greece, 91

Chapter 10 (pp. 171–183)

1 Alexander, *Once a Grand Duke*, 186
2 Lowe, 355
3 Hough, 110
4 Victoria, *Empress Frederick writes to Sophie*, 150
5 Maylunas & Mironenko, 35
6 Bing, 75–6
7 Maylunas & Mironenko, 52–3
8 Bing, 86
9 Maylunas & Mironenko, 92
10 Nicholas of Greece, 116
11 St Aubyn, 296
12 Alexander, *Once a Grand Duke*, 168
13 Vorres, 65
14 St Aubyn, 296
15 Lieven, 51
16 Lowe, 311
17 *ibid.*, 312
18 Lieven, 24
19 Lowe, 310
20 *The Times*, 5.11.1894

Chapter 11 (pp. 187–205)

1 Vorres, 67
2 Radziwill, 36–7
3 St Aubyn, 297
4 Magnus, 246
5 Pope–Hennessy, 308
6 Maylunas & Mironenko, 108
7 Seton–Watson, 549
8 Lieven, 72
9 Maylunas & Mironenko, 108
10 *ibid.*, 133
11 Almedingen, *Unbroken unity*, 47
12 Maylunas & Mironenko, 147
13 Alexander, *Once a Grand Duke*, 172
14 Almedingen, *Unbroken unity*, 48

15 Maylunas & Mironenko, 155
16 Harcave, 296
17 Maylunas & Mironenko, 161
18 Cornwallis–West, 183–4
19 *ibid.*, 186
20 Marie, Grand Duchess, 46
21 Maylunas & Mironenko, 222
22 Bing, 170
23 *ibid.*, 171
24 Marie, Grand Duchess, 18–9
25 *ibid.*, 55
26 *ibid.*, 56

Chapter 12 (pp. 206–223)

1 Marie, Grand Duchess, 57
2 Maylunas & Mironenko, 257
3 *ibid.*, 270
4 *ibid.*, 268
5 Alexander, *Once a Grand Duke*, 139
6 *ibid.*, 141
7 Maylunas & Mironenko, 274
8 Gooch & Temperley, 84
9 Maylunas & Mironenko, 302
10 *ibid.*, 314
11 *The Times*, 20.2.1909
12 Vorres, 98

Chapter 13 (pp. 224–237)

1 Marie, Grand Duchess, 211
2 *ibid.*, 219
3 Obolensky, 148
4 Paley, 19
5 *ibid.*, 35–6
6 Maylunas & Mironenko, 510
7 Paley, 388
8 Bing, 300
9 Paley, 53
10 *ibid.*, 56
11 Vorres, 152

Chapter 14 (pp. 238–260)

1 Paley, 59
2 Marie, Grand Duchess, 305
3 Van der Kiste & Hall, 136
4 Paley, 220
5 Kleinmichel, 153–4
6 Paley, 284
7 Kleinmichel, 151
8 Paley, 299
9 Alexander, *Always a Grand Duke*, 87–8
10 Pakula, 305
11 Paley, 314
12 Obolensky, 193
13 Yourievsky, 115
14 Vorres, 182
15 Vorres, 182
16 Channon, 320–1
17 LP, undated, *c.* 1877 (translated from Russian)

Bibliography

I MANUSCRIPTS

Royal Archives, Windsor
Letters in private possession

II BOOKS

Alexander, Grand Duke of Russia, *Always a Grand Duke*. Farrar & Rinehart, 1933

— *Once a Grand Duke*. Farrar & Rinehart, 1932

Almedingen, E.M., *The Emperor Alexander II*. Bodley Head, 1962

— *The Empress Alexandra, 1872–1918: a study*. Hutchinson, 1961

— *An unbroken unity: a memoir of Grand Duchess Serge of Russia, 1864–1918*. Bodley Head, 1964

Aronson, Theo, *A family of Kings: the descendants of Christian IX of Denmark*. Cassell, 1976

Battiscombe, Georgina, *Queen Alexandra*. Constable, 1969

Bing, Edward J. (ed.), *The letters of Tsar Nicholas and Empress Marie*. Ivor Nicholson & Watson, 1937

Buchanan, Meriel, *Queen Victoria's relations*. Cassell, 1954

Channon, Sir Henry, *Chips: the diaries of Sir Henry Channon*; (ed.) Robert Rhodes James. Weidenfeld & Nicolson, 1967

Chavchavadze, David, *The Grand Dukes*. Atlantic International, 1990

Clark, Ronald W., *Lenin: the man behind the mask*. Faber, 1988

Cornwallis-West, Mrs George (Lady Randolph Churchill), *The reminiscences of Lady Randolph Churchill*. Edward Arnold, 1908

Corti, Egon Caesar Conte, *The downfall of three dynasties*. Methuen, 1934

Cowles, Virginia, *The Romanovs*. Collins, 1971

Crankshaw, Edward, *The fall of the house of Habsburg*. Longmans, 1963

— *The shadow of the Winter Palace: the drift to revolution*. Macmillan, 1976

Cyril, Grand Duke of Russia, *My life in Russia's service – then and now*. Selwyn & Blount, 1939

Duff, David, *Hessian tapestry*. Frederick Muller, 1967

Gilliard, Pierre, *Thirteen years at the Russian court*. Hutchinson, 1921

Gooch, G.P. & Temperley, Harold, *British documents on the origins of the war 1898–1914: Vol. IV, The Anglo-Russian rapprochement, 1903–7*. HMSO, 1929

Graham, Stephen, *A life of Alexander II, Tsar of Russia*. Ivor Nicholson & Watson, 1935

Hall, Coryne, *Little Mother of Russias: A biography of Empress Marie Feodorovna*. Shepheard-Walwyn, 1999

Hamilton, Lord Frederick, *The vanished world of yesterday*. Hodder & Stoughton, 1950
Harcave, Sidney, *Years of the Golden Cockerel: The last Romanov Tsars 1814–1917*. Robert Hale, 1970
Haslip, Joan, *The lonely Empress: a biography of Elizabeth of Austria*. Weidenfeld & Nicolson, 1965
Hough, Richard (ed.), *Advice to a grand-daughter: letters from Queen Victoria to Princess Victoria of Hesse*. Heinemann, 1975
Jackman, S.W. (ed.), *Romanov relations: the private correspondence of Tsars Alexander I, Nicholas I and the Grand Dukes Constantine and Michael with their sister Queen Anna Pavlovna, 1817–55*. Macmillan, 1969
Joyneville, C., *Life of Alexander II, Emperor of all the Russias*. W.H. Allen, 1883
King, Greg, *Empress Alexandra*. Atlantic International, 1990
Kleinmichel, Baroness, *Memories of a shipwrecked world*. Brentano's, 1923
Kochan, Lionel, & Abraham, Richard, *The making of modern Russia*, 2nd ed. Jonathan Cape, 1983
Kornilov, Alexander, *Modern Russian history*, 2 vols. Skeffington, 1916
Lee, Sir Sidney, *King Edward VII: a biography*, 2 vols. Macmillan, 1925–7
Lieven, Dominic, *Nicholas II, Emperor of All the Russias*. John Murray, 1993
Lincoln, W. Bruce, *Nicholas I: Emperor and Autocrat of All the Russias*. Allen Lane, 1978
Loftus, Lord Augustus, *The diplomatic reminiscences of Lord Augustus Loftus, PC, GCB, 1862–1879*, 2 vols. Cassell, 1894
Lowe, Charles, *Alexander III of Russia*. Heinemann, 1895
Magnus, Philip, *King Edward the Seventh*. John Murray, 1964
Marie, Queen of Roumania, *The story of my life*, 3 vols. Cassell, 1934–5
Marie, Grand Duchess of Russia, *Things I remember*. Cassell, 1930
Martin, Ralph G., *Lady Randolph Churchill: a biography, 1854–1895*. Cassell, 1969
Martin, Theodore, *The life of HRH the Prince Consort*, 5 vols. Smith, Elder, 1874–80
Massie, Robert K, *Nicholas and Alexandra*. Victor Gollancz, 1968
Maude, Aylmer, *The life of Tolstoy*, 2 vols. Constable, 1908–10
Maylunas, Andrei, & Mironenko, Sergei, *A lifelong passion: Nicholas and Alexandra, their own story*. Weidenfeld & Nicolson, 1996
McClintock, Mary Howard, *The Queen thanks Sir Howard: the life of Major-General Sir Howard Elphinstone, V.C., K.C.B., C.M.G.* John Murray, 1945
Millar, Lubov, *Grand Duchess Elizabeth of Russia: new martyr of the communist yoke*. Nicodemus Orthodox Publications Society, 1991
Monypenny, W.F., & Buckle, G.E., *The life of Benjamin Disraeli, Earl of Beaconsfield*, 6 vols. John Murray, 1910–20
Morley, John, *The life of William Ewart Gladstone*, 2 vols. Macmillan, 1903
Mosse, W.E., *Alexander II and the modernization of Russia*. Tauris, 1992

Nicholas of Greece, Prince, *My fifty years*. Hutchinson, 1926
Nowak, Karl Friedrich, *Kaiser & Chancellor: the opening years of the reign of the Emperor William II*. Putnam, 1930
Obolensky, Serge, *One man in his time; the memoirs of Serge Obolensky*. Hutchinson, 1960
Orlova, Alexandra, *Tchaikovsky: a self-portrait*. Oxford University Press, 1990
Pakula, Hannah, *The last romantic: a biography of Queen Marie of Roumania*. Weidenfeld & Nicolson, 1985
Paléologue, Maurice, *The tragic romance of Alexander II of Russia*. Hutchinson, 1926
Paley, Princess, *Memories of Russia, 1916–1919*. Herbert Jenkins, 1924
Poliakoff, Vladimir, *The Empress Marie of Russia and her times*. Thornton Butterworth, 1926
Ponsonby, Sir Arthur, *Henry Ponsonby, Queen Victoria's private secretary: his life from his letters*. Macmillan, 1942
Ponsonby, Magdalen (ed.), *Mary Ponsonby: a memoir, some letters and a journal*. John Murray, 1927
Pope-Hennessy, James, *Queen Mary, 1867–1953*. Allen & Unwin, 1959
Poznansky, Alexander, *Tchaikovsky: the quest for the inner man*. Lime Tree, 1993
Redlich, Joseph, *Emperor Francis Joseph of Austria: a biography*. Macmillan, 1929
Rogger, Hans, *Russia in the age of modernisation and revolution 1881–1917*. Longman, 1983
St Aubyn, Giles, *Edward VII, Prince and King*. Collins, 1979
Seton-Watson, Hugh, *The Russian Empire 1801-1917*. Oxford University Press, 1967
Skott, Staffan, *Romanovs*. Bonniers, 1989
Stanley, Lady Augusta, *Later letters of Lady Augusta Stanley, 1864–1876*; (ed.) Dean of Windsor & Hector Bolitho. Jonathan Cape, 1929
Tarsaidze, Alexandre, *Katia, wife before God*. Macmillan, 1970
Tisdall, E.E.P., *The Dowager Empress* [Marie Feodorovna, 1847–1928]. Stanley Paul, 1957
Van der Kiste, John, *Princess Victoria Melita, Grand Duchess Cyril of Russia*. Alan Sutton, 1991
Van der Kiste, John, & Hall, Coryne, *Once a Grand Duchess: Xenia, sister of Nicholas II*, Sutton, 2002
Van der Kiste, John, & Jordaan, Bee, *Dearest Affie: Alfred, Duke of Edinburgh, Queen Victoria's second son*. Alan Sutton, 1984
Victoria, Queen, *The girlhood of Queen Victoria: a selection from Her Majesty's diaries between the years 1832 and 1840*; (ed.) Viscount Esher, 2 vols. John Murray, 1912
— *The letters of Queen Victoria: a selection from Her Majesty's correspondence between the years 1837 and 1861*, 3 vols; (ed.) A.C. Benson and Viscount Esher. John Murray, 1907

— *The letters of Queen Victoria: a selection from Her Majesty's correspondence and journal between the years 1862 and 1885*, 3 vols; (ed.) George Earle Buckle. John Murray, 1926–8
— *The letters of Queen Victoria: a selection from Her Majesty's correspondence and journal between the years 1886 and 1901*, 3 vols; (ed.) George Earle Buckle and Viscount Esher. John Murray, 1930–2
— *Dearest Mama: letters between Queen Victoria and the Crown Princess of Prussia, 1862–64*; (ed.) Roger Fulford. Evans Bros, 1968
— *Darling Child: private correspondence of Queen Victoria and the Crown Princess of Prussia, 1871–78*; (ed.) Roger Fulford. Evans Bros, 1976
— *Beloved Mama: private correspondence of Queen Victoria and the German Crown Princess, 1878–1885*; (ed.) Roger Fulford. Evans Bros, 1981
Victoria, Consort of Frederick III, German Emperor, *The Empress Frederick writes to Sophie, her daughter, Crown Princess and later Queen of the Hellenes: letters, 1889–1901*; (ed.) Arthur Gould Lee. Faber, 1955
— *Letters of the Empress Frederick*; (ed.) Sir Frederick Ponsonby. Macmillan, 1928
Volkoff, Vladimir, *Tchaikovsky: a self-portrait*. Robert Hale, 1975
Vorres, Ian, *The last Grand-Duchess; Her Imperial Highness Grand-Duchess Olga Alexandrovna*. Hutchinson, 1964
Vyrubova, Anna, *Memories of the Russian court*. Macmillan, 1923
William II, Ex-Emperor of Germany, *My early life*. Methuen, 1926
Yourievsky, Princess Catherine, *My book*. Eveleigh, Nash & Grayson, 1924
Youssupov, Felix, *Lost splendour*. Jonathan Cape, 1953
Zeepvat, Charlotte, *Romanov Autumn: Stories from the last century of imperial Russia*, Sutton, 2000

III ARTICLES

The European. Lutyens, Mary, 'Love-struck Tsar's sad race with the assassins'. 18-20 May 1990
Hampshire County Magazine. Pierce-Jones, V.G., 'Neglected Princess lies alone on Hayling'. July 1992
Imperial Russian Journal. Anon, 'The Grand Dukes and the Russian imperial navy'. Vol. III, No. 3, 1997
Sole, Kent M., 'The fate of the Romanovs: the survivors.' Vol. II, No. 1, 1995
Stover, Karla, 'Princess Catherine Yourievsky: Katia, 41 years a widow.' Vol. IV, No. 1, 1997
International Affairs. Obukhova, Olga, 'The Romanovs in Denmark'. July 1995
Slavonic & East European Review. Abrash, Merritt, 'A curious royal romance: the Queen's son [Alfred, Duke of Edinburgh] and the Tsar's daughter [Marie Alexandrovna]'. July 1969
Royalty Digest. Anon, 'Explosion in the Winter Palace: the attempt on the

life of the Czar' [Alexander II]. January 1993 [reprinted from *The Graphic*, 28 February 1880]
Goliczov, Roman Ilmar, 'Grand Duchess Marie Alexandrovna and music'. January 1997
— 'Prince Vladimir Meshcherski and the "death bed betrothal" of Grand Duke Alexander and Princess Dagmar'. May 1997
The Times. Kirby, Heather, 'Intimate revelations of a Tsar's passion'. 19 September 1984

IV Journals

Daily Telegraph
Punch
The Times

Index

Abbreviations: A II – Alexander II; A III – Alexander III;
N II – Nicholas II.
Nicknames are only given where mentioned in text.